Unreal Engine Lighting and Rendering Essentials

Learn the principles of lighting and rendering in Unreal Engine

Muhammad A.Moniem

[PACKT] PUBLISHING

BIRMINGHAM - MUMBAI

Unreal Engine Lighting and Rendering Essentials

First published: September 2015

Production reference: 1180915

Published by Packt Publishing Ltd.
Livery Place
35 Livery Street
Birmingham B3 2PB, UK.

ISBN 978-1-78528-906-4

www.packtpub.com

Cover image by Muhammad A.Moniem (muhammadamoniem@gmail.com)

Credits

Author
Muhammad A.Moniem

Reviewers
Kevin Adanan
Brendon Clifford
Javier Garcia-Lajara Herrero
Terry Matthes

Commissioning Editor
Edward Bowkett

Acquisition Editor
Usha Iyer

Content Development Editor
Shweta Pant

Technical Editor
Madhunikita Sunil Chindarkar

Copy Editor
Rashmi Sawant

Project Coordinator
Sanjeet Rao

Proofreader
Safis Editing

Indexer
Hemangini Bari

Production Coordinator
Komal Ramchandani

Cover Work
Komal Ramchandani

About the Author

Muhammad A.Moniem started in the industry at a very early age. He taught himself everything related to the game development process even before he joined college. After being a software engineer, he started to teach himself the art of game design and game art techniques. As a self-taught person, he was able to find his way into the industry very easily, which led him to be hired for big, medium, and small companies, titles, and teams. Throughout his career, he was able to contribute as a full-time or part-time employee or freelancer to games for a wide range of platforms, including Windows, Mac, iOS, Android, PS4, Xbox One, and OUYA. He has also worked with technologies, such as VR, AR, and Kinect. Finally, he was able to establish his own one-person game company/team as a part-time independent developer. A lot of his indie games got recognition or have been finalists at international indie game events, such as IGF, Indie Showcase, IGC, and Tokyo Game Show. He has written another Unreal Engine book before and he has also designed an amazing website, `www.mamoniem.com`.

He has also worked on *Learning Unreal® Engine iOS Game Development, Packt Publishing*, which is available at `https://www.packtpub.com/game-development/learning-unreal-engine-ios-game-development`.

Acknowledgments

I would like to thank all the people who helped me with this book. A special mention goes to all the team members of Epic games for their hard work on the Unreal Engine and for the great decision to make the engine and source free for everyone.

I would like to thank all the people at Packt Publishing who worked on this book. They helped me a lot and were patient when I couldn't give them enough time because of my personal obligations. Thanks for helping me and teaching me more about how to write a book.

I want to express my gratitude to my wife and kids, Lamiaa, Yussuf, and Mariam. You are my gifts. You are a very supportive family. Thanks to Loly for giving me the best environment to write this book in and thanks for believing in all my projects. Thanks to Joe and Mary for being noisy sweet kids all the way!

I would like to thank my parents for raising me and teaching me how to self-learn; it helped me a lot to learn and pass the knowledge to others.

Last but not least, thanks Egypt for being my home, safety, dream, and warm hug for a long time. Thanks for raising me and teaching me how to live. Thanks to every single person I met in Egypt; you definitely trusted and helped me learn and reach this level. Egypt, I will never be able to pay you back.

Dear God, thanks for being that Muhammad and thanks for everything. Please keep these wonderful people around me.

About the Reviewers

Kevin Adanan is an honors graduate from Teesside University, and he has worked on five games. He specializes in 3D art and has extensive experience in Unreal Engines.

Kevin is currently working as a 3D artist at 3D4Medical in Dublin, Ireland. He also works on independent games in his spare time.

You can contact him at `kevin.adanan@gmail.com`.

Knowledge and practice is everything when it comes to 3D art. No one can put in the hours of practice for you, but knowledge is a precious resource that is crucial to an artist's development. There is no better way to receive knowledge than from others. Without different people taking time (often long hours) out of their lives for no gain other than my personal development, I wouldn't be the artist I am today. With this in mind, I would like to thank, in no particular order, Shafeq Rahman, Deepak Gautam, David Cockburn, Andrew Walker, Vladimir Andreevsky, William Taylor Parker, Stephan Dammrau, Mark Byrne, and Matthew Lloyd.

Brendon Clifford is a graphics and engine programmer. He has worked to create extensive and robust game engines in order to use them as graphical frameworks and independent game projects. His graphical strengths include Particle Systems, material pipeline frameworks, lighting, and post processing.

In 2015, he graduated from DigiPen Institute of Technology with a bachelor of science degree in computer science in real-time interactive simulation, and he is a minor in mathematics. During his education, he shipped four game projects using a combination of Unreal Engine 4 and custom built game engines, such as the Prometheus Engine.

After graduating, he began working for Ember Entertainment as a gameplay programmer. He has worked to develop and maintain live games for the iOS and Android platforms.

I would like to thank my father, Patrick Clifford, and my brother, Jordan Clifford, for their support in my education and career. Through my work in Unreal Engine, I would like to thank the developers of my team: Chuck Silvers, Kevin Giang, and Jeff Quek.

Javier Garcia-Lajara Herrero was part of the booming video game industry in Spain, participating in the Commandos saga by Pyro Studios, where he developed as an artist, before continuing his career in different disciplines at Virtual Toys, Bitoon, and Unusual Studios.

He is now one of the professors at U-tad University of Technology.

He is always passionate about technical advancements. He now researches and develops new proposals in games, virtual reality, the aerial photogrammetry of objects, and environments with drones.

He has also reviewed other books, *Building Levels in Unity* and *Unity 3D UI Essentials*, both by *Packt Publishing*.

You can follow him on his Twitter @Prf_Moriarty

Terry Matthes grew up in central Canada (Winnipeg, Manitoba) where he studied computer science at the University of Manitoba. After working with the Web, he went back to school to study digital media design and 3D animation at Red River College. While in Winnipeg, he worked as a web developer and was later employed as a texture artist in long format animation.

After several years, he and his wife, Anna, moved to Montreal, Quebec, where he now works in the game industry. Some of his recent projects include the massive multiplayer game WildStar by Carbine, Mortal Kombat 9, and Mortal Kombat X, published by Warner Brothers, as well as several unreleased titles.

He never stops investigating and practicing new techniques. Working with Unreal Engine, he currently designs natural environments using a mix of the procedural terrain generation tools and ZBrush. Snapshots of his work can be seen on his blog at `www.terrymatthes.com`.

I would like to thank my wife, Anna. She has been a great support during many late nights spent working on this book. I would also like to thank my family and friends for pushing me to pursue my goals.

---

www.PacktPub.com

Support files, eBooks, discount offers, and more

For support files and downloads related to your book, please visit `www.PacktPub.com`.

Did you know that Packt offers eBook versions of every book published, with PDF and ePub files available? You can upgrade to the eBook version at `www.PacktPub.com` and as a print book customer, you are entitled to a discount on the eBook copy. Get in touch with us at `service@packtpub.com` for more details.

At `www.PacktPub.com`, you can also read a collection of free technical articles, sign up for a range of free newsletters and receive exclusive discounts and offers on Packt books and eBooks.

PACKTLIB™

`https://www2.packtpub.com/books/subscription/packtlib`

Do you need instant solutions to your IT questions? PacktLib is Packt's online digital book library. Here, you can search, access, and read Packt's entire library of books.

Why subscribe?

- Fully searchable across every book published by Packt
- Copy and paste, print, and bookmark content
- On demand and accessible via a web browser

Free access for Packt account holders

If you have an account with Packt at `www.PacktPub.com`, you can use this to access PacktLib today and view 9 entirely free books. Simply use your login credentials for immediate access.

Table of Contents

Preface

This book is meant to help you dive into the rendering features of Unreal Engine, regardless of your level of experience with the rendering pipeline of modern real-time graphics.

While this is a cross-platform engine, and not all platforms have equal configurations, we will discuss, from this point of view, which feature can be used with which platform, and how to scale your game to fit pretty much all the supported platforms.

During the course of this book, we will dive deep into all the available rendering features in the engine, how to enable them for your project, and how to debug and optimize their performance. We will not only discuss how to implement them, but also what makes them useful and effective for your projects.

What this book covers

Chapter 1, An Introduction to Lighting and Rendering, introduces you to the Unreal's rendering system with an introduction to the most important editors required to master the rendering process and an explanation of the light sources, their types, and properties.

Chapter 2, Understanding the Working of Materials, covers the Unreal Material editors, how to use them to build different types of materials, and how and when to use Unreal's Layered Materials.

Chapter 3, Cascade – a World Made of Particles, covers the Cascade editor, and how to use it in order to build the most complex and appealing Particle Systems. It also covers how to add some animations or controls and how or when to spawn particles.

Chapter 4, Precomputed Lights, explains how to use pre-computed lighting and lightmaps in order to save the runtime memory. Indirect Light Cache and Reflection Environment capturers are the keys to mastering pre-computed lighting, and all of them have been discussed in detail and broken into bits and pieces in this chapter.

Chapter 5, Dynamic Lights Versus Performance, shows that sometimes you have to get your lights to move, rotate and change color at runtime, and teaches you about all the dynamic light features, which include the Moveable Lights, Distance Fields, Ambient Occlusion, and the powerful Ray Traced Distance Field Soft Shadow.

Chapter 6, Post Processing Effects, teaches you that sometimes adding lights will never make the final rendered image as striking as possible, and covers how to use the Post Process effects to add a new layer and one more step toward the awesomeness of your product. All the different effects supported in Unreal Engine will be discussed in detail in this chapter.

Chapter 7, Render Performance Debugging, discusses how to debug the rendering features, how to use the console to debug the editor and/or the game, and shows you how sometimes the use of some render features causes a lag or crash. Lots of debugging tools are discussed, such as the GPU Visualizer, view modes, visualizers, FPS charts, and the console, in this chapter.

Chapter 8, The Unreal Scalability Settings, shows that while Unreal Engine is a cross-platform engine, sometimes you have to make your game accessible to more platforms, and covers the tools and techniques that allow you to adjust the performance and the quality to match the targeted platform.

Chapter 9, Adding Fog to Your Games, covers how to add the different fog types to your game. It also covers the difference between the fog types and how to master all the settings for each type.

What you need for this book

You need to have a Windows, Mac, or Linux computer with the minimum requirements of Unreal Engine. Also, you will need to have Unreal Engine installed (I used 4.8 while writing the book, which is the latest version at the time of writing), which is free to download, so go ahead and download it.

Apart from a good drink next to you and a good taste for colors, this is all you need to get started with this book!

Who this book is for

If you are building any type of content in Unreal Engine and looking forward to getting the most epic render quality over the best performance, then this book is for you.

In this book, you'll find a detailed explanation of each feature in the editor, how to enable and use the features, and which features are useful for which cases. Most importantly, you'll find out how to debug and optimize rendering for the best performance possible.

If you are a programmer or a game designer who wants to learn more about Unreal Engine's lighting and rendering essentials, or someone from outside the game industry who wants to master rendering Unreal Engine, this is the book for you. This book is friendly and anyone can build a striking production quality using Epic's technology, regardless of their background, target platform, or content type.

Conventions

In this book, you will find a number of text styles that distinguish between different kinds of information. Here are some examples of these styles and an explanation of their meaning.

Code words in text, database table names, folder names, filenames, file extensions, pathnames, dummy URLs, user input, and Twitter handles are shown as follows: "The final color will be equal to the source color if `OpacityMask` is greater than `OpacityMaskClipValue`."

New terms and **important words** are shown in bold. Words that you see on the screen, for example, in menus or dialog boxes, appear in the text like this: "In the **Transform** category, for every light, there is a property called **Mobility** that has only three types: **Static**, **Stationary**, and **Movable**."

> Warnings or important notes appear in a box like this.

> Tips and tricks appear like this.

Reader feedback

Feedback from our readers is always welcome. Let us know what you think about this book—what you liked or disliked. Reader feedback is important for us as it helps us develop titles that you will really get the most out of.

To send us general feedback, simply e-mail `feedback@packtpub.com`, and mention the book's title in the subject of your message.

If there is a topic that you have expertise in and you are interested in either writing or contributing to a book, see our author guide at `www.packtpub.com/authors`.

Customer support

Now that you are the proud owner of a Packt book, we have a number of things to help you to get the most from your purchase.

Downloading the color images of this book

We also provide you with a PDF file that has color images of the screenshots/diagrams used in this book. The color images will help you better understand the changes in the output. You can download this file from `http://www.packtpub.com/sites/default/files/downloads/9064OT_ColorImages.pdf`.

Errata

Although we have taken every care to ensure the accuracy of our content, mistakes do happen. If you find a mistake in one of our books—maybe a mistake in the text or the code—we would be grateful if you could report this to us. By doing so, you can save other readers from frustration and help us improve subsequent versions of this book. If you find any errata, please report them by visiting `http://www.packtpub.com/submit-errata`, selecting your book, clicking on the **Errata Submission Form** link, and entering the details of your errata. Once your errata are verified, your submission will be accepted and the errata will be uploaded to our website or added to any list of existing errata under the Errata section of that title.

To view the previously submitted errata, go to `https://www.packtpub.com/books/content/support` and enter the name of the book in the search field. The required information will appear under the **Errata** section.

Piracy

Piracy of copyrighted material on the Internet is an ongoing problem across all media. At Packt, we take the protection of our copyright and licenses very seriously. If you come across any illegal copies of our works in any form on the Internet, please provide us with the location address or website name immediately so that we can pursue a remedy.

Please contact us at `copyright@packtpub.com` with a link to the suspected pirated material.

We appreciate your help in protecting our authors and our ability to bring you valuable content.

Questions

If you have a problem with any aspect of this book, you can contact us at `questions@packtpub.com`, and we will do our best to address the problem.

1
An Introduction to Lighting and Rendering

If you are looking forward to making a 3D project with Unreal Engine, then you are definitely a person who is seeking high-end visual quality versus the best performance approach! Even if you are not looking forward to making something look realistic, then you need to make your game regardless the art style runs smooth and optimized, even with the most fabulous shading and rendering techniques.

Unreal Engine has been the best measurement of industry standards for the past 20 years, and a lot of the most famous and beloved games have been made with it. Unreal Engine has always been a witness to, and a participant of, the huge jumps in gaming and real-time rendering technology. With all this importance of Unreal Engine, I will be glad to introduce you to its techniques for achieving the best quality ever!

By the end of this chapter, you will:

- Understand Unreal's rendering pipeline and the 3D graphics pipeline in general
- Understand the job and the importance of the Material Editor and Cascade
- Know where to find the best rendering features in Unreal Editor
- Understand the light sources and its different types, and learn how to use and adjust them

An introduction to the Unreal rendering system

While Unreal Engine 3 used the forward lighting path to produce the final rendered image on the screen, Unreal Engine 4 is based on the deferred lights and shading path.

Deferred shading is a screen-space shading technique. It is called deferred because no shading takes place during the first pass of the vertex and pixel shaders. Instead, shading is "deferred" until the second pass.

So, what happens in that first pass?

On the first pass, only data that is required for the shading computations is gathered. Positions, normals, and materials for each surface are rendered to the **Geometry Buffer (G-buffer)** as a series of textures. Then, a pixel shader computes the direct and indirect lighting (from all the available light sources) at each pixel using the information of the texture buffers, in screen space. This is the most important element of the pipeline. Later on, we will discuss this in more detail. It is good to know that the order of the rendering pipeline is as follows:

- The depth pass
- The opaque geometry pass
- The lighting pass
- The translucency pass
- The post-processing pass

For example, Unreal renders the opaque geometry pass without light shading to several screen-space buffers using multiple render targets (on the left-hand side), which in this case is the depth, normal, and color, and all of them are written to separate buffers. These buffers are then combined to provide enough information for each light to light the pixels and show the final result (on the right-hand side):

The importance of using deferred shading with Unreal Engine 4 is that only one geometry pass is required, and each light is only computed for those pixels that it actually affects (no paths per light). This gives us the ability to render as many lights as possible in a scene without a significant performance overhead!

Lighting paths

Unreal Engine 4 supports different types of lighting paths. These types give you a variety of options that can be used to fit your game/project based on your aim to improve the quality and performance. The different light paths are as follows:

- **Static Lighting**: As the name suggests, this type of light doesn't react to changes during runtime. It is calculated through an individual asset called **lightmaps**, which can be edited to improve the lighting and shadow quality. This type of lighting has the lowest overall cost on the game performance, while keeping the lighting and shadow at a good/medium rendering quality. As a result of this, these types of lights can't even be moved at runtime due to their limitations.

  Since the light scene with this light will use lightmaps, the shadows will be baked as well to these lightmaps, which means that there will be no shadows following the dynamic objects in the scene (for example, characters).

- **Stationary Lighting**: It is also called partially static lighting, which can be achieved using the Stationary Lights, and it's name came from the fact that these type of lights need to be static and not move from their positions, while they still have the ability to change some of their attributes (such as their brightness or color) at runtime.

  Like the previous type, the stationary lights can store lightmaps as well, and reuse them. This gives it the opportunity to give a good performance while maintaining the best quality, and it can still make some changes at runtime.

- **Dynamic Lighting:** This type of lighting is achieved using the Movable Lights, and as the name suggests, these type of lights cast a completely dynamic light and shadow. You can change any of its attributes, as well as it's positioning and direction at runtime too. With all this power and not using any sort of recomputed lightmaps, you might have guessed that this type of lighting incurs a huge cost on the overall performance, even though it has the most accurate and believable look.

Now you know how and why to choose your lights. You don't have to run the entire project with a certain type of lighting. The great benefit of using Unreal Engine is called **Flexibility**. You can mix the three lighting types based on the level, cut scene, or conditions you have set, and keep the quality versus performance consistent throughout the project.

Using the Material and Cascade editors

In order to get the final rendered image, you have to go through lots of panels, windows, editors, and options. One of the most common editors you've to use throughout the process of creating any type of project based on Unreal Engine 4 is the Material Editor and the Particle Editor (Cascade).

The Material Editor

The Material Editor is Unreal's interface that is responsible for creating and changing the material assets. A material asset can be applied to any type of mesh (Static Meshes or Skeletal Meshes) and give it a visual look that defines the surface's type and its texture. Any type of Unreal visual element, not only meshes but also post-processing, decals, and particles get their materials done here.

Imagine that you have three objects that have the same shape, but one of them is made of wood, the other is made of gold, and the last one is made of steel. What makes them look like wood, gold, and steel? In simple words, their **Material** and their **Texture**. More specifically, the material, which is the asset, that defines how the surface is going interact with the lights. In the following screenshot, you can tell which object is made of wood, copper, and steel:

In Unreal Engine 4, there is a very impressive Material Editor that is responsible for this type of material asset editing process. With all its nodes, variables, and attributes, you will be able to achieve any type of material to match any type of surface.

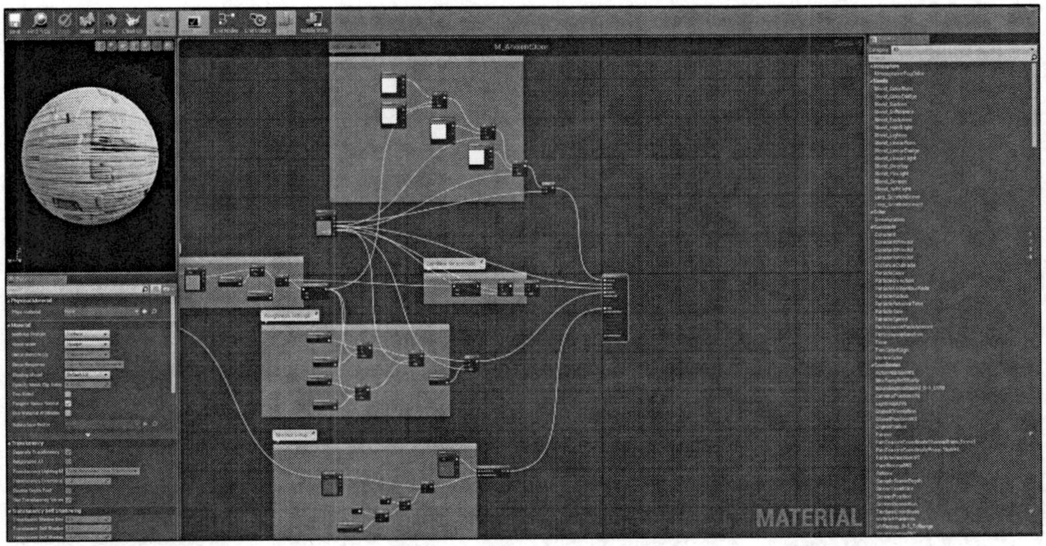

Unreal Engine 4 introduces you to a physically-based shading model. This means that you are not going to define your material attributes using the typical old school properties, such as the **Diffuse Color** or **Specular Power**; but you can instead use properties that are more connected to our real world, such as the base color, metallic, specular, and roughness.

Physically-based shading means that the engine approximates what light actually does as opposed to approximating what we intuitively think it should do. The end result is more accurate and looks more natural. The advantage of using physically-based materials is that they will work equally well in all lighting environments:

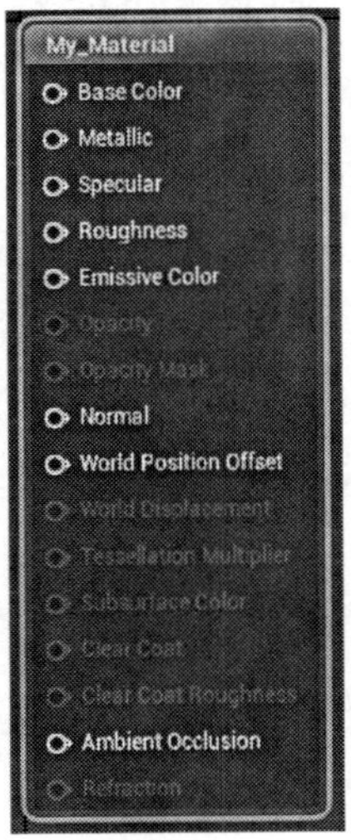

The Cascade editor

In Unreal Engine 4, creating particle effects is no longer a tedious process. With it's Cascade interface, you will be able to create and edit the most complex, visually appealing, GPU calculated, particle effects.

Cascade not only gives you the chance to create a typical particle effect, but with such a modular editor, each Particle System (particle blueprint class) can have multiple subsystems (different Particle Systems in a Particle System), which makes it more unique than any other Particle System, not only in the game engine, but also in 3D VFX applications. Especially, when it comes to the real-time feedback that gives you the power of saving time in order to reach the most complex and robust Particle Systems.

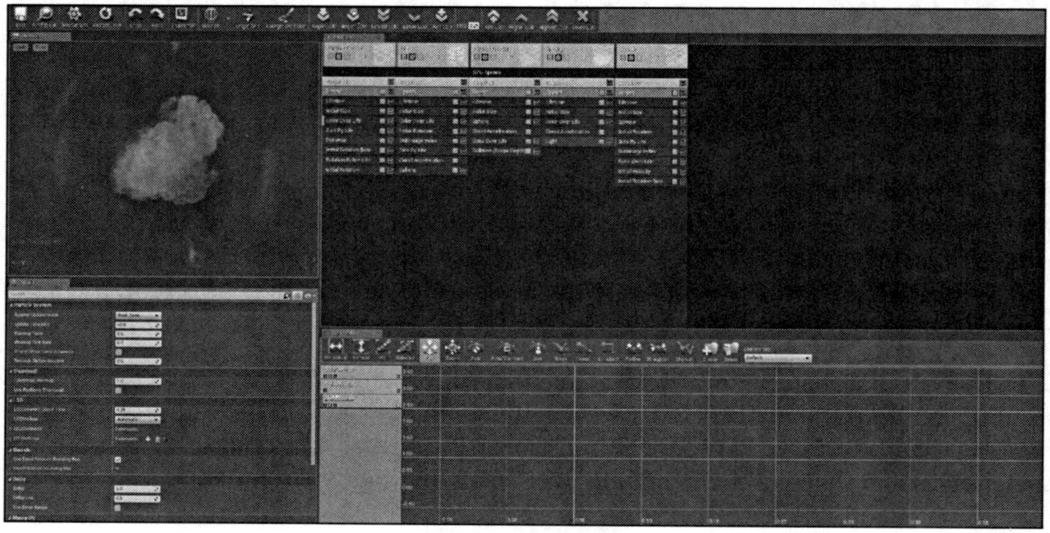

Working with light

The light sources in Unreal Engine are considered actors as well. This means that each light can be placed, moved, and/or get it's parameters edited. In order to get your environment looking as you desire, you have to keep throwing some lights around the scene and keep tweaking them. In the following few paragraphs, we'll discuss how to put them in and how to tweak them.

Using light sources

Lighting is an essential element in any Unreal scene. It helps you define the scene and tells the story or guides the player's path. Without lights in the scene, it will look dark and the player/viewer will not be able to recognize the mesh shapes or surface types. Depending on the type of the game, this might be the intent. So lighting should be described as a process for achieving a wide range of scene types, not just well-lit scenes. In order to put a light in an empty scene, you can follow different ways to place a light source regardless of its type. The most common ways are as follows:

- As a person who likes to fill the viewport on my screen while constructing my levels, I have never been able to get access to the interface panels and windows. Here comes the benefit of having the magical contextual menus in Unreal Engine 4. If you right-click on the viewport, you can select **Place Actor**, and finally, select a light. It doesn't matter where the light is added, as once it is added, you can then adjust its location in the world and its rotation angles like any other actor/object in your scene, but don't try to scale the light, as it has no effect! You can also pick it at any time, either by hitting its gizmo shape in the scene view or by selecting it from the scene outliner window:

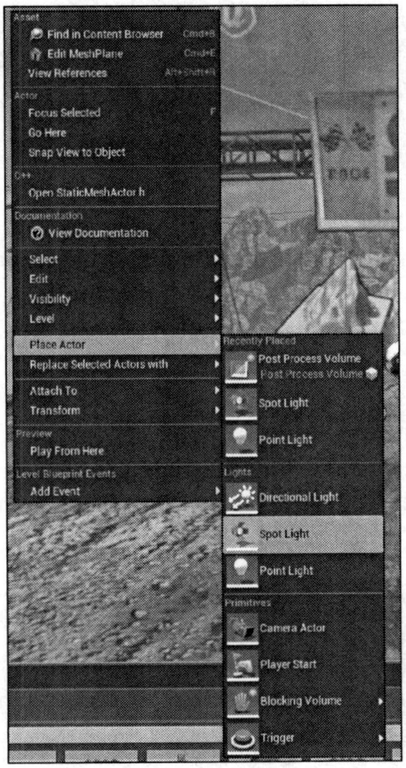

- In the case that you have to work with all the panels around your viewport, then from the **Modes** window, under the **Place** tab, select the **Lights** menu. From this menu, you can drag and drop a light into the scene.

This way guarantees that you can spawn the light at the correct position from the first mouse click, then you don't have to keep tweaking its position. You might need to tweak its rotation though.

Once you have a light in your scene, you will want to edit its options. To do this, select the light. Once you select the light, the information and settings will be displayed in the **Details** panel. We will now go through the options that can be found. Some options are available in all light types.

Light Mobility status

In the **Transform** category, for every light, there is a property called **Mobility** that has only three types: **Static**, **Stationary**, and **Movable**. Each of them has its own usage as well its own performance impact.

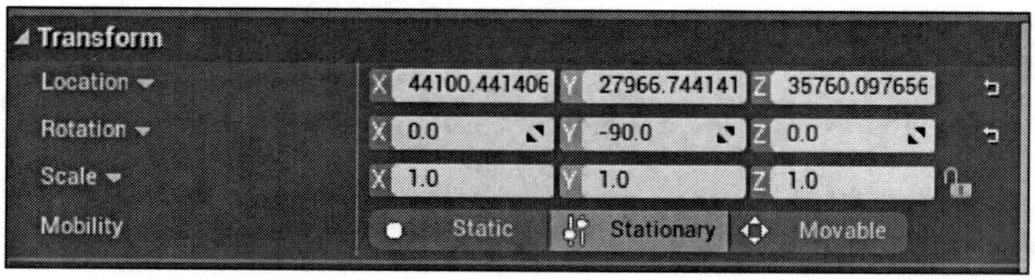

- **Static**: This is a static light that gets calculated only in lightmaps and after that it has no impact on the performance during a running game.

  As it is already baked, it cannot be changed or moved during runtime. They are baked into static lightmaps that do not interact with dynamic objects, such as characters, and this makes it a limited mobility type.

  Shadow Maps are also baked into static textures that do not interact with dynamic objects.

  As the shadows are already baked, you must keep in mind that if your shadows are using a high **Source Radius** (that causes a falloff effect as described earlier in this chapter), then you might need to increase the lightmap resolution (on the Static Mesh components or the Brush surfaces) to avoid aliasing or sharpness in order to save lots of the softness details to it, as this resolution value works on controlling the details of the baked lighting that static lights produce. However, you can use a very low lightmap resolution, but this is only recommended in case you are using a lower radius value. So this means that a large light with that mobility type needs a larger resolution, and this produces a larger lightmap although it takes a longer build time and it requires a higher memory space. That means in order to save memory, while building a level, always try to use static lights unless you are 100 percent sure that the light will have to be edited in some way at runtime.

  Also, using static lights is a great way to quickly block out the basic lighting in a level to give an impression of how you want it to look like.

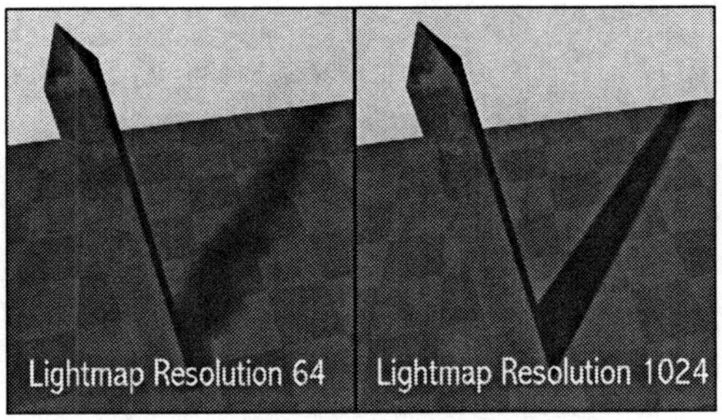

- **Stationary**: This is a half-static and half-dynamic light. It is a type of light that can change its color and brightness at runtime but can't move or rotate at runtime. As it is calculated only in lightmaps (once processed, it has no further impact on the performance), this makes it the best of the three mobility statuses. It has a nice look with the lowest performance cost, and this is what makes it the best fit for modern mobile devices.

  Keep in mind that the runtime changes to brightness only affect the direct lighting. Indirect (bounced) lighting will not change, as it is precalculated by the lightmaps.

While indirect lighting and shadowing from the Stationary Lights is stored in the lightmap, the direct shadows are stored in the Shadow Map. This is one of its known benefits that it can make use of the Distance Field shadows, which means that their shadows can remain detailed and smooth even with a fairly low lightmap resolution on the static mesh component.

While this light type can't support any runtime changes on the indirect lighting (the ones that are not baked on lightmaps), you still have the chance to scale the contribution of the indirect lighting via the **Indirect Lighting Intensity** option on a post-processing volume under the **Global Illumination** settings, and this will partly affect the indirect lighted areas.

- **Movable**: This is the highest quality light, but it also has the highest performance usage as well. It is a fully dynamic light that casts real-time shadows. It can change any of its properties during runtime, and this includes its position, rotation, color, brightness, falloff, radius, and every single property it has. None of the light they cast gets baked into the lightmaps, and currently, they cannot have any indirect lighting.

  As mentioned, it has an impact on the performance, but if you know how to control the rendered amount of meshes affected by the light and the triangle count of these meshes, then you will definitely be able to optimize your scenes to use real-time lights and shadows with the lowest possible cost.

  Movable lights should only be used for specific purposes with caution in order to save on memory. Unless you specifically need the light to actually move, then only use a stationary light.

  In fact, Unreal Engine 4 made it very easy to recognize light types in its viewport. In case you have lots of lights that cover your scene, you don't only have to recognize their colors from the gizmo shape, but you can also recognize some of the mobility status. Regardless of the color type or shape, it will always has a single icon if it is a **Static** or a **Stationary** light, while it will hold a small navigation crosshair gizmo if it is a **Movable** light.

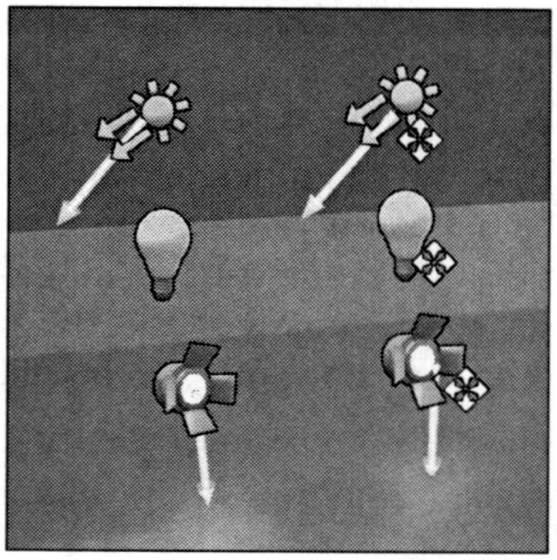

There is no hidden and tricky way to get a moveable light. In fact, any light in the Mods menu can be a movable dynamic light, just by switching its **Mobility** to be **Movable**. In the following table, you will see the difference between the three main light mobility types and their impact on performance versus quality:

	Static	Stationary	Movable
Quality	Medium	High	High
Performance cost	Low	Medium	High
Mobility	Low	Medium	High

The light settings

Regardless of the light source type, all of them have some parameters in common. After selecting any of the light sources from the scene view, by navigating to the **Details** panel, you will find a section called **Light Settings**, where you can find all the basic options required to change the size, feel, and look of a light effect in the scene. Here are a list of those light settings that will change the visual looking of your light sources:

- **Intensity**: The intensity is the value that controls how much energy the light outputs to the scene (the energy of the light photons). If you set the intensity of a light (Point Lights or Spot Lights emulate manufactured light sources, while the Directional Light emulates the sunrays), then the intensity value is measured in **lumens**, where 1,700 lumens (Unreal's light units) correspond to a 100 Watts light bulb.

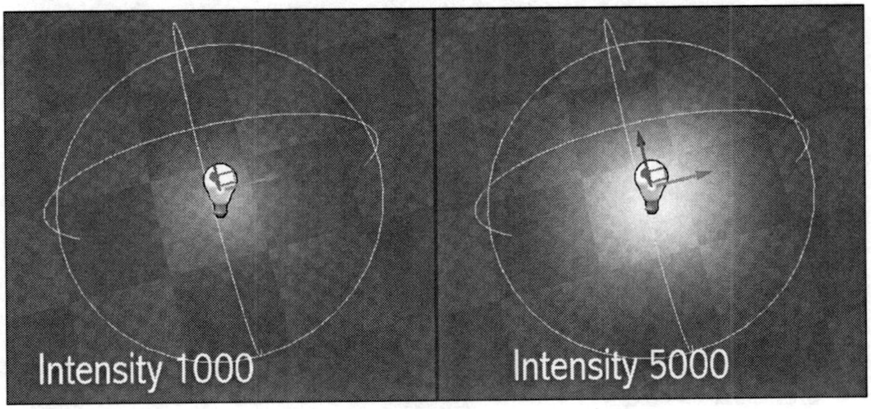

- **Light Color**: It is the most important value, not only because it changes the look but because it makes the design process easier. The **Light Color** is the color of the light. Once you set the value to any color, you will find that the light gizmo billboard on your scene has been changed to match the color you picked. This smart process makes it easy for you to select your light sources while having lots of lights lighting the scene.

- **Attenuation Radius**: Remember when we said that a light source can be scaled up or down with the scale tool like any other actor in the scene. This is because the extent of a light source is defined by the **Attenuation Radius**. This property only applies to point and spot light sources. This radius represents the outer bounds for the falloff of the light.

- **Source Radius and Source Length**: An object with a material that has some specularity usually will have some highlights when it gets exposed to a light source. These two values are meant to control the highlight shape. Typically, specular highlights have a spherical shape, but Unreal Engine allows you to extend this functionality further by modifying the radius and length of the specular highlight. This allows you to create unique area light shapes, such as light rods, that wouldn't be possible with point or spot light sourced lights.

  The light's **Attenuation Radius, Source Radius** and **Source Length** can be reasons for the frame rate to drop. So try to use these values wisely, and don't use them with a high value for the tall light sources you have. If it is necessary, use it for a couple of lights. It depends on the targeted platform at the end. Don't use them with more than one light with mobile targets.

- **Affects World**: This is a sort of disabling feature of the light, but it is kept in the scene hierarchy so that it can be enabled at some point later. Keep in mind that this value can't be controlled or changed via code or blueprints during runtime, as the light that has set it to true is considered as a deleted light. This feature is useful for testing the scene lighting without having to physically delete the lights that are added.
- **Cast Shadows**: This is a toggle true or false value that controls whether or not a light can cast shadows.

- **Indirect Lighting Intensity**: You can consider it a **Global Illumination** (**GI**) value of that light, as it will change the light contribution regarding the indirect lighted areas. Using a value of 0 will disable the effect, while a higher value will make the scene more lighted at these areas.

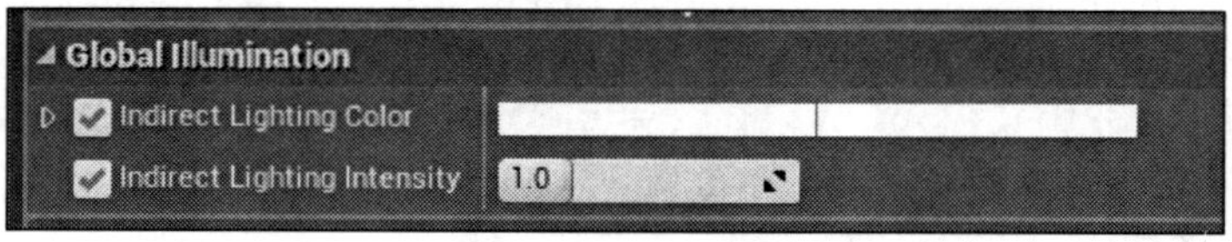

Light shapes

As you can see, lights can be classified based on different attributes. For example, they could classified based on the shadows emission status. They could be classified based on the status, dynamic or baked, or could be classified based on their mobility in the game, and their shape and emission type. Based on the shape and how the light is emitted from the source, Unreal Engine 4 has four types of light, and each of them has its own unique options and usage:

- **Directional Light**: The best description for this is that *it is the sunlight*. Usually, it is used to light an outdoor scene, as it works on simulating a light that is being emitted from an infinite distance.
- **Point Light**: This is is like a typical classic *light bulb* light that can emit light in all directions from its center point, and it is geometrically represented as a sphere.
- **Spot Light**: This is is like a normal manufactured spot. A spot light emits the light from a point source in a single direction. It is geometrically represented as a cone.
- **Sky Light**: This light is best used for open area lighting . It works on capturing the skybox of your level and uses its data to light the objects.

The Directional Light

As this light simulates a light source that is very far away and has infinite rays (like the sun), all shadows cast by this light will be parallel. It can be moved and rotated as its rotation has a huge effect on the final look of the scene:

Directional Light properties

The **Directional Light** has lots of unique settings, but it also has some shared settings with other light types. You might feel familiar with some of the properties, but a majority of them are brand new and unique to the **Directional Light** sources. Here is a list of the settings:

- **Light**: The **Light** section always includes the popular and shared options between the different light sources. If you try to change the light source type, or switch back and forth between two different light types, you will see that this section has the same parameters always:
    - **Intensity**: The total light power
    - **Light Color**: The lighting color
    - **Atmosphere sunlight**: This defines the location of the sun in the sky based on this light source's location
    - **Affects World**: This disables or enables the light effect (not accessible during runtime)
    - **Casts Shadows**: The shadows casting status of the light source
    - **Indirect Lighting Intensity**: This increases and decreases the indirect lighting caused by the light
    - **Min Roughness**: This is the minimum roughness effective for this light, which is used for softening specular highlights
    - **Shadow Bias**: This controls how accurate the shadows from this light are
    - **Shadow Filter Sharpen**: This is the amount of the sharpen filter applied to the shadows produced by this light source
    - **Cast Translucent Shadows**: This controls whether the light is allowed to cast dynamic shadows through translucent objects
    - **Dynamic Indirect Lighting**: This controls whether the light should be injected into the **Light Propagation Volume**
    - **Cast Static Shadows**: This controls whether the light should cast static shadows
    - **Cast Dynamic Shadows**: This controls whether the light should cast dynamic shadows
    - **Affect Translucent Lighting**: This controls whether the light affects translucency or not

- **Light Shafts**: In order to add more realism and depth to the scene, we can use light shafts that will make sure that the Directional Light source will simulate the real-world effect of crepuscular rays:
    - **Enable Light Shaft Occlusion**: This controls whether to occlude the fog or the atmosphere inter scattering with the screen-space blurred occlusion from this light
    - **Occlusion Mask Darkness**: This is the amount of darkness from the occlusion masking
    - **Occlusion Depth Range**: Everything closer to the camera other than this distance will occlude the light shafts
    - **Enable Light Shaft Bloom**: This controls whether to render a light shaft bloom for the light
    - **Bloom Scale**: This is the size of the additive bloom
    - **Bloom Threshold**: The scene color must be larger than this in order to create the bloom in the light shafts
    - **Bloom Tint**: The color to tint the bloom comes from this light's light shafts
    - **Light Shaft Override Direction**: This changes the light shafts' direction, and sets it to a direction that differs from the original light direction
- **Distance Field Shadows**: The **Distance Field Shadows** options might not work or give any results at all. It requires you to enable the **Generate Mesh Distance Fields** in the project settings under the **Rendering** settings. Perhaps restarting the editor as well. Listed here are the different types of **Distance Field Shadows**:
    - **Distance Field Shadow Distance**: This is the distance at which the ray traced shadow cascade should end.
    - **Light Source Angle**: This is the light source angle in degrees.
    - **Use RayTraced DistancedField Shadows**: Enable this option if you want to use the ray traced distance field shadow. They have less aliasing artifacts than the normal Shadow Maps.
- **Lightmass**: In order to save the performance, you will definitely need to use the lightmaps. In each light source, you can set some lightmass (lightmaps) per light source, which will help you increase or decrease the lightmaps' build time:
    - **Light Source Angle**: The angle that the directional light's emissive surface extends relative to a receiver.

- **Indirect Lighting Saturation**: The saturation value for the areas gets affected indirectly by the light. A value of 0 will completely desaturate this light in Lightmass at those areas.
- **Shadow Exponent**: This controls the falloff of shadow penumbras.

- **Cascaded Shadow Maps**: While **Cascaded Shadow Maps (CSM)** is the most common shadowing model for a more realistic and anti-aliased shadows, it is mostly based around the distance from the camera. There are some detailed settings per light source that you can set in order to have more control over the shadowing quality:
    - **Dynamic Shadow Distance Movable Light**: This controls the distance from the movable light in which you will see **Cascading Shadow Maps**. Beyond this, you will see only precalculated Shadow Maps.
    - **Dynamic Shadow Distance Stationary Light**: This controls the distance from the Stationary Light in which you will see Cascading Shadow Maps. Beyond this, you will see only precalculated Shadow Maps.
    - **Num Dynamic Shadow Cascades**: This controls the number of cascades that you should split the view frustum into for the whole scene.
    - **Cascade Distribution Exponent**: This controls how the cascades are distributed in the largest exponent or in a smaller exponent.
    - **Cascade Transition Fraction**: This controls the size of the fades between cascades and each other.
    - **Shadow Distance Fadeout Fraction**: This controls the size of the fade out region at the far extent of the dynamic shadow's influence.
    - **Use Inset Shadows for Movable Objects**: (Stationary Lights only) This allows you to use per-object inset shadows for movable components, even though the Cascaded Shadow Maps are enabled.
- **Light Function**: The **Light Function** is a type of material that can be applied to filter the light's intensity, which gives you some hard time to reach results, just using some material nodes:
    - **Light Function Material**: The light function material to be applied to this light
    - **Light Function Scale**: This scales the light function projection
    - **Fade Distance**: The distance at which the light function will be completely faded to the value of **Disabled Brightness**

- **Disabled Brightness**: The brightness factor applied to the light when the light function is specified but disabled based on the **Light Function Fade Distance**

The Point Light

This is a kind of a real light bulb, and it can emit light in all directions (equally).

Point Light properties

A light bulb will never act like a Directional Light source like the sun. In this section, you can find the different Point Light settings that you can tweak. While some options are shared with the Directional Light as we discussed earlier, the majority of the other parameters are unique and only used with the Point Light sources.

- **Light**: The **Light** section always includes the shared options between the different light sources as we discussed earlier in the Directional Lights section:
    - **Intensity**: The total light power
    - **Light Color**: The lighting color
    - **Attenuation Radius**: This bounds the light's visible influence
    - **Source Radius**: The radius of the light source
    - **Source Length**: The length of the light source
    - **Affects World**: This disables or enables the light effect (not accessible during runtime)
    - **Casts Shadows**: The shadow casting status of the light source.
    - **Indirect Lighting Intensity**: This increases and decreases the indirect lighting caused by the light
    - **Use Inverse Squared Falloff**: Enable this option if you want to use physically-based inverse squared distance falloff, where **Attenuation Radius** is only clamping the light's contribution

  - **Light Falloff Exponent**: This controls the radial falloff of light when the previous option is disabled
  - **Min Roughness**: This is the minimumin roughness effective for this light, which is used for softening specular highlights
  - **Shadow Bias**: The accuracy of the light's resulted
  - **Shadow Filter Sharpen**: The amount of the sharpen filter applied to the shadows produced by this light source
  - **Cast Translucent Shadows**: Enable this option if the light casts dynamic shadows through translucent objects
  - **Affect Dynamic Indirect Lighting**: This controls whether the light should be injected into the **Light Propagation Volume**
  - **Cast Static Shadows**: Enable this option if the light should cast static shadows
  - **Cast Dynamic Shadows**: Enable this option if the light should cast dynamic shadows
  - **Affect Translucent Lighting**: This controls whether the light affects translucency or not

- **Light Profiles**: The **Light Profiles** are a more effective way toward achieving realistic light effects from the Point and Spot light sources. It is a curve that defines the light intensity in an arc that will sweep around an axis:
  - **IES Texture**: The **IES Texture** is used for the light profile. IES files are ASCII though Unreal represents them as textures, they are not image files.
  - **Use IES Brightness**: This enable you to use the IES files brightness in Lumens to determine the brightness. When it is disabled, the light will use it's brightness to determine how much light to produce.
  - **IES Brightness Scale**: The size of the IES brightness.

- **Lightmass**: In order to save the performance, you will definitely need to use the lightmaps. As with all the other light sources, you can set some lightmass (lightmaps) per light source, which will help increase or decrease the lightmaps' build time.
  - **Indirect Lighting Saturation**: The saturation value for the areas that get affected indirectly by the light, a value of 0 will completely desaturate this light in Lightmass at these areas.
  - **Shadow Exponent**: This controls the falloff of shadow penumbras.

- **Light Function**: **Light Function** settings are a set of options that will be applied to filter the light's intensity, which gives you some hard time to reach results, just using some material nodes:
    - **Light Function Material**: The light function material to be applied to this light
    - **Light Function Scale**: This scales the light function projection
    - **Fade Distance**: The distance at which the light function will be completely faded to the value in **Disabled Brightness**
    - **Disabled Brightness**: The brightness factor applied to the light when the light function is specified but disabled based on the **Light Function Fade Distance**
- **Distance Field Shadows**: In order to get more shadowing details, you might need to use the **Use RayTraced DistanceField Shadows**, which was presented at UE4.5.
- **Use RayTraced DistanceField Shadows**: Enable this option if you want to use the ray traced distance field shadow. They have less aliasing artifacts than the normal Shadow Maps.

The Spot Light

A **Spot Light** emits the light in a shape (mostly, a cone shape):

Spot Light properties

Spot lights are like any other light sources in the Unreal Editor. They have different settings that can be set in order to change the final result of the light source and its behavior and impact over the scene elements.

- **Light**: The set of **Light** options are general light options that can be used with any light source types. The majority of the settings here are shared between the different light sources:
    - **Intensity**: The Total light power
    - **Light Color**: The lighting color
    - **Inner Cone Angle**: This sets the inner cone angle of the Spot Light
    - **Outer Cone Angle**: This sets the outer cone angle of the Spot Light
    - **Attenuation Radius**: This bounds the light's visible influence
    - **Source Radius**: The radius of the light source
    - **Source Length**: The length of the light source
    - **Affects World**: This disables or enables the light effect (not accessible during the runtime)
    - **Casts Shadows**: The shadow casting status of the light source
    - **Indirect Lighting Intensity**: This increases and decreases the indirect lighting caused by the light
    - **Use Inverse Squared Falloff**: Enable this option if you want to use physically-based inverse squared distance falloff, where **Attenuation Radius** is only clamping the light's contribution
    - **Light Falloff Exponent**: This controls the radial falloff of light when the previous option is disabled
    - **Min Roughness**: This is the minimumin roughness effective for this light, which is used for softening specular highlights
    - **Shadow Bias**: The accuracy of the light's resulted
    - **Shadow Filter Sharpen**: The amount of the sharpen filter applied to the shadows produced by this light source
    - **Cast Translucent Shadows**: Enable this option if the light should cast dynamic shadows through translucent objects
    - **Affect Dynamic Indirect Lighting**: This controls Whether the light should be injected into the **Light Propagation Volume**
    - **Cast Static Shadows**: Enable this option if the light should cast static shadows

    - **Cast Dynamic Shadows**: Enable this option if the light should cast dynamic shadows
    - **Affect Translucent Lighting**: This controls whether the light affects translucency or not

- **Light Profiles**: It is the lighting industry standard way of diagramming and curving the brightness and falloff in order to visually control the intensity of light as it would behave as a real world light:
    - **IES Texture**: The IES Texture is used for the light profile. IES files are ASCII though Unreal represents them as textures, they are not image files.
    - **Use IES Brightness**: Enable this option to use the IES files' brightness in Lumens to determine the brightness. When disabled, the light will use it's brightness to determine how much light to produce.
    - **IES Brightness Scale**: The size of the IES brightness.
- **Lightmass**: Here are listed some options that will affect the light behavior while baking the lightmaps to be used later at runtime:
    - **Indirect Lighting Saturation**: This is the saturation value for the areas that get affected indirectly by the light. A value of 0 will completely desaturate this light in lightmass at these areas.
    - **Shadow Exponent**: This controls the falloff of shadow penumbras.
- **Light Function**: The options here are related to the light behavior with the light function materials that will eventually have an impact on the light intensity:
    - **Light Function Material**: The light function material to be applied to this light
    - **Light Function Scale**: This scales the light function projection
    - **Fade Distance**: The distance at which the light function will be completely faded to the value of **Disabled Brightness**
    - **Disabled Brightness**: The brightness factor applied to the light when the light function is specified but disabled based on the **Light Function Fade Distance**

Distance Field Shadows:

- **Use RayTraced DistancedField Shadows**: Enable this option if you want to use the ray traced distance field shadow. They have less aliasing artifacts than the normal Shadow Maps.

The Sky Light

The Sky Light captures the distant parts of the scene and then applies it back again as a light to the scene. The Sky Light will capture the scene only when you rebuild the lighting.

Sky Light properties

As the **Sky Light** term sounds different than all other light sources, the sky light has it's own light options. But still share some of the **standard** options. Here are a list of the Sky Light options:

- **Light**:
  - **Intensity**: The total light power
  - **Light Color**: The lighting color
  - **Affects World**: This disables or enables the light effect (not accessible during runtime)
  - **Casts Shadows**: The shadow casting status of the light source
- **Distance Field Ambient Occlusion**: The **Distance Field Ambient Occlusion** (**DFAO**) is a method used for shadowing the **Movable Sky Lights**, where it generates a medium scale **Ambient Occlusion** from **Signed Distance Field Volumes** that are precomputed around each rigid object:
  - **Occlusion Max Distance**: This is the maximum distance that the occlusion of one point will affect another. The higher values increase the cost of the **Distance Field Ambient Occlusion**.
  - **Contrast**: The contrast applied to the computed Ambient Occlusion. A value of 0 means no contrast increase, while a value of 1 means a very high contrast increase.
  - **Min Occlusion**: This is useful to prevent the occlusion from going fully black when desired.
  - **Occlusion Tint**: The color of the occluded areas.

- **Sky Light**: The Sky light options are only available when you select a Sky Light source. It is mostly responsible for capturing the scene in order to do the sky lightening calculations.
- **Recapture Scene**: Press this button to recapture the image the Sky Light is using to light the scene.

Summary

Now, you have learned about the Unreal Engine's rendering process for one frame in a game and what makes the Unreal rendering system so powerful and more special than any other engine. We also learned how to use lights, and tweaking them became an easy process for you. We also covered the core differences between the different light sources. Both the Cascade and Material Editor are the most powerful features that support the Unreal Engine's final rendered images, and you have the main goal behind each of them.

With a brief introduction of the Material Editor, it is the time to get deeper into it, and learn how to produce some special materials. If you are ready now, let's move to the next chapter, where you will start learning how to make your surfaces look more believable and material defined.

2

Understanding the Working of Materials

In simple words, the material's main job is to provide the definition of a surface, while a material is a form of shader that can be used to specify parameters to render on a surface. A material is an asset type like any other asset that Unreal Engine has and supports. While the animation asset can be applied to skeletal meshes, the material asset can be applied to any mesh type in order to define the surfaces and control the look of the scene. Once the light rays from the light source hit the surface of a mesh, the material writes information to the G-buffer and the lighting shaders to perform calculations from this information.

A surface can be defined as either opaque or translucent, and it provides properties to control their color, roughness, transparency, and refraction, and a lot of other properties that are able to reproduce, emulate, and define any surface that you can find in the real world with the help of textures, bitmaps, and expression nodes. You can even invent new surface types that never existed.

By the end of this chapter, you will be able to:

- Use the Material Editor efficiently, and learn all about its panels, buttons, and functionalities
- Understand and edit any material properties or inputs
- Assign materials to the different surface types with a range of methods
- Use the Dynamic material instancing
- Use the Unreal Engine's powerful Layered Material
- Understand the construction of a node or an expression
- Build you first material in Unreal Engine

Understanding the Material Editor

The Material Editor is a handy way that Unreal Engine 4 provides for its users to easily create the most complex and outstanding materials. While a material should be written in a pure HLSL code, Unreal Engine's material editor provides you with a set of node/expressions that is needed to be connected together in order to construct a network that represents a material. Each node/expression is part of the HLSL code, which has its own functionality. Putting the different nodes together in one network will end up with a HLSL code in the backend of the engine that is represented by a material in the editor.

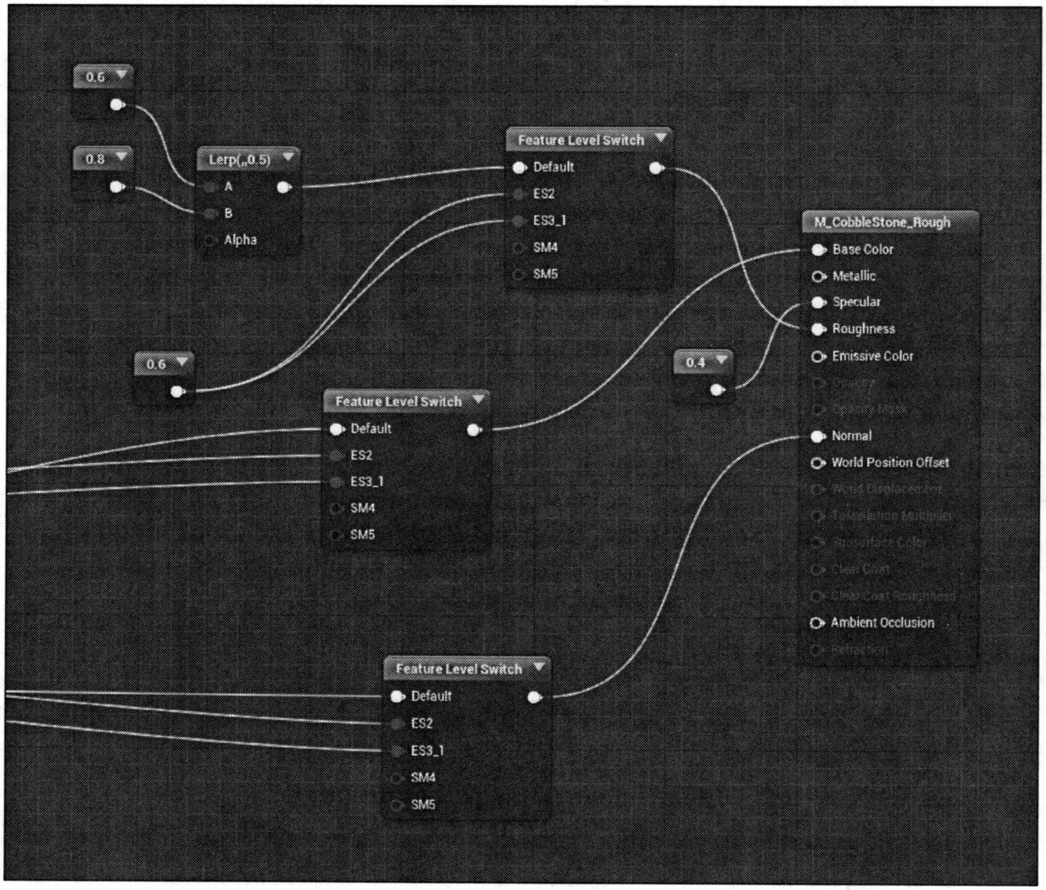

The easiest way to access the Material Editor is by double-clicking on one of your materials. If you don't yet have materials, you can just add a one from the context menu by right-clicking on the content browser and selecting **Material**.

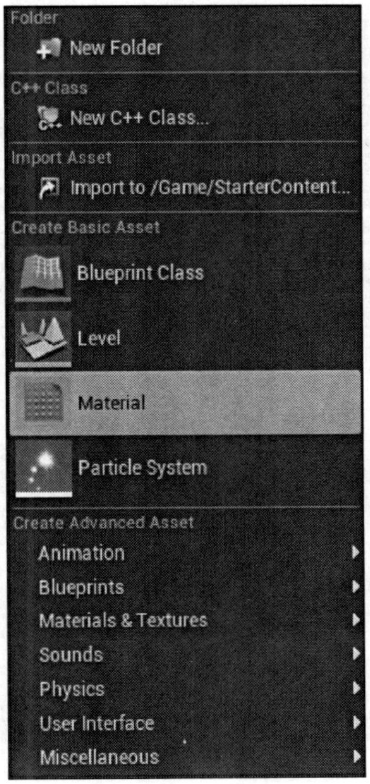

Once you open the Material Editor, you will see that it is divided into specific areas; each of these areas are designed to achieve a specific goal in the process of creating a material network:

- The top bar is used for debugging, saving, loading, or compiling materials.
- The top part of the left panel is a live display of the material. Consider it as a tiny viewport, where you can change its viewing properties.
- The lower-left panel is the **Details** panel, which lists all the properties of a node if selected, or the properties of the material itself.
- The middle area is the graph, where you add, move, remove, and connect the nodes.

- The right panel, which is called **Pallet**, is the nodes' home. In this panel, you can find all the nodes and expressions that can be used to build a material with Unreal Engine 4. If you want to get a larger area of the graph, you can close this panel, and you can still access all the nodes' list by right-clicking on anywhere in the graph area.

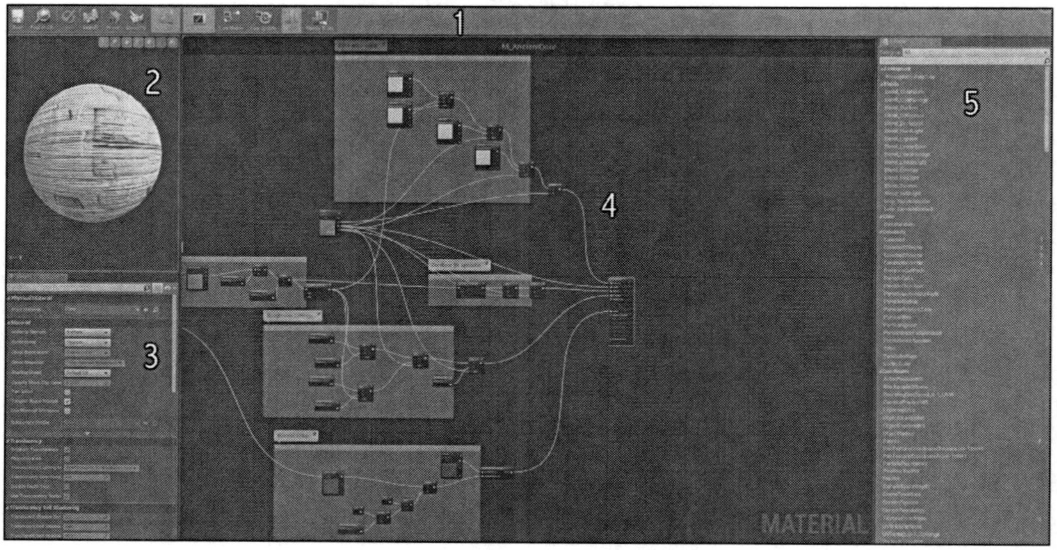

Increasing the efficiency with the Material Editor

As you might have noticed, as with all other Unreal's editors, there is too much stuff on the interface, so all of them are set in order to help you be productive and provide you with an easy way to reach the most common and required functionalities. Here are some of the important tips that you really need to understand and use in your daily material editing process in order to save time and produce a more organized, bug free, and readable material:

- **Adding comments**: While a material graph is just a huge spaghetti of connected nodes, you will need to somehow add details to it or areas to organize it. Comments are a great way to document what your material network is doing. Creating them will allow you to build a bounding box around a group of nodes titled with whatever comment you put. This can be simple and yet very important as you learn and develop more and more complicated materials. The more complicated the material is, the more nodes and wires will be cluttered and overlapped. Basic names and grouping can clean this up and make a material easier to read, understand, and edit.

Often, if there is a problem and the material isn't working correctly, it can be very difficult to track it through a messy material layout and figure out where the error lies. Adding a comment to the material graph can be done in the following two ways:

- Select some nodes that you want to create comments for, right-click on them, and choose **Create Comment from Selection** from the context menu. This will end up with a comment area and its text will be highlighted for you to change.

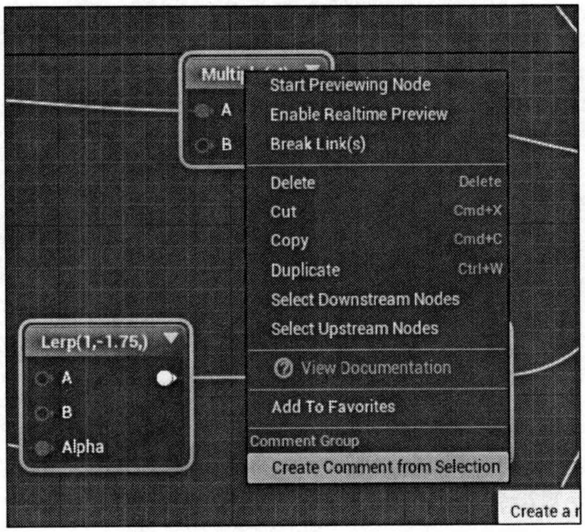

Select some nodes that you want to create comments for, and directly hit *C* from the keyboard in order to quickly add a comment.

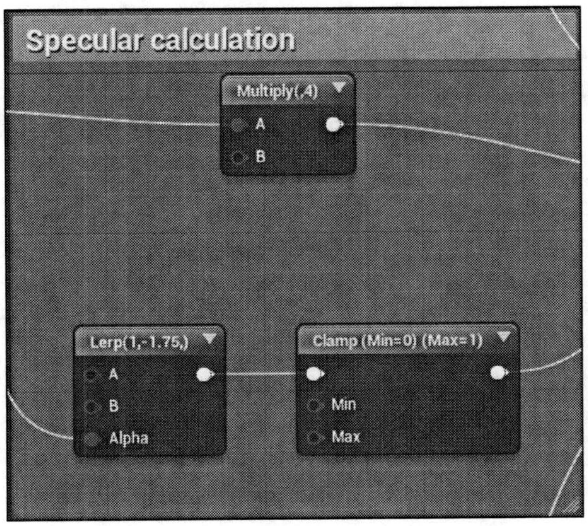

- **Adding descriptions:** Every material node contains a **Description** property named **Desc**, which is available in the **Details** panel. This property is a way to add a description of what that node is doing. Keep in mind that this type of a note is a per node note. Unlike the previous one, this one can't be added to several nodes at once.

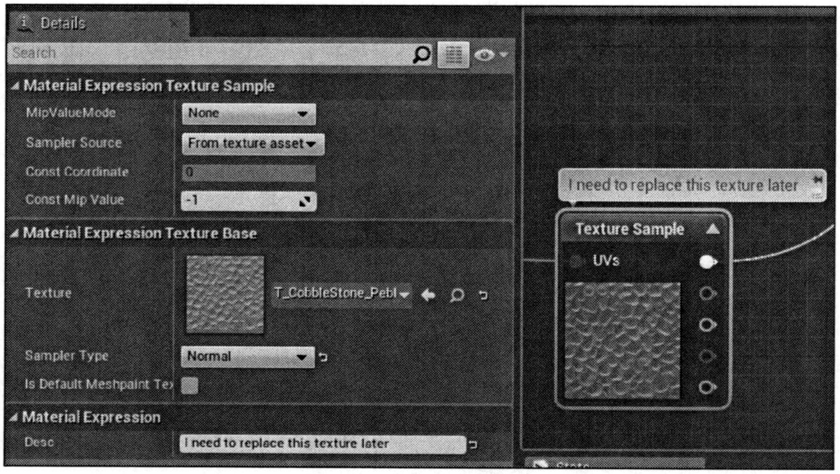

- **The live functionalities**: While the three options from the top bar seem to perform the same functionality, in fact, each of them has its own function and a different goal.

While making changes to a material network, it will be useful to get immediate feedback from each change (regardless of the change type or size) in real time. With these three features of the material editor, you'll be able to get a direct visual feedback of your changes.

The difference between these three options may not be apparent at first. The **Live Preview** displays the final material result on a mesh surface (mostly, a sphere, but you are free to change it). **Live Nodes** allow any constant changes that the nodes makes at real time. While **Live Update** allows you to have a per node shader recompilation, once you get some changes, these changes might be a creation of new nodes, deletion of nodes, node connections and disconnections, and changes in properties (yes, it has a performance overhead). This means that whenever a change is made, all the nodes will recompile themselves.

- **The search feature:** Have you ever thought of going crazy about building your material graphs? What if you ended up with a super complex and detailed material? Of course, this is something awesome regarding the quality. What about productivity?! How can you be super quick on editing, updating, or replacing nodes in such a material graph?

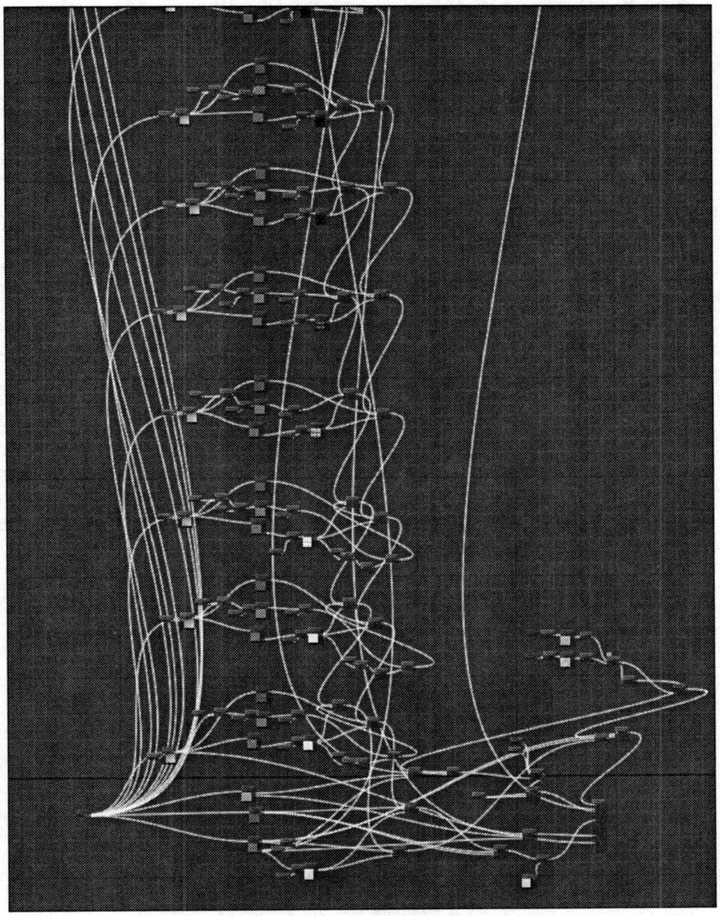

With the search panel presented in the Material Editor, it will be a super easy task. Once you know what exactly you are looking for, you can easily put your hands on it.

You don't have to search for the node name itself, but a hint or a piece of text related to it might be enough. You can not only look for the node name or a piece of it, but also look for a node **Desc** (remember point 2 of the efficiency?) and comments as well.

In order to display the **Search** panel, which is hidden by default, you need to navigate to the **Window** menu, and choose **Find Results** from it.

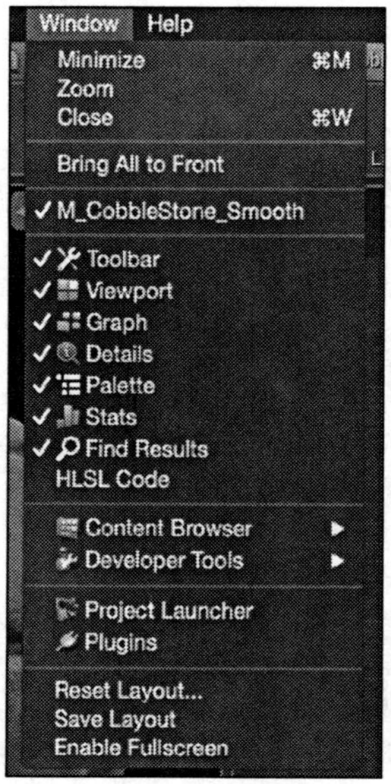

By just adding a piece of the node name or its description, the search panel will list all the nodes that share the search hint.

Double-clicking on the targeted result will directly zoom the graph to the proper node and frame it for you. It's never been easy like that!

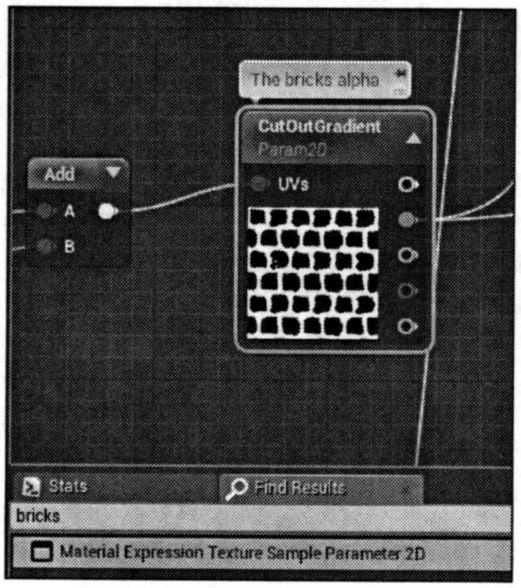

Dynamic material instances and material instances

Material instancing is used to change the visual look of a material asset (offline or at runtime via the dynamic nodes) without incurring an expensive recompilation of the material.

In order to be able to achieve this type of a concept, you have to be a very organized person; usually artists and developers build assets and materials without taking too much care of the names of the given assets or nodes. With such a target in mind (the dynamic material instances), you have to know the names that you are using very well. For example, in the following basic material graph, I gave the color node a name called **Base Color**:

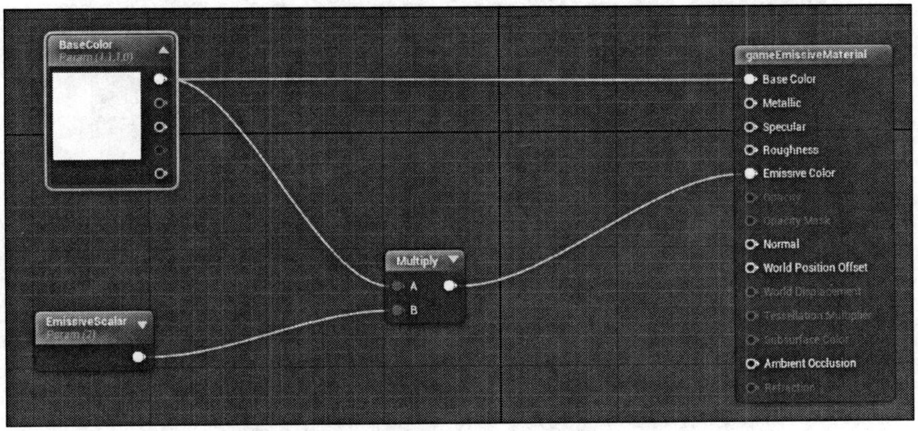

Now any time you want to make any changes at runtime in this material, you have to use the logic node called **Create Dynamic Material Instance** in order to create an instance of a given material. Of course, you need to set the mesh that holds the material as your **Target**.

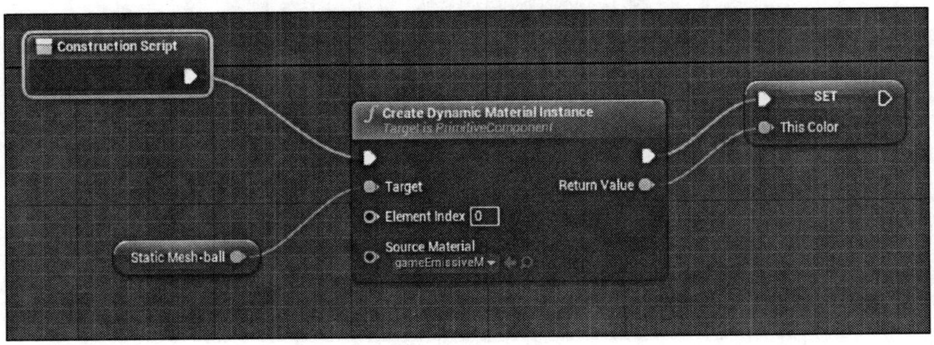

Now, you have the instance, and you are ready to make changes whenever you want. As in my example, I wanted to change the color of the **BaseColor** node that is connected to the **BaseColor** slot of the **BaseNode** material. At runtime, if you want to change that color to another color, you just have to node a logic node called **Set Vector Parameter Value**, and then connect the color to a Target, which is the name of the parameter that I was insisting to use (**BaseColor**), and finally, the new value of the color as a **Value**.

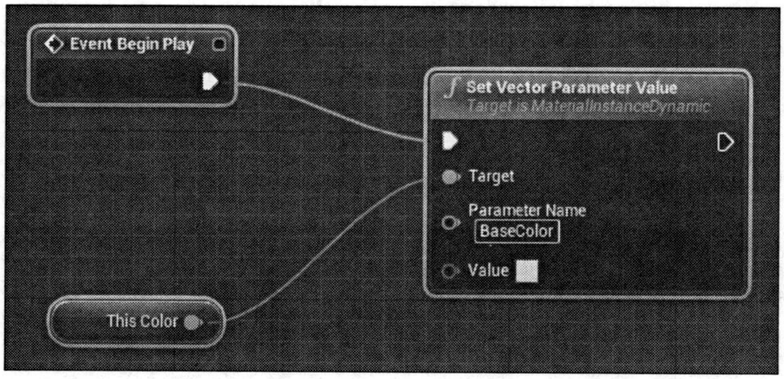

Is that everything?

Of course not. This is how to do it at runtime, but if you want to prepare it offline (during editing in the edit mode), then you will have to use a different type of a material asset called **Material Instance**, which can be found at the **Material & Textures** section of the **Add** menu in the Content Browser.

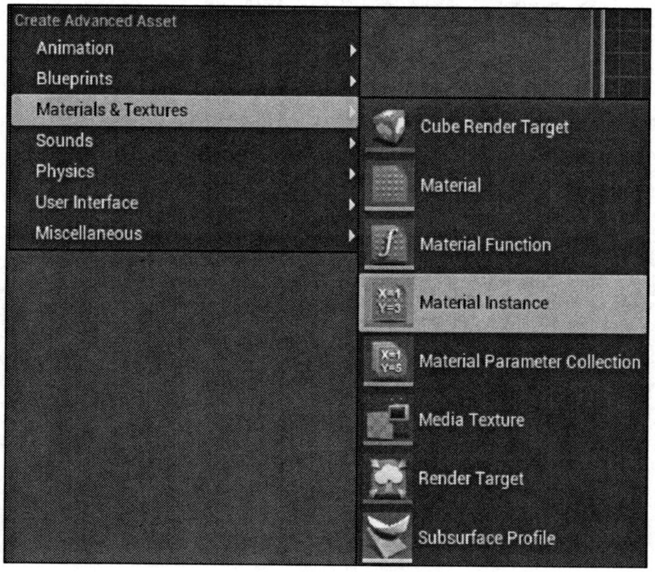

Getting acquainted with the properties and inputs of the Material Editor

Any material asset has a main material node, which you find in the material graph by default once you open it. The different behaviors of a surface is just a bunch of properties that you set on the material itself, as well as the way you connect to the Material Expression node network that defines the proper material behavior.

The final outcome of a material is determined by the node behavior that is hooked up to the material node pins (the main material node itself). Pins are automatically assigned default values. Pins that are highlighted will effect the current surface and faded out parameters will have no effect on the surface. The main material node has a lot of details by default, as well as a list of inputs that you need to fill in order to correctly define the surface. With this in mind, let's check both the value types in more detail.

Properties

Once you select the main material node, the left details panel will display all the properties that you can define.

> Note that with the consistent updates the engine gets, some of the properties listed here might disappear, or you might find some new properties in your engine version, that are not covered in this book.

With this in mind, let's see what properties are included in the main material node.

The Physical Material property

The **Physical Material** is associated with this material. The Physically-Based Shading Model has provided Unreal with a definition of physics properties. The physics material has no influence over how a material will look like eventually.

The Material

The main material node settings, while it looks simple, has a great impact on the material look. Using the following options in this section, you can plan the whole future of a material asset:

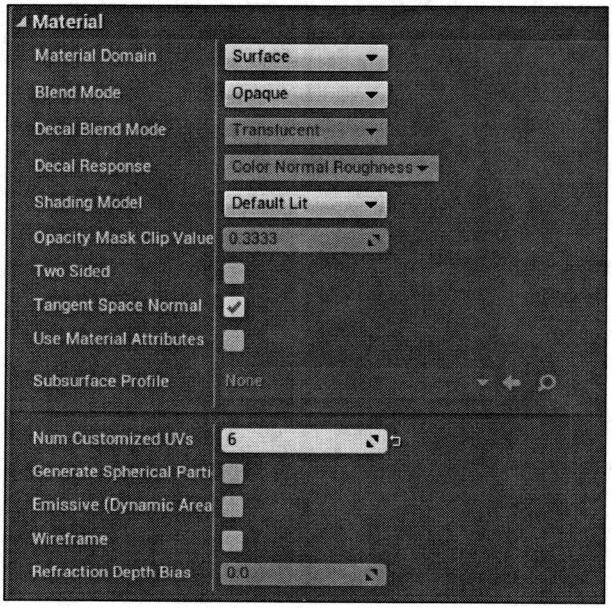

- **Material Domain**: This setting allows you to designate how this material is going to be used. Some materials require additional instructions for the rendering engine to consider (such as the decals). The **Material Domain** includes the following options:
    - **Surface**: A surface domain is a material applied to a geometric object (either a static or skeletal)
    - **Deferred Decal**: A projected quad applied to the geometric surface of the scene
    - **Light Function**: This setting is used when you are going to create a material for use with a light function
    - **Post Process**: This setting is used if your material is used as a post process material
- **Blend Mode**: This describes how the output of the current material will blend over what is already being drawn in the background. It allows you to control how the engine will combine this material (source color) with what is already in the frame buffer (destination color) when rendered.

The available blending modes are as follows:

- **Opaque**: The material will draw on top of the background. This blend mode is compatible with lighting, which means final color will be equal to the source color.
- **Masked**: The final color will be equal to the source color if `OpacityMask` is greater than `OpacityMaskClipValue`. It has the same properties as opaque but will not render any pixel that has lower opacity than the clipping value.
- **Translucent**: It is better to be used if the surface needed to have some transparency. This blend mode is *not* compatible with dynamic lighting.
- **Additive**: This blend mode is *not* compatible with dynamic lighting as the final color is equal to the sum of source color and dest color.
- **Modulate**: This blend mode is *not* compatible with dynamic lighting or fog, unless this is a decal material, as the final color is equal to the product of source color and dest color.

- **Decal Blend Mode**: This defines how to GBuffer channels that get manipulated by a decal material pass.
- **Decal Response**: This defines how the material reacts on DBuffer decals (affects look, performance, and texture/sample usage). Non DBuffer decals can be disabled on the primitive (for example, a **Static Mesh**)
- **Shading Model:** Shading models determine how material inputs (for example, **Emissive**, **Diffuse**, **Specular**, and **Normal**) are combined to make the final color:
  - **Unlit**: The material is defined by the **Emissive** and **Opacity** inputs only. It does not respond to light.
  - **Default Lit**: The default shading model.
  - **Subsurface**: This is used for subsurface scattering materials, such as wax and some skin types.
  - **Preintegrated Skin**: This is used for materials similar to human skin.
  - **Clear Coat**: This is used for materials that have a translucent coating on top such as a clear coat car paint or lacquer.
  - **Subsurface Profile**: This is used for materials similar to human skin. It requires the use of a **Subsurface Profile** in order to work correctly.

Keep in mind that, based on the **Shading Model**, some inputs are going to either be enabled or disabled in order to allow you to start connecting some logic to it.

- **Opacity Mask Clip Value**: This is the value which the **OpacityMask** input of masked materials will clip against per-pixel. Any value higher than **OpacityMaskClipValue** will cause the pixel to be drawn (opaque), and any value lower will fail and the pixel will be discarded (transparent).
- **Two Sided**: The normal will be flipped on back faces, which means that the lighting will be calculated for both the front faces and the back faces. This is used on foliage to keep from having to double up the number of polygons. Keep in mind that the two-sided materials do not work correctly with static lighting.
- **Tangent Space Normal**: This is calculated from the surface of the object, with the *z* axis always pointing directly away from the surface. World space normals use the world coordinate system to calculate the pixel angle, ignoring the surface's original orientation. Tangent space normal maps tend to look primarily blueish, while world space maps are more vividly rainbow-colored.
- **Decal Blend Mode**: This value defines the **Blend Mode** that will be used when the **Material Domain** property is set to **Deferred Decal**. The different **Blend Modes** are as follows:
    - **Translucent**: This will cause the decal to blend the **Base Color**, **Metallic**, **Specular**, **Roughness**, **Emissive color**, **Opacity**, and **Normal**.
    - **Stain**: This only blends the **Base Color** and **Opacity**. It is useful for decals that only change color, such as a dry spray paint on a wall.
    - **Normal**: This only blends **Normal** and **Opacity**.
    - **Emissive**: This only blends the **Emissive** and **Opacity** channels. It is usually used to make things glow.
- **Use Material Attributes**: Setting this value will cause the material main node to be condensed down to a single input that is named **Material Attributes**. It is useful for when you need to work with multiple **Layered Materials**.
- **Subsurface Profile**: This sets the **Subsurface Profile** used in the material.
- **Num Customized UVs**: This sets the number of customized UV inputs to display. The unconnected customized UV inputs will just pass through the vertex UVs.
- **Generate Spherical Particle Normal's**: If a Particle System uses this material, then this option produces surface normals that remain spherical as you rotate around that Particle System. It is highly recommended with volumetric Particle Systems because the sprites always rotate to face the camera, and this option will give you the illusion that a particle has an actual volume.
- **Emissive(Dynamic Area Light)**: If enabled, the material's **Emissive Color** is injected into the **Light Propagation Volume**.

- **Wire Frame**: This enables the wire frame of the mesh that the material is applied to.
- **Refraction Bias**: This offsets the depth of the refraction test. It is useful when refraction values cause unwanted nearby objects from rendering into the Material.

Translucency

Translucency is a set of transparency that allows light to pass through an object. The photons can be scattered at either of the two interfaces where there is a change in the index of refraction or internally. This means that a translucent medium allows the transport of light, while a transparent medium not only allows the transport of light, but also image formation.

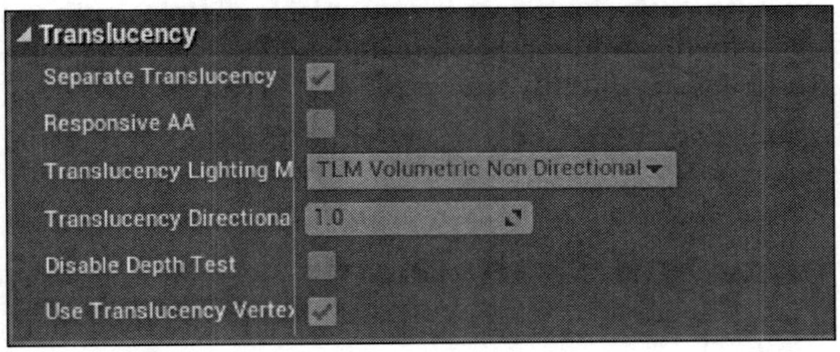

A brief description of the options available under Translucency are as follow:

- **Separate Translucency**: This defines whether the material should be rendered in the **Separate Translucency** pass or not.
- **Responsive AA**: By setting this property to true, the AA algorithm is used to provide more definition for the small moving objects (such as particles) that can sometimes get obliterated by anti-aliasing.
- **Translucency Lighting Mode**: This allows you to have control over the lighting mode used by **Translucency** in the material. This is especially useful for Particle Systems that make use of translucency, such as self-shadowing smoke or steam:
    - **TLM Volumetric Non Directional**: Lighting will be calculated for a volume, without directionality. Use this on particle effects, such as smoke and dust. This is the cheapest lighting method, and the material normal is not taken into account.
    - **TLM Volumetric Directional**: Lighting will be calculated for a volume with directionality so that the normal of the material is taken into account.

> Note that the default particle tangent space faces the camera, so use the console (this will be discussed in *Chapter 7, Render Performance Debugging*) in order to enable the show flag **bGenerateSphericalParticleNormals** to get a more useful tangent space.

- **TLM Surface**: Lighting will be calculated for a surface. Use this on translucent surfaces, such as glass and water. See *lit translucency* for more information.

- **Translucency Directional Lighting Intensity**: This is useful for increasing the influence of the normal on the lighting result for translucency. If the value is larger than 1, then this increases the influence for the normal, and if the value is smaller than 1, then this makes the lighting more ambient.
- **Disable Depth Test**: This allows the material to disable depth tests, which is only meaningful with translucent blend modes. Disabling depth tests will make rendering significantly slower since no occluded pixels can get Z-culled.
- **Use Translucency Vertex Fog**: If set to true, translucent materials will be fogged.

Translucency Self Shadowing

As mentioned earlier, when we defined translucency, do you think that it makes sense that if the object could cast some shadows on itself in those translucent areas?

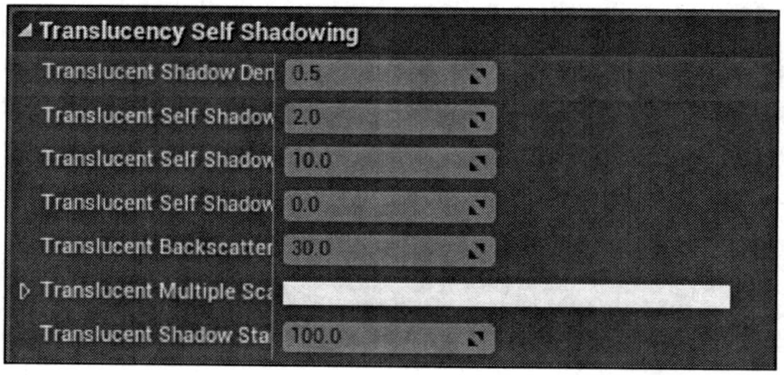

- **Translucent Shadow Density Scale**: This sets the density of the shadow cast onto other surfaces by the translucent material. You can consider it as a master scale for shadowing.
- **Translucent Self Shadow Density Scale**: This sets the density of the shadow this material casts on itself.

- **Translucent Self Shadow Second Density Scale**: This is a second self shadow density that can be set for variation. An internal gradient is created between this value and the **Translucent Self Shadow Density Scale**.
- **Translucent Self Shadow Second Opacity**: This sets the opacity value for secondary self shadowing. It is a way to scale the gradient effect between a self shadow and a second self shadow.
- **Translucent Backscattering Exponent**: This controls the backscattering that is used if the material uses the **Subsurface Shading** model along with **Translucency**. The larger the values, the smaller and brighter backscattering highlight it will result. Keep in mind that this value is only used in volumetric translucent shadows that come from a directional light - only a directional light!
- **Translucent Multiple Scattering Extinction**: This gives a colored extinction value for objects that have a volumetric translucent shadow.
- **Translucent Shadow Start Offset**: This is a world-space offset for the self shadow created in a translucent volume. The higher the number, the farther the shadow moves away from the lighting source.

Usage

You *can not only make* a material and then apply it directly to a mesh; you can also define what type of surfaces or visuals that will be using the newly created material asset. This is a good feature in Unreal Engine that makes the materials more responsive and optimized for a specific job from the *beginning*.

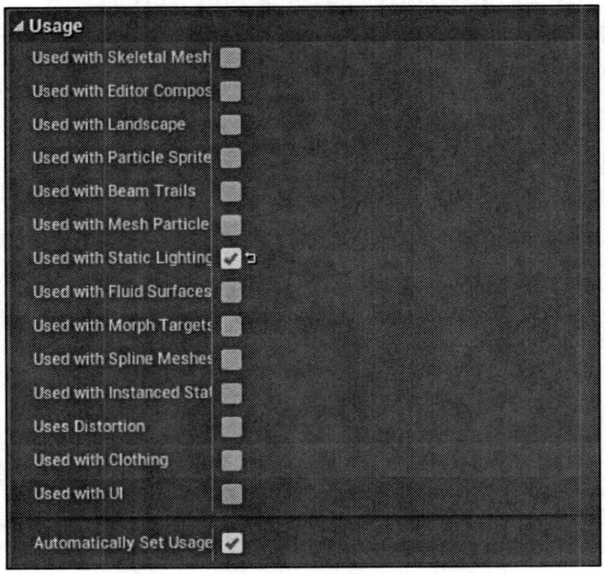

- **Used with Skeletal Mesh**: Set this property if the material is placed on a **Static Mesh**.
- **Used with Editor Compositing**: Set this property if the material is used with the editor UI.
- **Used with Landscape**: Set this property if the material is used on a landscape surface.
- **Used with Particle Sprites**: This is used if this material is placed on a Particle System.
- **Used with Beam Trails**: Set this property if the material is used with Beam trails.
- **Used with Mesh Particles**: Set this property if the material and its instances can be used with mesh particles. This will result in the shaders required to support mesh particles being compiled, which will increase the shader compile time and memory usage.
- **Used with Static Lighting**: Set this property if the material is considered for **Static Lighting**, such as if it uses an **Emissive** effect that will affect lighting.
- **Used with Fluid Surfaces**: Fluid surfaces are no longer supported in Unreal Engine 4. You might not find this option in future.
- **Used with Morph Targets**: Set this property if this material is applied to a **Skeletal Mesh** that has **Morph Targets**.
- **Used with Spline Meshes**: Set this property if the material is applied to **Spline Meshes**.
- **Used with Instanced Static Meshes**: Set this property if the material is going to be applied to **Instanced Static Meshes**.
- **Used with Distortion**: Distortion is no longer supported in Unreal Engine 4. You might not find this option in future.
- **Used with Clothing**: Set this property if the material is applied to Apex clothing mesh (Apex does not support some platforms, such as Mac).
- **Used with UI**: Set this property if this material and any Material Instances can be used with Slate UI and **UMG** (**Unreal Motion Graphics**).
- **Automatically Set Usage in Editor**: This checks whether to automatically set usage flags based on what the material is applied to in the Editor.

Mobile

If that material is going to be used in a mobile game, why not apply some options that might make it run with better performance?

- **Fully Rough**: This forces the material to be completely rough and, by doing so, saves a number of shader instructions and one texture sampler.
- **Use Lightmap Directionality**: If set to true, the material will use the lightmap directionality and per pixel normals. If set to false, lighting from lightmaps will be flat.

Tessellation

Tessellation is used to manage datasets of polygons presenting objects in a scene and dividing them into suitable structures for rendering. For real-time rendering, data is tessellated into triangles, and the main goal of using it is that it allows the details to be dynamically added and subtracted from a 3D mesh and its silhouette edges based on control parameters (usually, *the camera* distance).

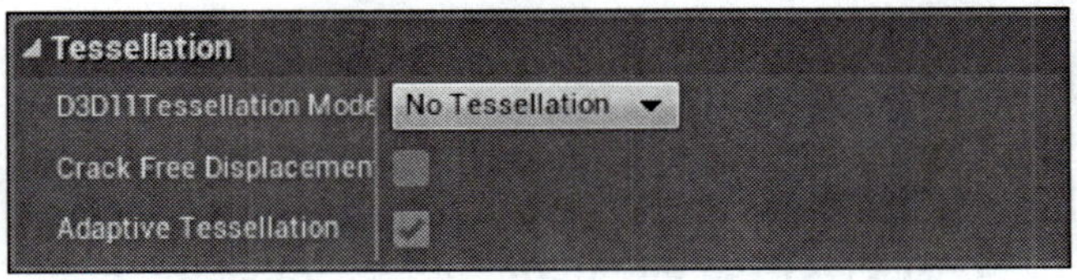

A brief description of the options available under Tessellation are as follow:

- **D3D11Tessellation Mode**: If the material supports tessellation, then this controls the type of tessellation that will be employed by your material, if any:
    - **No Tessellation**: The mesh will not tessellate. This is where you can enable or disable the feature for the material.
    - **Flat Tessellation**: This is a simple form of tessellation. This adds more triangles without smoothing the mesh.
    - **PN Triangles**: This is a simple spline-based tessellation, which is more expensive, but it is the best to display the most accurate and tiny details.
- **Crack Free Displacement**: This enables a displacement algorithm that fixes any cracks that may appear in the mesh. This is more expensive than the previous one.
- **Enable Adaptive Tessellation**: This tessellation method tries to maintain the same number of pixels for each triangle.

Post Process Material

Unreal Engine not only features post-processing effects over the final rendered frames, but also features very complex post-processing effects based on a material graph full of post-processing nodes. Here is a list of the options that should be set if the material is targeting a post-processing material:

- **Blendable Location**: If this material is used as a **Post Process Material**, and the material is used to modify the color of the **Post Process**, then this property allows you to control whether the material is calculated before or after the **Tonemapping**.
- **Blendable Priority**: This is a priority value that is used for any other materials that can be applied to the Post Process, using it will give you the opportunity to set the advantage between the different **Post Process Materials**.

Lightmass

The lightmass is the Unreal Engine's name of the prebaked Lightmaps methods used. We will discuss how to use them and how to build them in *Chapter 4, Precomputed Lights*. You have to know that even a material holds some parameters and options to define the quality of these prebaked lightmaps.

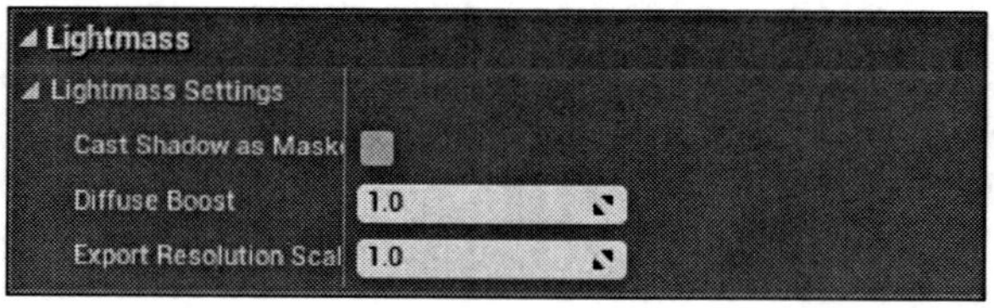

A brief description of the options available under Lightmass are as follow:

- **Cast Shadow as Masked**: If set to true, the lit translucent objects will cast shadows as if they were using the masked lighting mode. It works on producing sharper shadows on translucent objects.
- **Diffuse Boost**: This is a multiplier for the amount of influence the diffuse component of the material has on static lighting.
- **Export Resolution Scale**: Increasing this value will allow you to get more details (it is more expensive as well) as it is a multiplier for the resolution at which this material's attributes are exported.

Material Interface

The **Material Interface** options are mostly options related to the editor. This means that the end result of the material will not be affected at all.

The **Preview Mesh** property allows you to choose a **Static Mesh** to preview the material.

Thumbnail

Unreal Engine does not only care about the visual quality and look of the game, but it also cares about the visual appeal of the editor. Here is a list of the options that you may require in order to control the final look of the material's thumbnail in the content browser panel of the editor. For some people, it might seem like a simple set of options, while for others it might seem like a very specific set of options. In my personal view, I would say that you should work on a large project first, and then judge its importance!

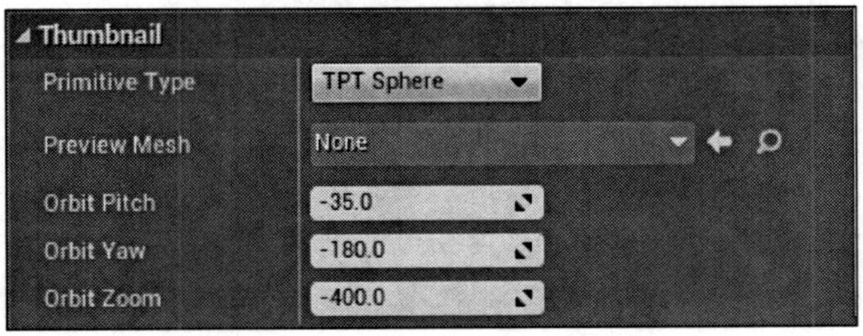

A brief description of the options available under Thumbnail are as follow:

- **Primitive Type**: This sets the shape primitive type that is used in the thumbnail preview
- **Preview Mesh**: If the **Primitive Type** is set to TPT **None**, then you can select a mesh that is used in the thumbnail preview
- **Orbit Pitch**: This sets the pitch of the orbit camera around the object
- **Orbit Yaw**: This sets the yaw of the orbit camera around the object
- **Orbit Zoom**: This is the offset from the bounds sphere distance from the object

BaseMaterial inputs

The main material node inputs are not hidden somewhere, or not triggered by selecting the node (as the case with the properties), all the inputs are visually displayed, and this is the first thing you will see after loading the material into the materials editor. With this in mind, here is a list of the different input types that are included in any main material node:

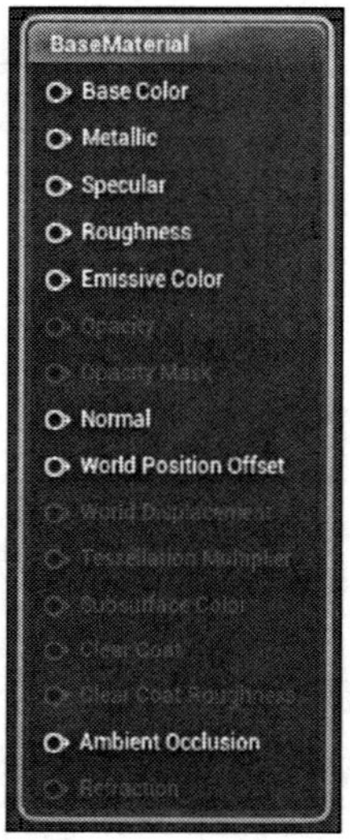

A brief description of the options available under BaseMaterial are as follow:

- **Base Color**: This represents the overall color of the material. It takes in a Vector3 (RGB) value, and each channel is automatically clamped between 0 and 1.

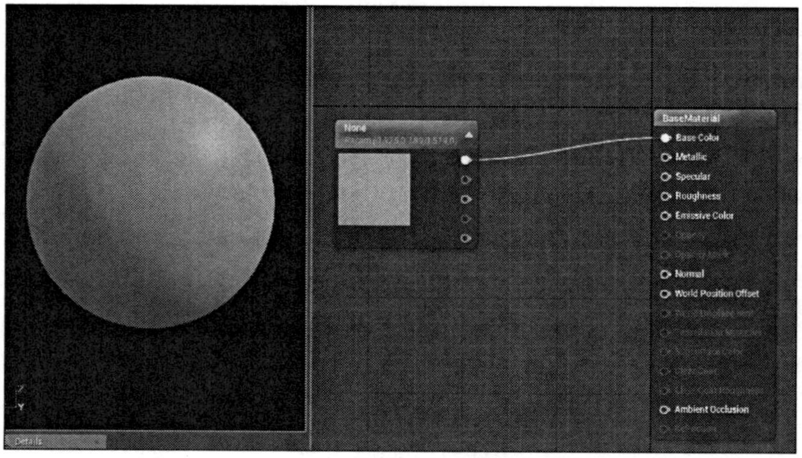

- **Metallic**: This controls how much the surface looks like a metallic surface. Nonmetals have metallic values of 0, while metals have metallic values of 1.0. For pure surfaces, such as a pure metal, pure stone, pure plastic, and so on, this value will be 0 or 1; not anything in between. When creating hybrid surfaces such as corroded, dusty, or rusty metals, you may find that you need some value between 0 and 1.

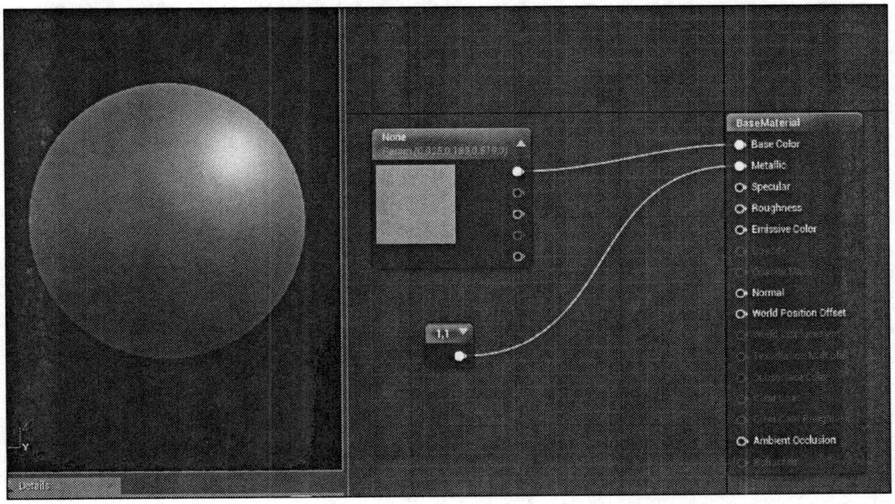

- **Specular**: By default, this has a value of 0.5 even if it is not connected to any other nodes, as this value is used for most normal cases. It has a value between 0 and 1 and is used to scale the current amount of specularity on nonmetallic surfaces. Keep in mind that if you set your surface as a metal with the previous value, then this value will have no effect on it.

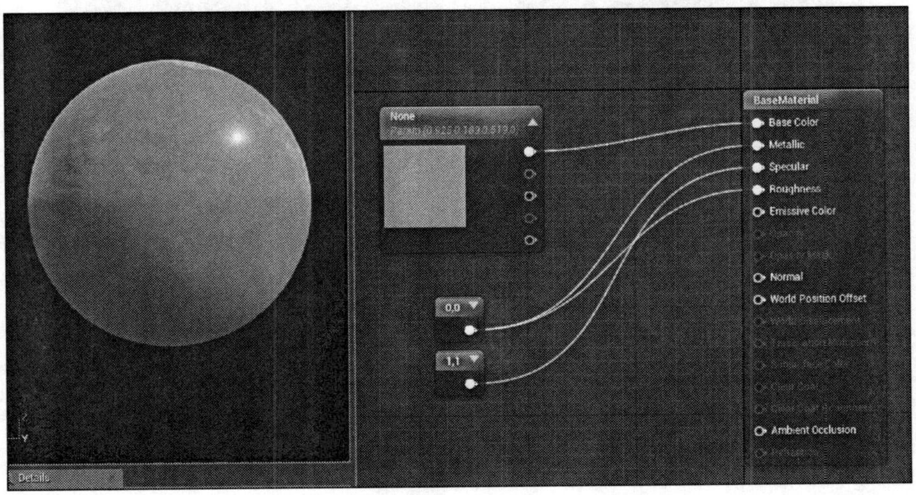

- **Roughness**: This controls how rough the material is. A rough material will scatter the reflected light in more directions than a smooth material. This can be seen in how blurry or sharp the reflection is or in how broad or tight the specular highlight is. A roughness of 0 is a mirror reflection (gives a smooth result), while a roughness of 1 is completely matte or diffuse (gives a rough result).

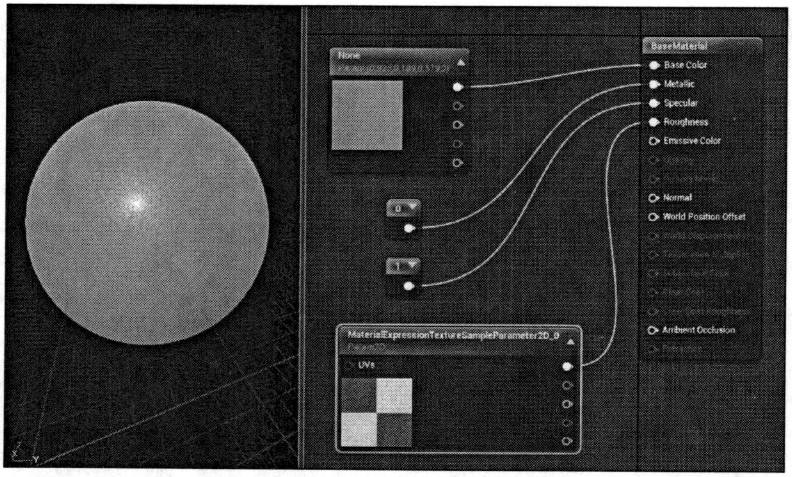

- **Emissive Color**: This controls which parts of your material will appear to glow because they emit the light.

> Keep in mind that values higher than 1 are allowed as long as HDR lighting is supported.

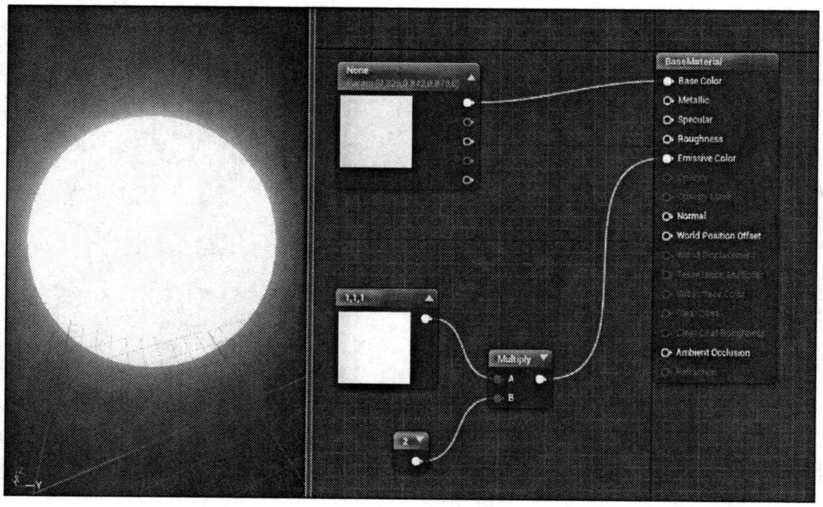

- **Opacity**: This can only be used when using the **Translucent Blend Mode**. It allows you to input a value between 0 and 1. While the value of 0.0 represents a completely transparent area, the value of 1.0 represents a fully opaque area.

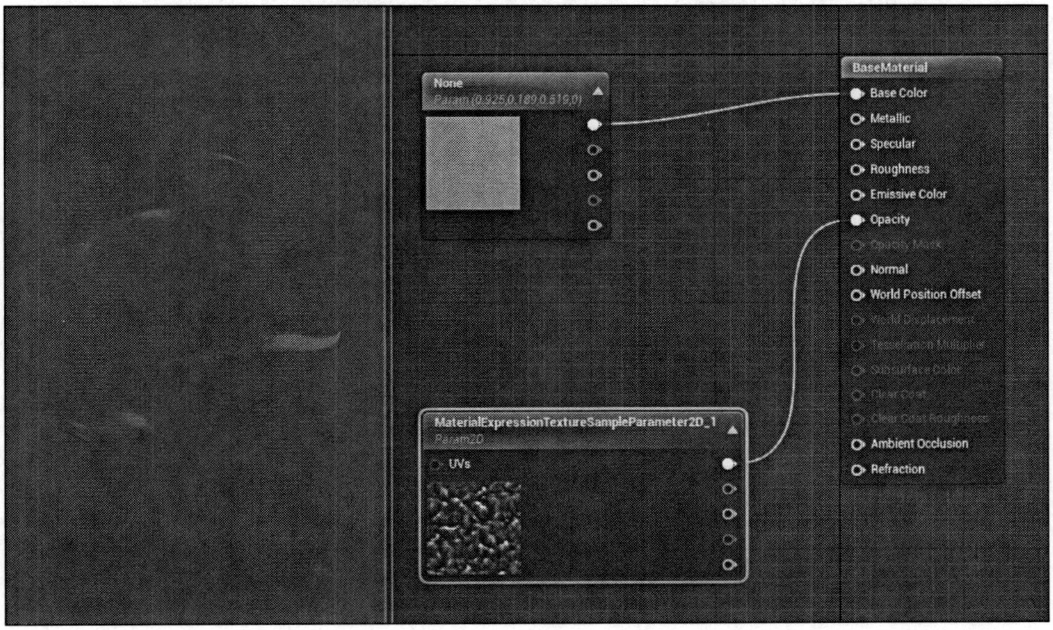

- **Opacity Mask**: This is similar to **Opacity** but is only available when using the **Masked Blend Mode**. It takes in a value between 0.0 and 1.0, but unlike Opacity, varying shades of gray are not seen in the result.

  When in Masked mode, a material is either completely visible or completely invisible. This is useful when creating materials, such as fences or wiring, that would normally require complex geometry.

- **Normal**: This takes in a normal map (texture/image), which is used to provide physical details to the surface by perturbing the "normal," or facing direction, of each individual pixel.

In the following screenshot, you can see the details caused using the normal map (the blue image), which provides tremendous additional details, and gives you the illusion that the surface contains more polygons than are actually being rendered. Normal maps are generated from the more advanced applications, such as modeling applications, for example, ZBrush or Mudbox.

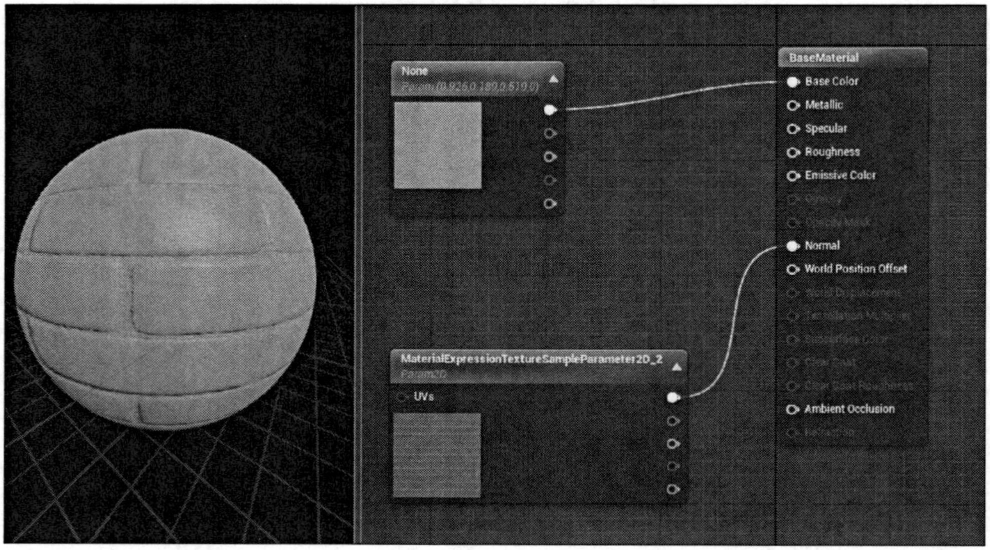

- **World Position Offset**: It allows the vertices of a mesh to be manipulated in world space by the material. It is useful for making objects move, change shape, rotate, and a variety of other effects. This is useful for things, such as fake waves or lava without the need to use any fluid surfaces (that is not supported by Unreal and hard to achieve).
- **World Displacement**: This works very much like the **World Position Offset**, but this uses **Tessellation** vertices instead of the base vertices of the mesh. In order to enable it, you need to enable the **Tessellation** property on the material as this input is based on tessellation.
- **Tessellation Multiplier**: This represents the amount of tessellation along the surface and allows more details to be added where needed. You need to enable the **Tessellation** property on the material in order to enable that input.

- **Subsurface Color**: The **Subsurface Color** input is only enabled when the **Shading Model** property is set to **Subsurface**. This input allows you to add a color to your material to simulate shifts in color when light passes through the surface. For instance, human characters might have a red subsurface color on their skin to simulate the blood beneath its surface.
- **Clear Coat**: Enable and use it in order to simulate multilayer materials that have a thin translucent layer of film over the surface of the material such as car paint.

  In addition to this, the Clear Coat Shading Model can also be used with either metal or nonmetal surfaces. The Clear Coat Shading Model opens up two new material inputs on the main material node.
- **Clear Coat Roughness**: This is the roughness for the clear coat layer.
- **Ambient Occlusion**: This is used to help simulate the self-shadowing that happens in crevices of a surface. Normally, it is connected to an AO map, which is often generated in 3D modeling applications, such as Mudbox, ZBrush, Blender, Maya, 3Ds Max, and so on.
- **Refraction**: This represents the index of refraction of the surface. This is useful for things, such as glass and water, which refract light that passes through them. You can use a value for the entire surface, or you can generate a map from a 3D application, just like the Normal map and the AO map.

> If you are a beginner to the topic of rendering and materials, then you can see that the amount of options can be quite daunting. It's best to just learn about **Base Color**, **Metallic**, **Roughness**, **Normal**, and possibly Ambient Occlusion, to begin with. These are the basics for the majority of solid assets. You can learn about the other paramaters later. The other options don't come into play unless you are creating a living thing (humans and so on) or something organic (plants and so on).

Applying and using materials

There are different ways to apply a material to a mesh or a surface, and based on the surface type, you can choose the method to use. In general, almost all the Unreal surface types accept applying materials in edit mode or during runtime via C++ code or the blueprint logic.

The most widely used methods are as follows:

1. Left-click and hold to drag the material from the content browser, and move your mouse toward the viewport that will produce a small icon representing the material. Once you are on the proper surface, you can release the mouse button, and this will directly apply the material to its main material slot.

2. With any mesh type (**Static**, **Skeletal**, or **Moveable**), after selecting the targeted mesh that will trigger the details panel to display all its components and properties, you can use the materials element slot located in the properties for the mesh.

3. With any mesh type (**Static**, **Skeletal**, or **Moveable**), you can right-click on it, choose **Properties** from the context menu, and then you can continue by applying the material to the material's element slots.
4. With any mesh type (**Static**, **Skeletal**, or **Moveable**), you can simply find the material's element slots in its editor. For example, the **Static Mesh** editor is where you can import and edit the import settings of a **Static Mesh**; Persona Skeletal Mesh editor is where you can import and edit the animated mesh.
5. With a brush surface, by selecting the material from the content browser and clicking on the brush surface that will activate its details panel, you will find a button called **Apply Material**. Click on it to directly apply the material to that brush.

> Note that this method might not be available anymore as the engine evolves.

Here are important notes about assigning materials:

- If you want a material to become the default for a given Mesh, make sure to set the material in that Mesh's properties, either by right-clicking on it and choosing **Properties** from the Content Browser, or by double-clicking on the Mesh in the Content Browser and setting the material using the asset editor (such as the Static Mesh editor or Persona) that appears.
- Changing a material from an asset editor or from the Content Browser will affect the asset itself. While changing it using the details of a Mesh already placed in the scene hierarchy will only affect the placed copy of the Mesh as an individual instance of the material asset.

The material nodes

Nodes are the units used to a material's network graph in **Unreal Engine 4**. Each material expression is just a black box/rectangle that performs a single operation on one or more inputs, and then outputs the results of that operation to be used next with a different black box (node/expression).

Certain material expressions are parameters, which means that their values can be modified in **Edit** mode or at runtime in some cases. These nodes can have a unique name, via the **Parameter Name** property in the **Details** panel (among lots of other parameters that varies based on the node type). This name will be useful later at runtime when the material starts to create instances (if your gameplay logic works that way).

While each node or expression serves a different goal and has different inputs, outputs, and properties, but all of them share the same base structure, which is shown in the following screenshot:

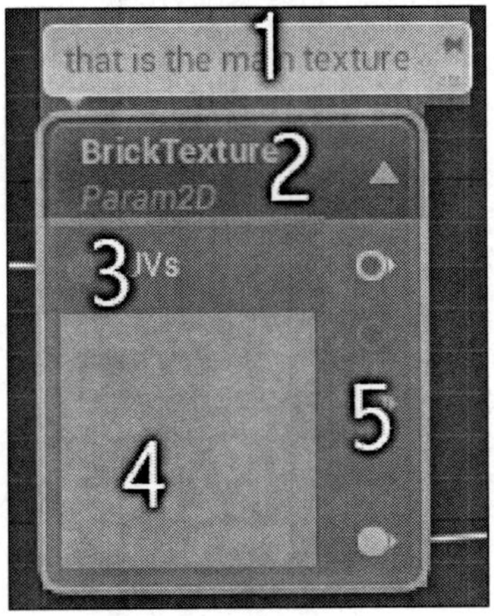

The numbers in the preceding image highlights the following elements:

- **Description**: All material's expressions have a common **Desc** property. It is just a piece of text entered in this property that will be displayed in the Material Editor just above the expression in the workspace.
- **Title bar**: This displays the given name (by yourself) and/or the pertinent information about the properties of the material node type.
- **Outputs:** This links the results of the material expression operation.
- **Preview:** This displays a preview of the value(s) that are output by the material expression. It is automatically updated when the real-time update is enabled. You can manually update the preview using the Spacebar.
- **Inputs**: This takes in the value(s) to be used by the material expression.

In order to learn about the different types of the hundreds of expressions and nodes supported by Unreal Engine 4, you can refer to the Unreal documentation's at `https://docs.unrealengine.com/latest/INT/Engine/Rendering/Materials/ExpressionReference/index.html#expressionindex`.

The powerful layered material

The most raw definition of this is that it is just materials within materials.

It is a method to create a single material that has a series of layers, and each layer is an independent sub-material.

Using the **MakeMaterialAttributes** node and **BreakMaterialAttributes** node, functions can also be used to define a material, entirely in a function. Then, by bringing these functions into a final material, you have a layered material.

You can consider Layered Materials to be an extension of Material Functions in the Material Editor. Functions, as you may recall, are self-contained node networks that perform a specific operation, just like any other node that has its different purpose.

In the preceding image, we created a simple chrome material in a Material Function, via a Make Material Attributes node. This function can now be used as a Material Layer and can be blended with other Material Layers.

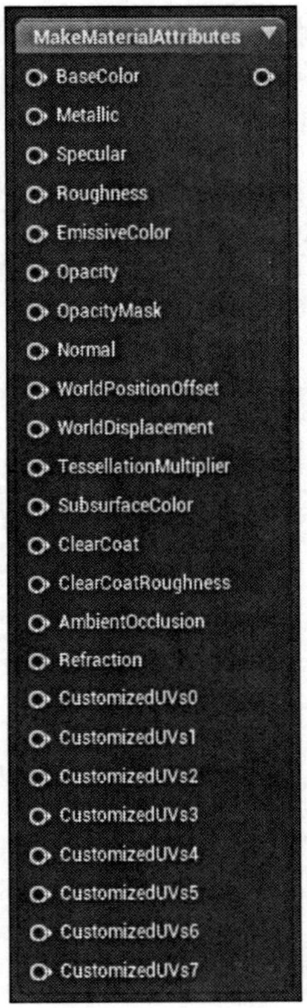

> Keep in mind that a Layered Material (or in a more formal way, a Make Material Attribute) cannot be applied directly to any mesh; you need to bring your Material Layer functions to a new material, which can then be applied to your objects.

So, in order to create and apply a Layered Material, you need to perform the following steps:

1. Create your new material asset in the content browser.
2. Create a new Material Function in the Content Browser, and copy/paste all your Material Function nodes into it.
3. Connect it to a **MakeMaterialAttributes** node, and connect it to the **Function** output.

4. Drag and drop the function from the Content Browser into the Material Editor.
5. Use the Material Layer Blend functions to blend multiple Material Layers together.

Your final object can now have multiple Material Layers distinctly blended across its surface.

The benefits of using Layered Materials are that they are reusable as they utilize the Material Functions. This allows you to set up a library of material archetypes, or materials that define a basic real-world surface type.

They also allow you to create the most complicated material and keep it much more manageable for future updates.

In the **Pallet** panel of the Material Editor, there is a list of various Material Layer Blend functions. In order to give you the ability to make a huge variation of behaviors, these functions are different and cover a wide range of usability requirements. These functions are as follows:

- **MatLayerBlend_AO**: This blends an Ambient Occlusion map over the surface
- **MatLayerBlend_BaseColorOverride**: This enables the Base Color replacement
- **MatLayerBlend_BreakBaseColor**: This outputs the Base Color from the Material Layer
- **MatLayerBlend_BreakNormal**: This outputs the Normal from the Material Layer
- **MatLayerBlend_Decal**: This blends a decal sheet over the Material using the 2nd UV channel
- **MatLayerBlend_Decal_UV3**: This blends a decal sheet over the Material Layer using the 2nd UV channel
- **MatLayerBlend_Emissive**: This blends an Emissive texture over the Material Layer
- **MatLayerBlend_GlobalNormal**: This blends a Normal texture over the Material Layer
- **MatLayerBlend_LightmassReplace**: This replaces the Base Color in lightmass in order to allow changes in the indirect lighting maps
- **MatLayerBlend_ModulateRoughness**: This multiplies the Material Layer's **Roughness** by an incoming texture
- **MatLayerBlend_NormalBlend**: Using a mask texture, this blends the normal texture across the surface and controls where the normal will appear via that mask texture

- **MatLayerBlend_NormalFlatten**: This diminishes the effect of the normal map
- **MatLayerBlend_RoughnessOverride**: This replaces the roughness texture of a Material Layer
- **MatLayerBlend_Simple**: This provides a simple linear interpolation "Lerp", which is a blending solution for two Material Layers
- **MatLayerBlend_Stain**: While blending the Top Material over the Base Material, the Base Color and Roughness values from the Top Material are the ones to be used
- **MatLayerBlend_Standard**: This blends all the attributes of the two Material Layers
- **MatLayerBlend_Tint**: Tinting the Material Layer by inputting a tint color and a mask to control the tint's location
- **MatLayerBlend_TintAllChannels**: This is a typical tint, but affects specular
- **MatLayerBlend_TopNormal**: This gives the priority to the normal of the Top Material after it blends all the attributes of both the Materials

A material network example

Now with all of this in mind, let's see how easy it is to build an outstanding wall bricks material. After creating a new material asset in the Content Browser, you open it in the Material Editor:

1. Add a **Texture Sample** node that allows you to load a texture file, which is basically an image. Use this node to load the diffuse image of the material. Finally, connect it's output color to the Base Color of the main material node.
2. By adding a **Multiply** node that works on multiplying the Texture to a floating value (0.5), and connecting the final result of the **Multiply** node to the **Specular** input of the main material node, you'll be able to make it a bit shiny.
3. Duplicate the previous node (the Texture sample), and set its properties to load the normal map that you generated from your 3D application. Then, connect this node to the **Normal** input of the main material node.
4. By adding a **Vector Parameter** node, setting its color to something between gray and white, and connecting it to the **Roughness** input of the main material node, you'll be able to control the roughness value via colors and not via floats as usual.
5. Finally, save your material and see how it looks in the **Preview** panel, or by applying it to an object with one of the methods that you already know.

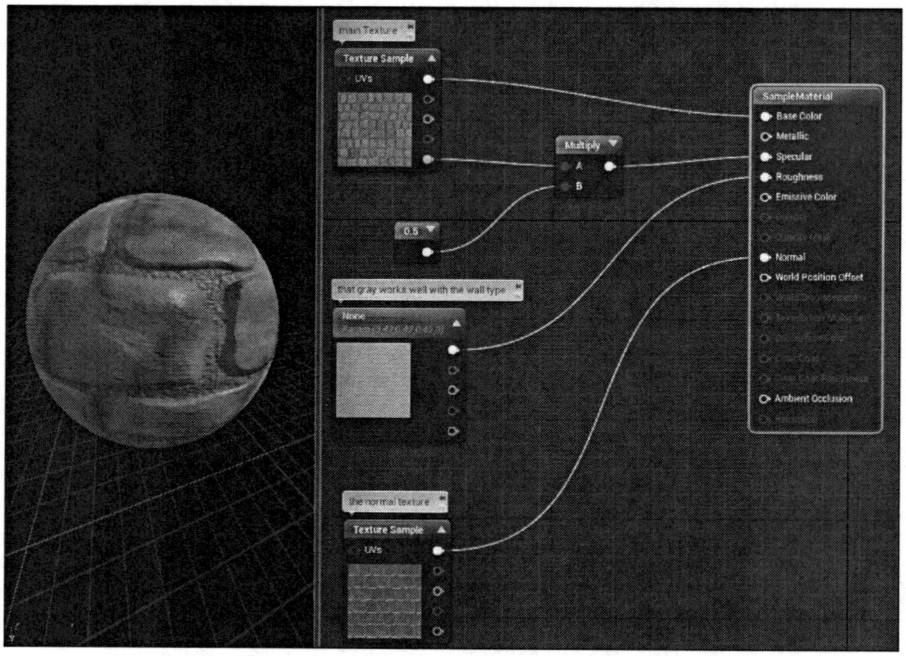

In case you are not happy to see the material wrapped on a spherical surface, which in some cases does not help you visually understand it, you can always switch between the different meshes to be used as a preview. Just select the one you want from the top mini bar of the preview panel of the Materials Editor.

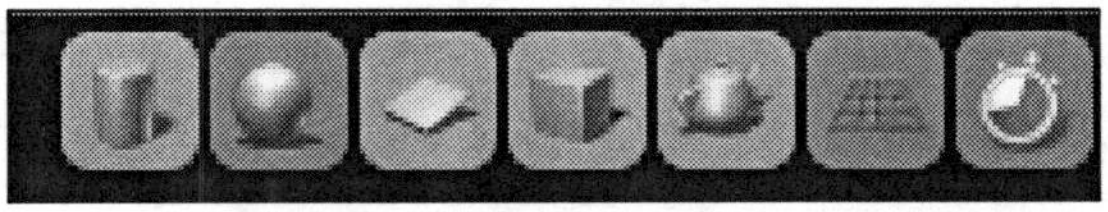

Summary

You have now learned the Unreal Engine's powerful Material Editor in detail, how to use it, and how to make the best use out of it. With the power of some hidden small features, such as comments or descriptions, you will be able to build organized networks for yourself or your team members. Knowing that the main material node is something essential, as it is the center pillar of the materials you are going to make, understanding its properties and inputs will give you the power of imagination to start building a whole new world of materials.

Understanding the Layered Material is something essential nowadays, as it is the most interesting and visually appealing material in your favorite game and is probably built using a layered material concept.

Getting your hands on the most common and powerful nodes and material expressions will give you the opportunity to start combining stuff together to build new materials that you've never been able to build before.

With all of this in mind, you can learn about cascade and Particle Systems in Unreal Engine in the following chapter. With your knowledge of the Material Editor, you will learn how to use materials to serve the Particle Systems' visual look. However, it is heavily recommended that you settle down for a couple of days and work on building pretty much all the materials you have in mind, moving forward after you have got used to the process of creating material networks.

3

Cascade – a World Made of Particles

Games without particles! I don't think so!

Have you ever imagined someone in a shooting game without actual gunfire, or even a cutscene where it is raining without drops? It would spoil the whole experience.

In Unreal Engine, there is a very powerful, modular particle editor called **Cascade**. It is capable of handling anything from a simple demo, to a game project, or something more cinematic. This editor will give you the opportunity to create (or even invent) outstanding visual effects that fit the real world or even more beyond your imagination.

What makes Cascade more interesting than any other particle editor is its modular-based system with real-time feedback. With this, while editing you can see the final results, there's no need to wait, patch, or even run the game to test it. This gives you the chance to create and prototype a wide variety of unique effects efficiently within a few minutes, or seconds in some cases.

By the end of this chapter, you'll be able to:

- Use the Cascade editor efficiently and know all its panels, buttons, and functionalities
- Understand the different types of modules
- Understand the core of building the most complex Particle Systems
- Understand how to use a particle blueprint in a game
- Get the best performance by optimizing the Particle Systems
- Build a Particle System example

The Cascade editor

As introduced earlier, Cascade is a property editor in Unreal Engine that is responsible for creating and editing the Particle Systems. Accessing Cascade is as easy as accessing the Material Editor. By double-clicking on a Particle System asset in the Content Browser, you will be able to launch Cascade in a second:

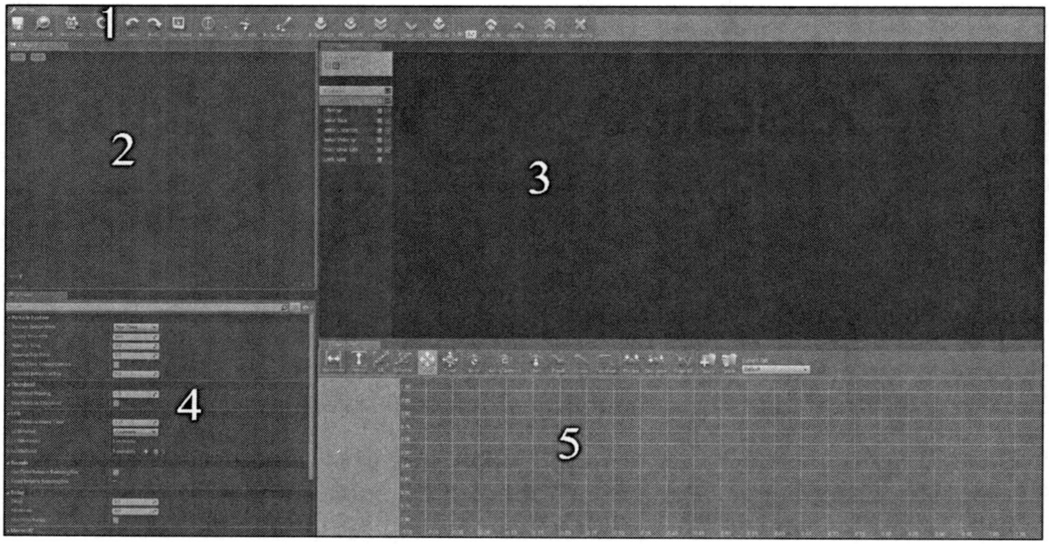

Once you have launched the editor, you'll find that it is designed in the same way as all the other Unreal editors, and the different areas give you easy access to all the required functionalities to achieve the goal of that editor. The good thing about Unreal is that everything you want is just in front of your eyes, and you don't have to navigate through tons of huge menus with tons of submenus. The main areas that the Cascade editor is comprised of are discussed in the following sections.

The toolbar

The toolbar contains the buttons for the most common tools, functionalities, and visualization orders that you'll need all the time. Some of the buttons might be hidden in the UI due to the screen size, but in general, the toolbar always contains the following buttons:

The description of the buttons in the toolbar is as follows:

- **Save**: This saves the changes in the Particle System.
- **Find in CB**: This points to the current Particle System asset in the Content Browser.
- **Restart Sim**: This restarts the simulation in the Viewport panel.
- **Restart Level**: This restarts the Particle System in general, which means not only in the Viewport, but also in all the instances in the level.
- **Undo**: This undoes the previous operation.
- **Redo**: This redoes the previous undone operation.
- **Thumbnail**: This saves the current frame from the Viewport panel's camera as the thumbnail image for the Particle System to be displayed in the Content Browser.
- **Bounds**: This toggles the on/off display of the bounding shapes of the current Particle System in the Viewport panel.
- **Origin Axis**: This toggles the On/Off origin axis in the Viewport panel.
- **Background Color**: This changes the color of the Viewport panel's background. It is black by default, but it is very useful if your Particle System is black in color, then by changing the background color, you'll be able to get a better understanding.
- **Regen LOD, Duplicating Highest**: LOD means the Level of Details (LODs), and this regeneration button works on regenerating the lowest LOD by duplicating the highest LOD.
- **Regen LOD**: This regenerates the lowest LOD using values that are a preset percentage of the highest LOD's values.
- **Lowest LOD**: This loads the lowest LOD.
- **Lower LOD**: This loads the next lower LOD.
- **Add LOD before current**: This adds a new LOD before the current one.
- **Current LOD**: This selects the current active LOD, if you have set up LODs.
- **Add LOD after current**: This adds a new LOD after the current one.
- **Higher LOD**: This loads the next higher LOD.
- **Highest LOD**: This loads the highest LOD.
- **Delete LOD**: This deletes the current LOD.

The Viewport panel

The Viewport panel is just a small viewport that is meant to give you a real-time visual feedback of the final look of the Particle System. As with any other viewport in the engine, it has some viewing options on the top buttons, just like the main level viewport in the Unreal editor. It is also responsive to the shortcuts, which means that you can still navigate in it in the same way you'd navigate in your level, using the mouse buttons, or even some shortcuts, such as hitting *F* to focus on the Particle System:

The viewing options include the following:

- **View Overlays**: This toggles between the different data readouts, which gives you a lot of information about the current Particle System:
    - **Particle Counts**: This shows how many particles have been emitted from each emitter in the current Particle System.
    - **Particle Event Counts**: This shows how many events have been triggered in each emitter in the current Particle System.
    - **Particle Times**: This shows how long each emitter of the current Particle System has been active.
    - **Particle Memory**: This toggles the display of a Particle System's memory usage, both for the template and for each instance.

- **View Modes**: The different options in this menu allow you to switch between the different draw modes in the Viewport panel. They are mostly the same as the ones in the Level Editor Viewport:
    - **Wireframe**: The **Wireframe** view mode shows the wireframe of the particles. If the emitter uses sprites, you will see two polygons, which make up each sprite.
    - **Unlit**: The **Unlit** view mode shows the result of the particles without lighting or post processing.
    - **Lit**: The **Lit** view mode shows the result of the particles with lighting and post processing.
    - **Shader Complexity**: This displays the feedback on how many instructions are required for a particular shader. The color green has the lowest value, and the color red has the highest value.
- **Detail Modes**: The **Detail Modes** submenu allows you to switch the viewport window between low, medium, and high in detail. These correlate to the engine detail modes, which allow you to see how a Particle System will appear in each different mode. If you use any one except the high mode, you will see a visual text on the left-hand side of the Viewport panel, telling you that you are looking at a specific one, just to save you from thinking that you are seeing the best quality right now:
    - **Low**: This previews the Particle System as it would appear when the system detail mode is set to low.
    - **Medium**: This previews the Particle System as it would appear when the system detail mode is set to medium.
    - **High**: This previews the Particle System as it would appear when the system detail mode is set to high.
- **Background Color**: This opens the color picker where you can change the color of the Viewport panel's background. It is just the same one you used to find in the toolbar.
- **Orbit Mode**: This toggles the camera behavior between orbiting around the Particle System and free moving in the Viewport pane.
- **Origin Axis**: This toggles the visibility for the origin axis gizmo. It works like the one found in the toolbar. The origin axis is always located in the lower-left corner.

- **Vector Fields**: This toggles On/Off for any vector fields applied to the Particle System.
- **Grid**: This toggles On/Off for the viewport grid. This makes it easy to define the Particle System in space.
- **Wireframe Sphere**: This shows a wireframe sphere representing the spherical radius of the Particle System.
- **Post Process**: This toggles the visibility of the global post process. It is not always useful, but sometimes, it helps you understand what it would look like if your game had some post-processing effects.
- **Motion**: This toggles whether the Particle System remains stationary or revolves around the center of the grid.
- **Motion Radius**: This uses its input field to set the radius of revolution for the **Motion** setting.
- **Geometry**: This shows or hides the default test mesh.
- **Geometry Properties**: This brings up the **Geometry Properties** window, where you can adjust the properties of the default geometry, adjust the placement, swap out the mesh used, and many other options.
- **Bounds**: This toggles On/Off for the Particle System bounds, just like the one in the toolbar. These are shown as both a bounding box and bounding sphere.
- **Set Fixed Bounds**: This activates fixed boundaries for the Particle System, and automatically sets the values to the largest setting calculated so far.

Here are listed a set of different timing options that helps you in reviewing the particles behaviors over time:

- **Play/Pause**: This plays or pauses the simulation of the current Particle System.

- **Realtime**: If checked, the simulation plays in real time. If unchecked, the simulation only plays when something updates in the Viewport panel.
- **Loop**: If checked, either the Particle System plays once, or it will restart once it reaches the end.
- **AnimSpeed**: With it's submenu, you will be able to adjust the playback speed percentage between **100**, **50**, **25**, **10**, and **1**.

The Emitters panel

As a Particle System is made out of one or more particle emitters, this is the place where you can add, select, edit, and arrange your emitters. Think of it as an empty graph area. This is where you can put the actual content. As this is just an area for all the emitters, you can call it *the Emitter List* as most people do:

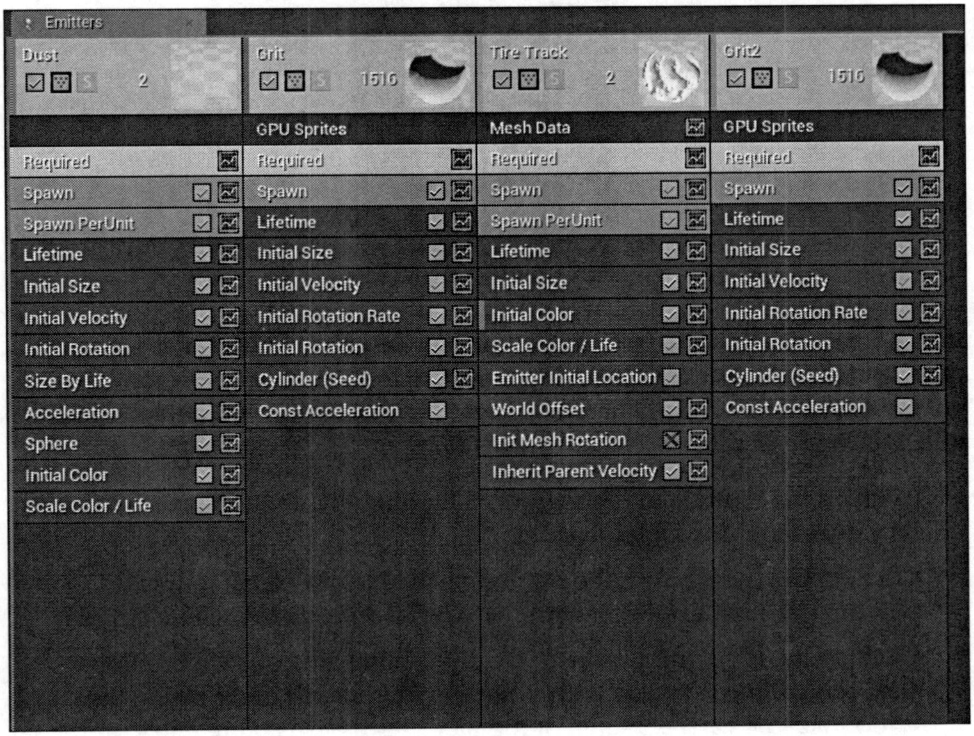

It contains a horizontal arrangement of all the emitters in the current Particle System. Each column represents a single particle emitter, and each is made up of an emitter block at the top, followed by any number of module blocks. The emitter block at the top contains the basic properties of the emitter, such as the name, editor color, detail amount, and type for the emitter. It is also used to quickly enable/disable the emitter, or even set it to solo mode to see it only in the Viewport panel, while the modules beneath it control the various aspects and behaviors of the particle:

Required, Spawn, Lifetime, Initial Size, Initial Velocity, Color Over Life, Initial Rotation, SubImage Index, Sphere, Drag, and **Size By Life** are the modules that control the emitted particle's behaviors. There are three ways to interact with each module, which are as follows:

- Click on the module in the emitter to highlight it, and then start changing its values from the **Details** panel.
- Click on the checkbox in the module to enable or disable it quickly so that you can get a better understanding of its effect over the whole emitter.
- Click on the little graph icon on the right-hand side of each module to start controlling its value with a curve that you will draw inside the Curve Editor. As you can see, some of the modules have a colored strip at the far left (red or green), and this one tells us that the module already has a curve controlling it.

Once you create a particle emitter, you will end up with some particles moving around, and that's an expected behavior with a modular Particle System editor. In fact, a base emitter must have the raw modules that control its particles with the minimal requirements. As everything is as per your choice, these initial modules can be totally removed if you want. They are essential in most cases:

If you want to add more modules to start with in order to have more control over the behavior you want for your emitter or Particle System, you can do so by right-clicking on the emitter, and triggering the magical menu of the modules, which will be discussed later in this chapter:

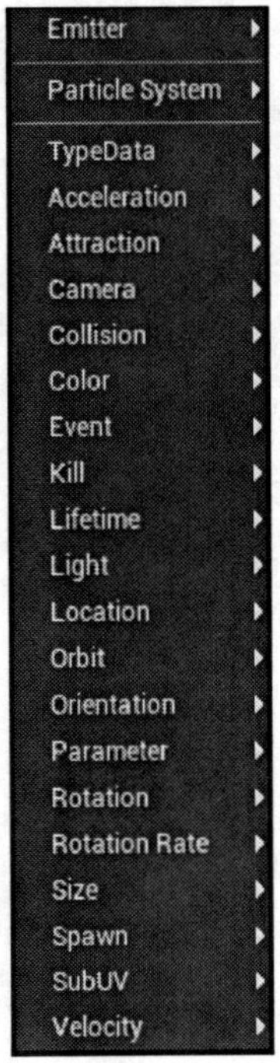

The Details panel

By default, if you do not select any of the emitters in the emitters list area, this panel will display the overall properties for the Particle System itself. However, as a sensitive window, it will automatically change its content based on your selection. Try to select the **Emitter** to see what it can display, and then try to select one of the modules. It will always change its content:

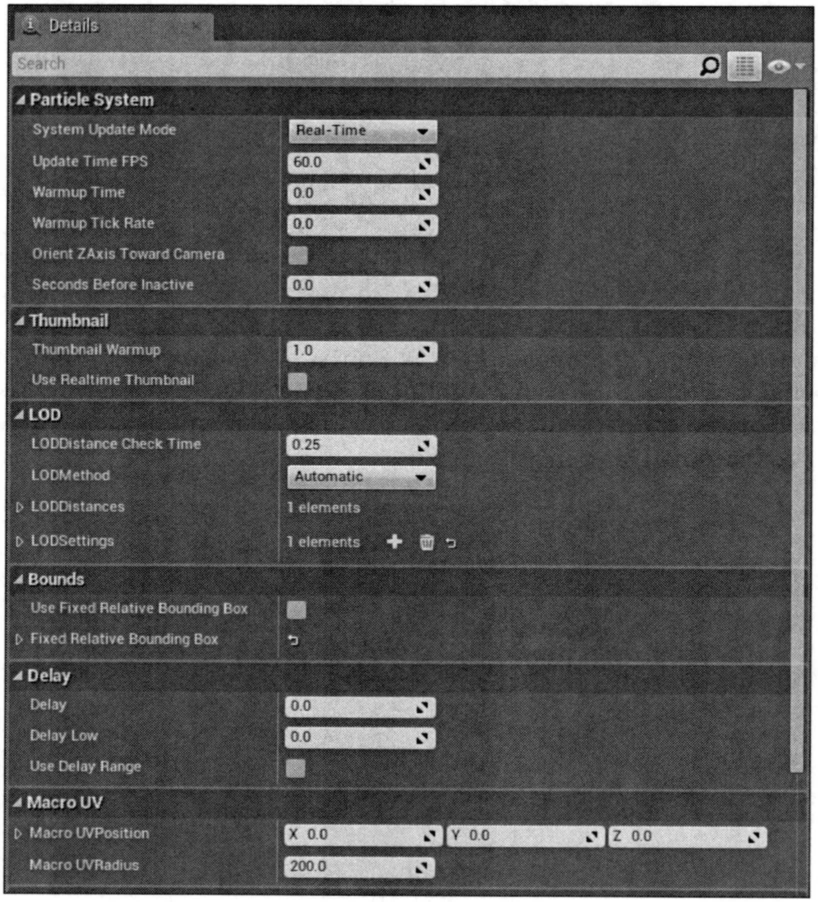

Now after learning about how the **Details** panel works, let's start to breakdown all the parameters that you can find there—almost all of them, starting with those related to the whole Particle System, and then those related to the particle emitter. The modules are different and the parameters for each are completely different, but there are a couple of attributes that are always the same in all the modules. Let's see all of these juicy properties.

The Particle System

This is a complete particle effect that is made up of one or more particle emitters. By allowing multiple emitters in a system, you'll be able to create particle effects that all belong to a single Particle System. Then, you can use that Particle System by spawning or inserting it into the level:

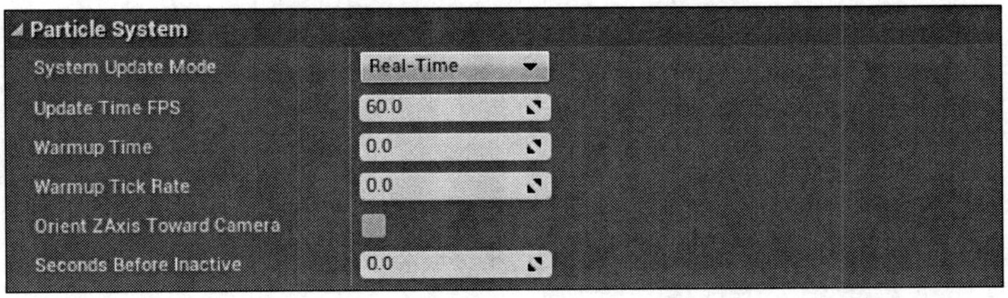

The Particle System contains the following public parameters:

- **System Update Mode**: This defines the method the Particle System should use to update all its emitters. The two modes available are as follows:
    - **Real-Time**: This updates the emitters in real time.
    - **Fixed-Time**: This updates the emitters at a fixed time step. This will lock the system to the update time of the game and is performance dependent. By setting the value of Update Time FPS, you'll be able to control it. A lower frame rate lowers the update time of the system, which means giving a slower Particle System, while a higher frame rate speeds it up.

      Try to not use this method a lot. It is better to use this method when the Particle System needs to give a certain behavior that is tied with something else that can be slower or faster than the rest of the game. For example, tying the emitter to an animation clip.
- **Update Time FPS**: The time-step is used when operating in FixedTime.
- **Warmup Time**: This is the amount of time taken to warmup the system at launch. It allows you set an emitter to start at its behavior peak. While it is super useful in a lot of cases, it can affect the performance, so use this sparingly especially at high values. It can be used with Particle Systems that you want to start while the map initially loads, for example, a fire already there or a cloud in the sky. So rather than start building the fire or the cloud once the particle has spawned, it will start in the middle of its behavior and the cloud will already exist.

- **Warmup Tick Rate**: This controls the time step for each tick during the system warmup (in the previous parameter). Increasing its value will improve the performance. A value of 0 means the default tick time.
- **Orient ZAxis Toward Camera**: Setting this to true will force the local *z* axis of the Particle System to be oriented toward the camera at all times.
- **Seconds Before Inactive**: If the Particle System is not rendered for this amount of time (in seconds), the Particle System will go inactive and no longer be ticked. Using the value of zero will prevent the system from ever being forced to be inactive.

Thumbnail

It is more about the editor and the Content Browser. As you can see, any of the assets can have their own thumbnails, which in some cases are animated, such as particles or flipbook animations. Here is a list of the options that will give you more control of how to display your Particle System thumbnail in the Content Browser:

The options available under **Thumbnail** are as follows:

- **Thumbnail Warmup**: The amount of time to warm-up the system before catching the thumbnail render when **Use Realtime Thumbnail** is checked.
- **Use Realtime Thumbnail**: If set to true, the thumbnail displayed in the Content Browser for the Particle System asset will be automatically captured using the default camera position and reflect the current settings and appearance of the Particle System instead of using the saved thumbnail.

  Use Realtime Thumbnail for rendering can slow down the performance of the Content Browser.

LOD

Particles are not different than any of the other Unreal asset types; all of the supported Unreal Engine's assets should have **LOD** to allow them to save the **performance**. In this section, there are some options that give you more control over the Particle System's level of details:

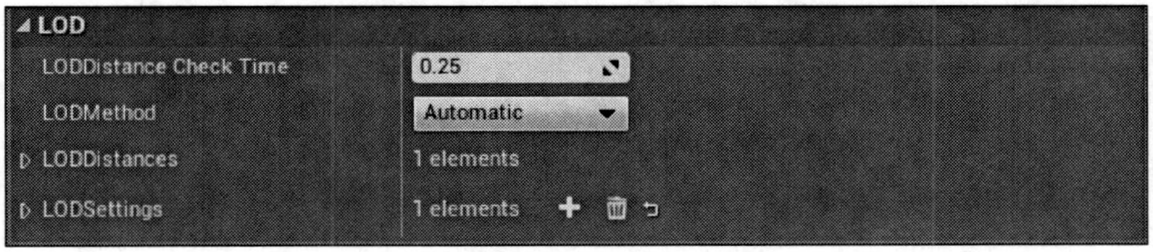

The options available in **LOD** are as follows:

- **LODDistance Check Time**: This is how often (in seconds), the Particle System should perform a distance check to get the LOD level
- **LODMethod**: This list contains options to define the method the system should utilize to select the appropriate LOD levels:
    - **Automatic**: This sets the LOD level based on the LOD distance and checks the time automatically
    - **DirectSet**: The game will set the LOD level for the system to use directly
    - **ActivateAutomatic**: The LOD level is determined at activation time, then left alone unless directly set by the gameplay logic
- **LODDistances**: This is an array of distances you can define in order to determine which LOD level to utilize while setting the **LODMethod** to **Automatic**
- **LODSettings**: This is an array of values used to determine a few settings to use for each individual LOD

Bounds

Any actor or object in the Unreal world has its own bounding box. This box shape is responsible for displaying the bounds of the object. However, when it comes to particles, it has two bounds to be displayed. The first type, which is the normal one, is displayed as an actor, just like anything else. The second type is only available with the particle editor from the top bar. Here, we will discuss the options for the last type when the view mode is changed into the bounding box:

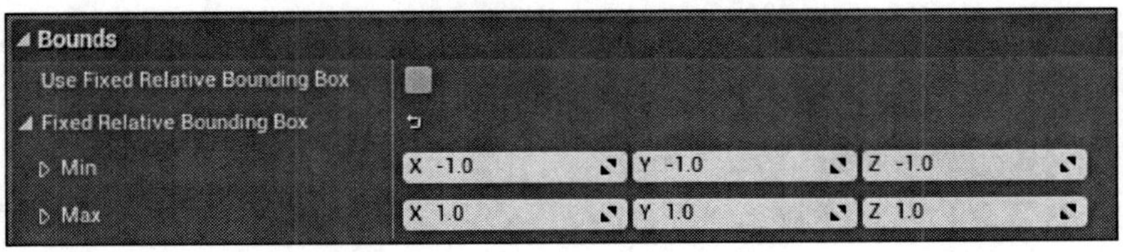

The options available in **Bounds** are as follows:

- **Use Fixed Relative Bounding Box**: If this is set to true, the logic will utilize the **Fixed Relative Bounding Box** as the bounds for the Particle System.
- **Fixed Relative Bounding Box**: This allows you to set bounding boxes for the Particle System. This is a good choice to make in order to reduce the overhead of performance while performing the bounds, updating each frame.You might need to right-click on the **Toggle Bounds** button on the toolbar, and in this dialog box, fill in the currently used values of the dynamic box in Cascade. This will give you some values that you can use to start tweaking your **Mix** and **Max** values of the **Fixed Bounding Box**.

Delay

The **Delay** set of options give you more control over the time behavior of the Particle Systems you have. You might need some effects to be time-triggered or time-bounded, and here, you can set those values:

The options available in **Delay** are as follows:

- **Delay**: The amount of time, in seconds, the Particle System should wait before it gets activated. It also represents the highest value of the range to use for choosing a random delay value when the **Use Delay Range** option is active.
- **Delay Low**: This represents the lowest value of the range to use for choosing a random delay value when the **Use Delay Range** option is active.
- **Use Delay Range**: If set to true, a random value between **Delay Low** and **Delay** is chosen for the actual delay value to use.

Macro UV

The Macro UV options are used when the particle material uses the Macro UV material node. Both the node and the options work together to allow you to use a single texture for all the particles, and pan it across in order to display an animation effect over all the particles:

The options available in **Macro UV** are as follows:

- **Macro UVPosition**: The local-space position relative to the Particle System is used as the center point to generate the UV texture coordinates for the ParticleMacroUV material expression.
- **Macro UV Radius**: This is the world-space radius that determines the distance from the **Macro UVPosition**, where the UV texture coordinates generated for the ParticleMacroUV material expression will begin tiling.

Occlusion

When it comes to rendering particles, you have to be wise enough to not affect the performance, especially when it is not a GPU-based Particle System.

The **Occlusion** set of options give you the power of setting an occlusion bounding box that will handle when particles shouldn't be rendered.

Keep in mind that as Unreal Engine always uses the occlusion information from the previous frame, you might have some delay at some point:

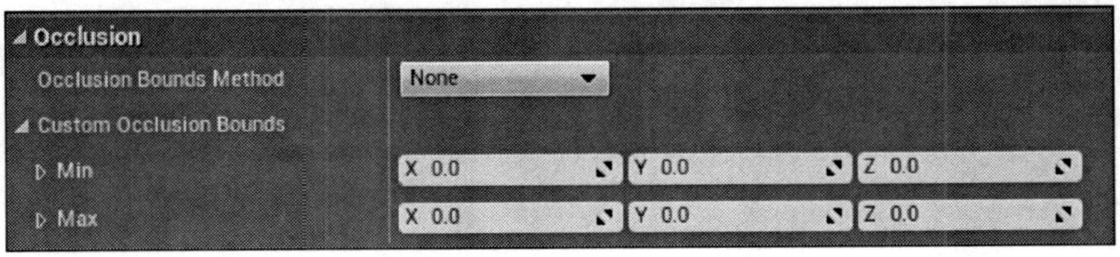

The options available in **Occlusion** are as follows:

- **Occlusion Bounds Method**: This method is used to calculate the occlusion of the Particle System:
    - **None**: The occlusion is not calculated for the Particle System
    - **ParticleBounds**: The bounds of the ParticleSystemComponent is used to calculate the occlusion for the Particle System
    - **CustomBounds**: The Custom Occlusion Bounds (the next value) values are used to calculate the occlusion for the Particle System
- **Custom Occlusion Bounds**: These bounds are used to calculate the occlusion when using the **CustomBounds** Occlusion Bounds method

Materials

The following screenshot shows the option available in **Materials**:

The **Named Materials Slots** option is an array of named material slots used by the emitters of this Particle System. An Emitter can use this array of materials rather than its own material.

The particle emitter

A particle emitter is a unit used to build a Particle System. The particle emitter contains the following parameters:

- **Particle**: The first set of options is related to the particle emitter itself. This set of options is mostly exclusive to define your particle emitter from other particle emitters within the same Particle System (remember a Particle System can have several emitters):

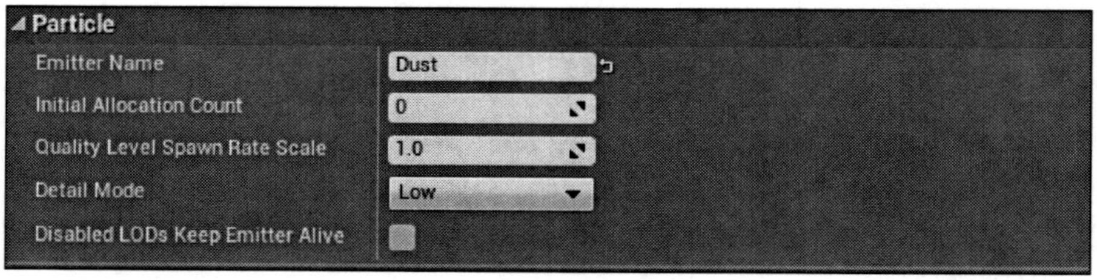

    - **Emitter Name**: This is the name of the emitter.
    - **Initial Allocation Count**: This value allows you to declare the number of particles that should be allocated at the initialization of the emitter. If it is 0, the calculated peak count is used.
    - **Quality Level Spawn Rate Scale**: You can use this value to scale down the spawn rate of the emitter when the engine is running in medium or low detail mode.
      It can be used to optimize the particle draw cost in a split-screen mode.
    - **Detail Mode**: This has three options for detail quality. It is different than the one we mentioned earlier. This time the detail's measured for only this emitter, not the whole system. The three options are **Low, Medium**, and **High**.

- **Disabled LODs Keep Emitter Alive**: Set this to true if your current LOD is disabled, and you want the emitter to be kept alive and not be considered as completed.

- **Cascade**: As we mentioned earlier, Cascade is the name of the particles editor in Unreal Engine. So to find a menu with the same name would simply imply that it is related to the editor itself more than the game or the final product. In this section, you can make some changes that will have an impact on the visual look for debugging in the editor only, and none of the following options will affect the final game:

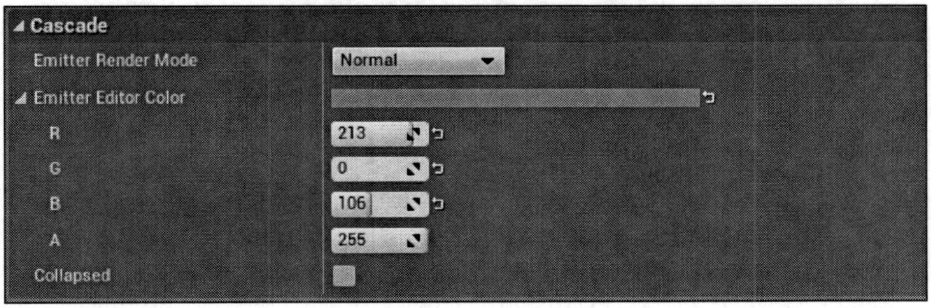

  - **Emitter Render Mode**: This method is used when rendering the emitter's particles.
  - **Normal**: This renders the emitter's particles as intended.
  - **Point**: This renders the emitter's particles as a 2 x 2 pixel block without scaling.
  - **Cross**: This renders the emitter's particles as a cross of lines.
  - **None**: The emitter's particles are not rendered.
  - **Emitter Editor Color**: The edits the color of the particle emitter block when collapsed, in the Curve Editor and debug rendering modes, as well as the strips at the emitter's title when it is not collapsed.
  - **Collapsed**: If set to true, the particle emitter will appear collapsed in the Emitter List in the editor. Double-clicking on the particle emitter block gives the same result.

The particle modules

The particle module is the base of all modules (regardless of the type or functionality, each module has its own parameters list and Cascade parameters list).

This means that all the modules will contain the following properties:

- **Cascade**: As mentioned earlier, as long as the options are titled with the word **Cascade**, it means they are editor-only options. Here is a small set of options used for more usability while working:

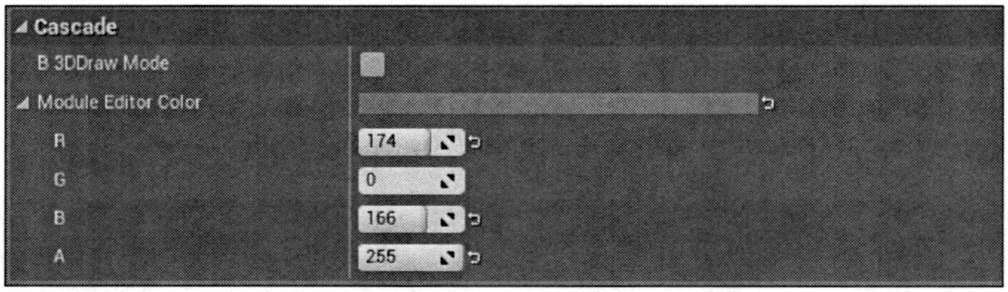

The options available under **Cascade** are as follows:

  - **B 3DDraw Mode**: If set to true, any 3D visualization helpers for the module, for example, the wireframe geometry depicting the extents of an initial location module, will be displayed.
  - **Module Editor Color**: This is the color the module will utilize in the graph editor.

The Curve Editor

One of the most powerful features of the Cascade editor is the typical Unreal Curve Editor editor panel (like the one used in the Matinee Editor). At first glance, you might think that this is not the proper place to have a curve editor. Once you know why it is there and how to use it, you'll definitely appreciate its existence:

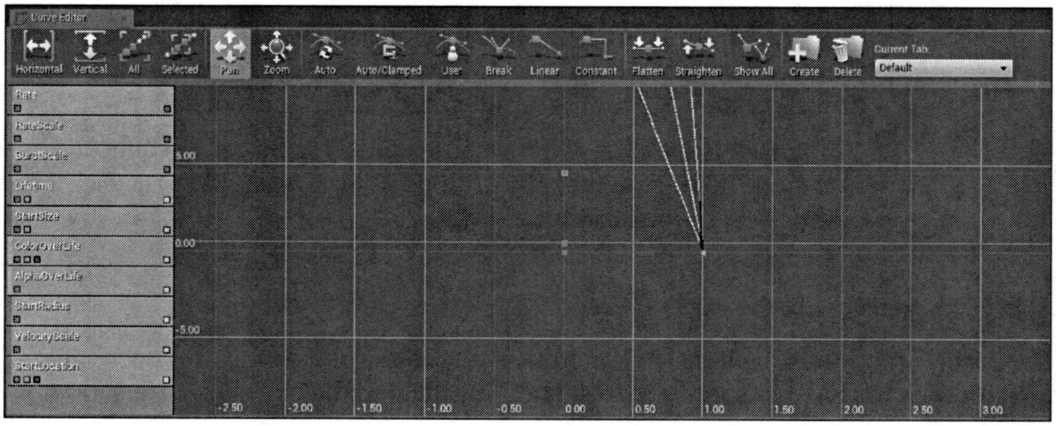

The curve panel allows you to adjust any of the module's values that need to be changed, along the life of a particle, or even along the whole life of an emitter. Using this editor, you'll be able to have the following types of values:

- Constant vales that will never be changed
- Dynamic values that always change over time

As you can see in the following screenshot, the Curve Editor is divided into specific areas, just like any other animation Curve Editor that comes with Unreal Engine:

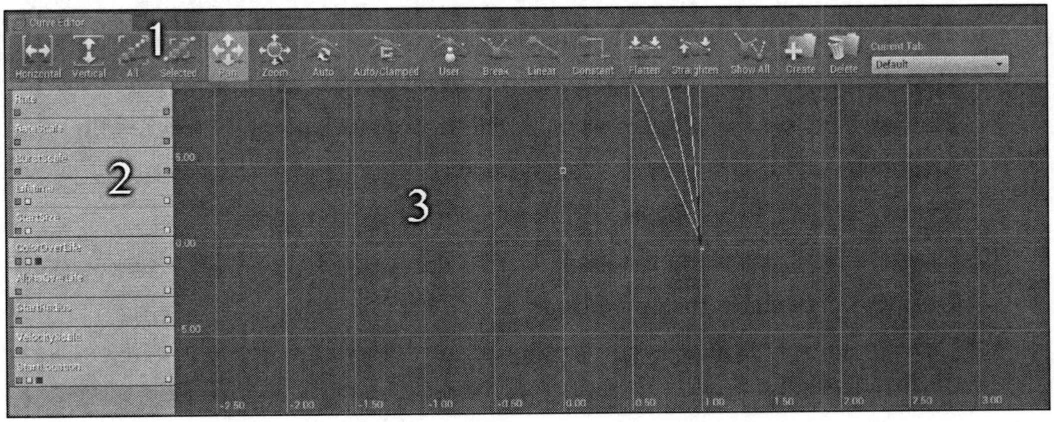

Any module property can be edited in a curve inside the curve editor, but the only condition required to achieve this is that the property needs to have a distribution type that utilizes a curve. A distribution type, such as **DistributionFloatConstantCurve**, is used to control float values. As you can see in the preceding screenshot, the Curve Editor is simply divided into three main areas.

The Toolbar

The toolbar is a bar full of buttons that gives you an easy access to the functionalities while drawing curves:

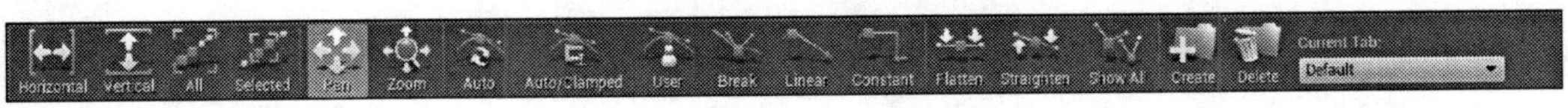

- **Horizontal**: This fits the graph view to the current visible tracks horizontally
- **Vertical**: This fits the graph view to the current visible tracks vertically
- **All**: This fits the graph horizontally and vertically to the current visible tracks
- **Selected**: This fits the graph horizontally and vertically to the selected points of the current visible tracks

- **Pan**: This switches the Curve Editor to the Pan and Edit mode
- **Zoom**: This switches the Curve Editor to the Zoom mode
- **Auto**: This sets InterpMode (Interpolation mode) for selected keys to Auto-curve mode
- **Auto/Clamped**: This sets InterpMode for selected keys to Auto-curve mode
- **User**: This sets InterpMode for selected keys to user curve mode (user-modified tangents)
- **Break**: This sets InterpMode for selected keys to Curve Break mode
- **Linear**: This sets InterpMode for selected keys to Linear mode
- **Constant**: This sets InterpMode for selected keys to Constant mode
- **Flatten**: This sets selected keys/points tangents to flattened horizontally
- **Straighten**: This straightens selected keys/point tangents, when broken
- **Show All**: This turns the on/off display of all key tangents
- **Create**: This creates a new tab
- **Delete**: This deletes the current tab
- **Current Tab**: This allows you to choose the current tab if you've created multiple tabs

The Track List

The **Track List** displays all the tracks you have in a Particle System. (In short, a list of the modules that are using curves to control their parameters.)

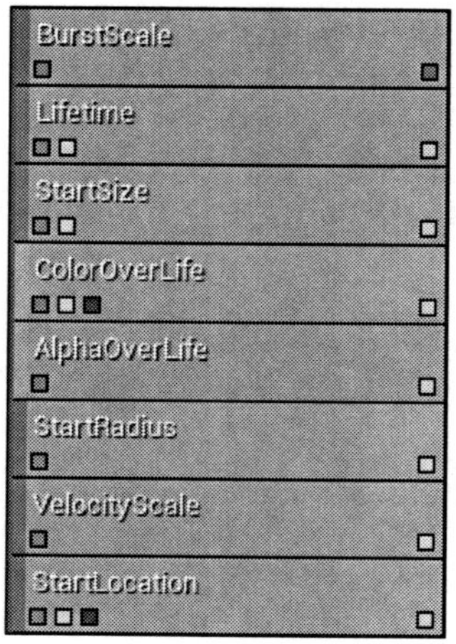

It is a list where you can find all of the curves currently loaded into the current tab. Each track in the Track List has a name that represents the name of the property associated with the track. Also, each track in the list has a visibility switch button for each curve in the track and an overall visibility switch button to turn On/Off all of the sub tracks. In order to remove a track from the list, the easiest way is by right-clicking on a track in the Track List, which will trigger the Track List context menu, which has only two options:

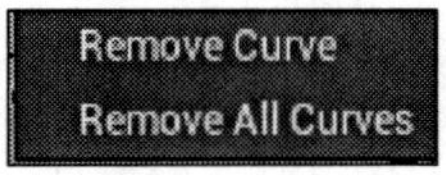

The options available in the context menu are as follows:

- **Remove Curve**: This removes the current track from the Curve Editor
- **Remove All Curves**: This clears all the tracks loaded in the Curve Editor from all the tabs

The Graph

The graph is a vast area with a vertical (value) and horizontal (time) axis for drawing all your curves:

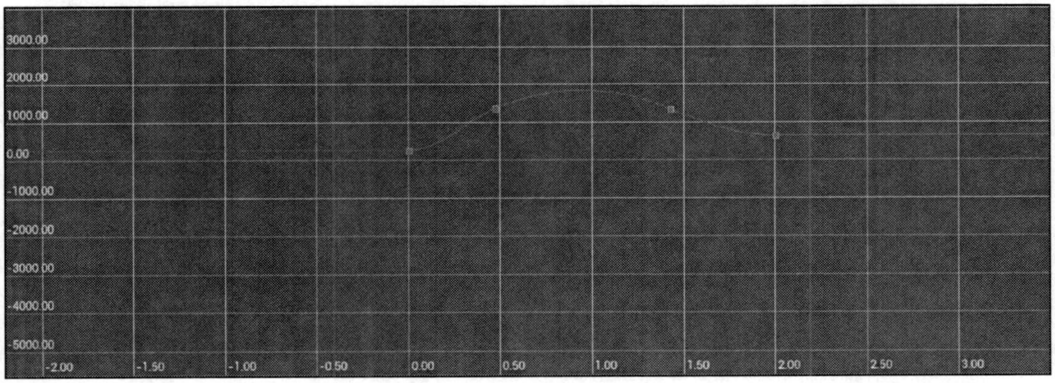

The most important and unimportant part of the Curve Editor panel! It sounds contradictory, but it is the truth. You can make an amazing Particle System using Cascade and without using graphs made by the curve editor at all, and it will still look amazing. However, at the same time, you might not be able to do anything without graphs. It depends on the visual look you are seeking, the game look, and the complexity that the Particle System should have.

It is a just typical graphical representation of the value (the vertical axis) over time (the horizontal axis). All the curves are made out of keys; if you have one key only, then you don't have a curve, but if you have more than one key, then you have a curve that connects these keys together. The keys are displayed as points (this is the reason why you will find me calling them keys sometimes, while others call them points), which can be selected and manipulated to visually edit the curve. These keys can have different interpolation modes applied to them in order to directly change the look of the key, which will change the way in which one key will lead to the following one.

Right-clicking on the graph brings up the graph sensitive context menu. While clicking on an empty area will give a general option in the context menu, clicking on a key/point will give you a different context menu. Right-clicking on the empty space will display the following options:

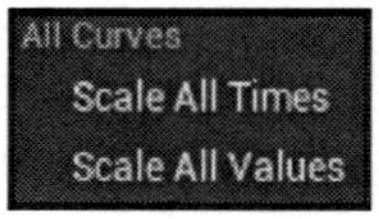

- **Scale All Times**: This scales the time values (horizontally) of all points of all the visible tracks.
- **Scale All Values**: This scales the values (vertically) of all points of all the visible tracks. While right-clicking on a key, it will display the following options:

  - **Set Time**: This manually sets the time of the key.
  - **Set Value**: This manually sets the value of the key.
  - **Delete**: This deletes the selected key/keys.

The interpolation modes

The interpolation mode buttons control the applied interpolation method that will be used on the curve point to allow a key on the curve to use that method to reach the next key. Some of these modes resulting constant curves, while others can be adjusted more freely. Methods, such as Break, Auto, and User, will produce white handles for you, and you can use these handles to take more control over the resulted curve between keys.

Here is a list of the different interpolation modes supported by Unreal:

- **Auto**: As you can see in the following screenshot, the Auto tangent mostly tends to set the handles of the two sides of the key to match the lines of the curve:

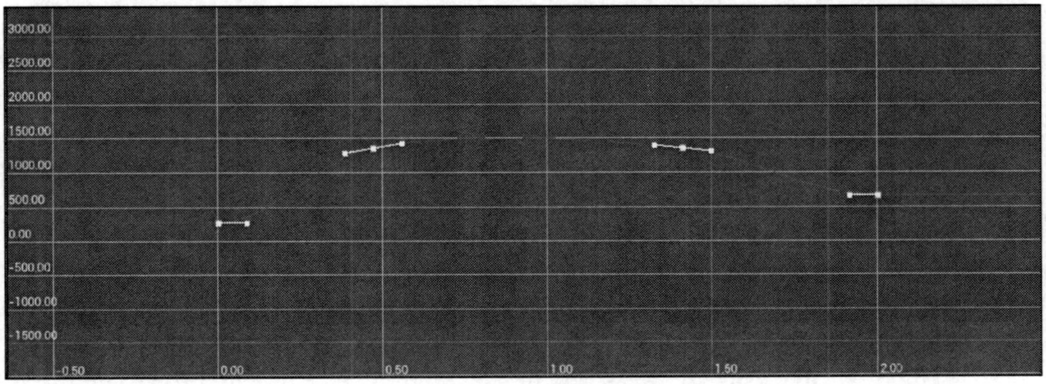

- **Auto Clamped**: In the Auto Clamped tangents, it is different, mostly, the handle will tend to be straight, but at the same time, it tries to adjust the curve to match one of the two handles of each key:

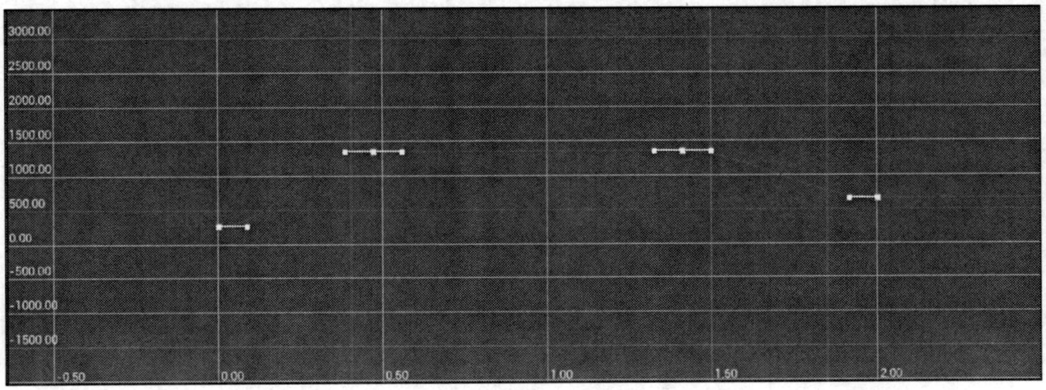

- **User**: A User is a set of custom tangents that you can modify to match the desired behavior.

- **Break**: Break tangents is super common, and it is mostly known for its bouncy behavior. Using this type will guarantee that moving one handle will not affect the other handle in the same key:

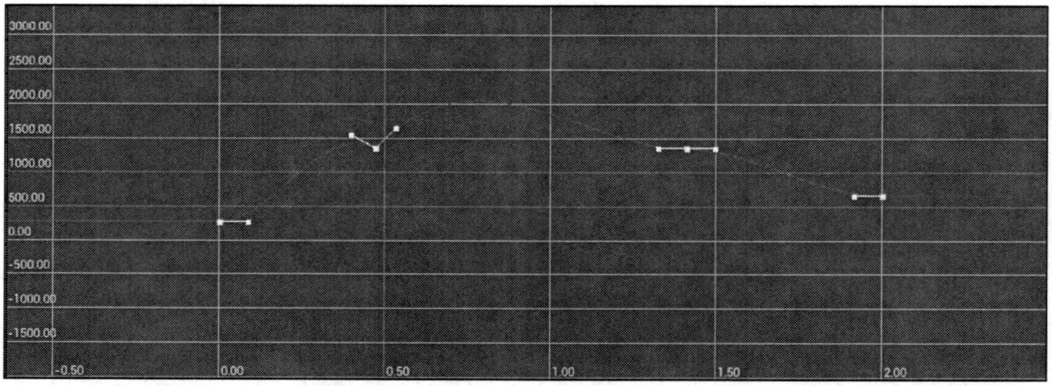

- **Linear**: As its name suggests, the linear tangents will mostly hide the handles of the keys. It is not hidden, but it is moved in a way so that it has no curvy effect in order to give the linear manipulation:

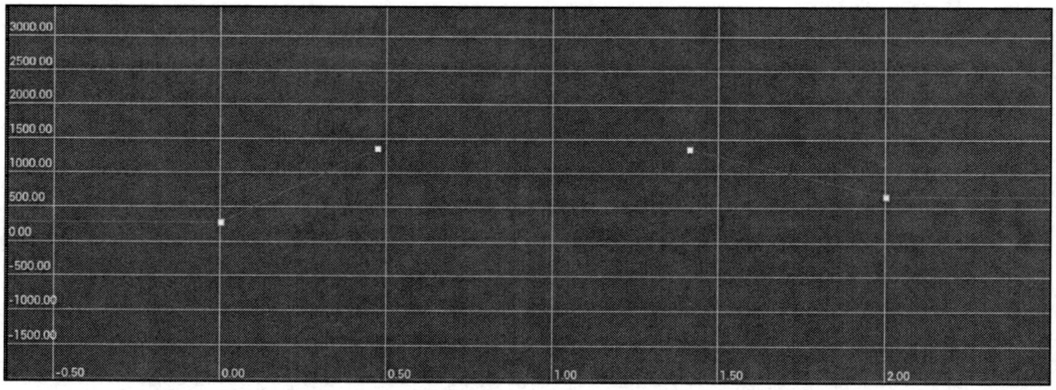

- **Constant**: The Constant, Snappy or Stepped -- it has lots of different names; this type of tangent will make the transition between the keys happen at once. So this means that there are no manipulations, but there are no smooth transitions. It just jumps from A to B to C, and so on:

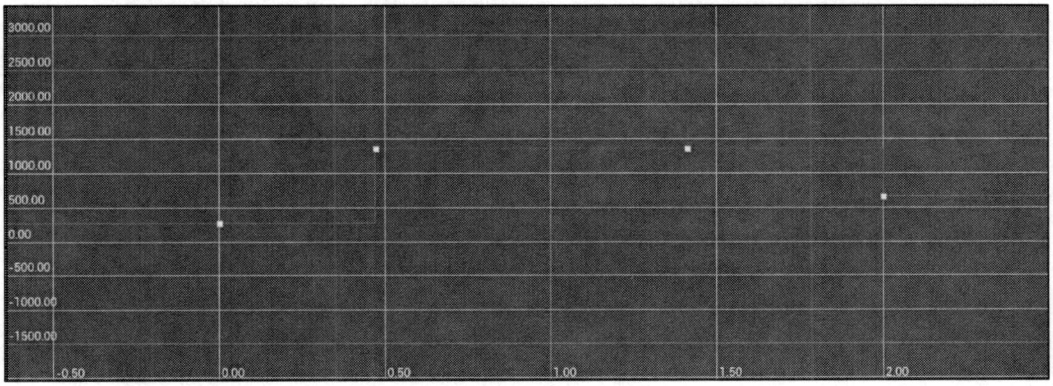

Adding, removing, and organizing curves

While breaking down the emitters, we mentioned earlier that a small button in each module can control it via a curve. So, to add a module to the Curve Editor, you just need to click on the little green box with a curve, which appears on the left-hand side of the module. This will produce a colored curve directly in the curve editor. You can still remove it by simply pressing the button again. The color that is used to draw the curve is a randomly generated color; you can change it by selecting the module and editing its color from the **Details** panel:

- **Adding curve to the graph**: By clicking on the previously mentioned curve icon in an emitter module, this option will send any available curves for that module down to the Curve Editor.
- **Removing curve from the graph**: In order to pull curves from the graph once you are done editing them, you just need to right-click on the block for the curve in the Curve Editor list, and choose **Remove Curve** from the context menu.
- **Organizing the Curve Editor with tabs**: Have you ever thought of having around a hundred tracks in one Particle System that are made up of multiple emitters? Yes, it is possible, and in some cases, with the most complex systems, you might need to go beyond the first hundred. In that case, you can start adding tabs, which are mostly described as folders.

Just like adding folders in the scene hierarchy, in order to organize it, you can add tabs as folders to include as many curves as you wish, and then give a general name for the tab.

- **Creating a new tab is easy**: It can be created by clicking on the Toolbar shortcut button or even by deleting another shortcut button:

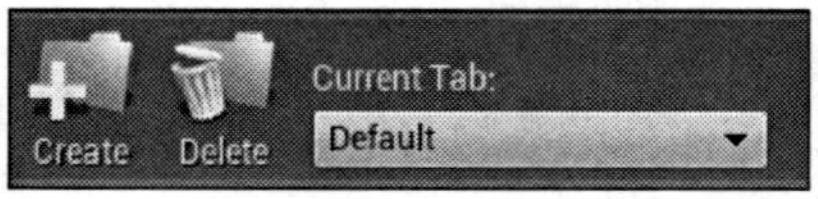

The different types of modules

By right-clicking on any of the emitters your Particle System has, you will see the famous, long menu in the Cascade editor. The **Emitter** context menu includes some parameters related to the emitter itself, but most importantly, it contains all the modules that can be used:

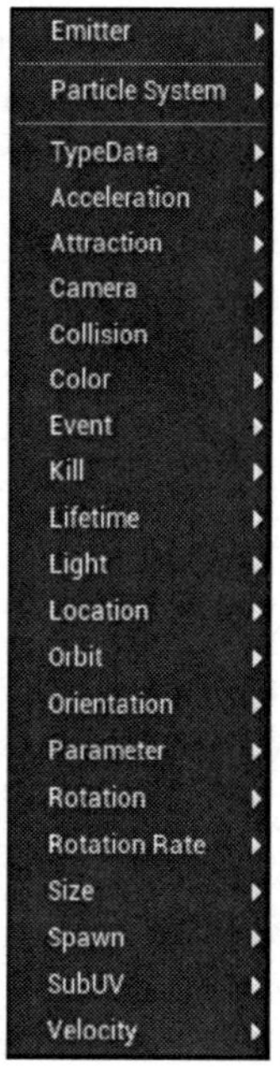

As mentioned earlier, the modules are the building blocks that make up an emitter. They control each and every aspect of a particle's lifetime. While the emitters are the main units that build the whole Particle System, the module is the main unit that builds a particle emitter. Modules are used to control the various aspects of the particles that are released by an emitter.

There are different modules that can be added to the particle emitters. These modules are broken up into various categories based on their usage. The supported categories are as follows:

- **TypeData**: All the particle emitters are made sprite emitters by default. However, there are other types of emitters that can replace them from the TypeData modules. These different modules represent different types of particles, such as beam, GPU, mesh, and ribbon:
    - **Sprite**: This is the default emitter type where it uses sprite particles.
    - **Beam**: This type of emitter indicates where it should output beams, connecting particles and the source.
    - **GPU**: This type of emitter indicates where the particle's simulation will be on the GPU.
    - **Mesh**: This type of emitter indicates where the emission will use Static Meshes instances instead of the sprite particles.
    - **Ribbon**: This type of emitter indicates where the emitter outputs trails, connecting the particles.
- **Acceleration**: This module controls the particle's acceleration effects, such as drag forces and constant acceleration force.
- **Attraction**: This module controls the particle's movement by attracting particles to various points in space.
- **Camera**: This module controls how the particles will move according to the camera space.
- **Collision**: This module controls how to handle the collisions between particles and geometries.
- **Color**: This module controls the color of the particles.
- **Event**: This module controls the triggering of particle events, which can in turn cause a variety of in-game responses.
- **Kill**: This module controls the particle's destruction.
- **Lifetime**: This module controls how long particles should live.
- **Light**: This module governs the particle lights.
- **Location**: This module controls where the particles will be born relative to the location of the emitter actor.
- **Orbit**: This module allows the screen-space orbital behavior in order to add extra motion to effects.
- **Orientation**: This module allows a rotational axis of the particles to be locked.

- **Parameter**: This module can be parameterized or controlled via external sources, such as Blueprints and Matinee.
- **Rotation**: This module controls the rotation of particles.
- **Rotation Rate**: This module controls the changes in the rotation speed.
- **Size**: This module controls the scale of particles.
- **Spawn**: This module is used to add specialized particle spawn rates, such as spawning particles per units.
- **SubUV**: This module allows you to use animated sprite sheets to be displayed on a single particle.
- **Velocity**: This module controls the velocity of each particle.

These are all the categories that you can find in the Cascade module's context menu. Feel free to start using the different ones from each category in order to learn about the slight differences between each of them. You can also check the particles system's reference guide from the Epic homepage, which is a good way to learn about the differences between each module:

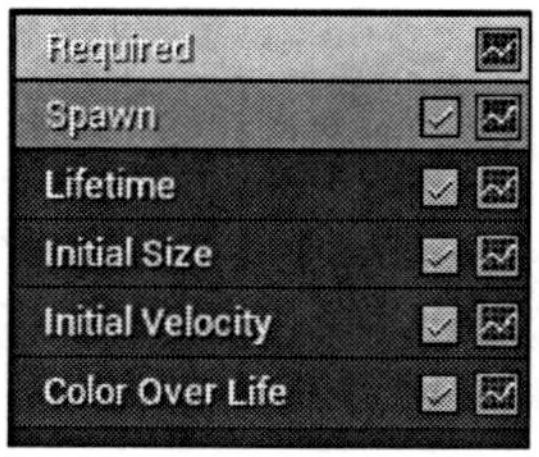

Some other modules also exist on a particle emitter by default regardless of its type. Any particle emitter is added to a Particle System, and it is always created with the default modules:

- **Required**: This contains the properties that are necessary for a Particle System, such as the material, how long the emitter should emit particles, the emission origin, and a lot of other properties:

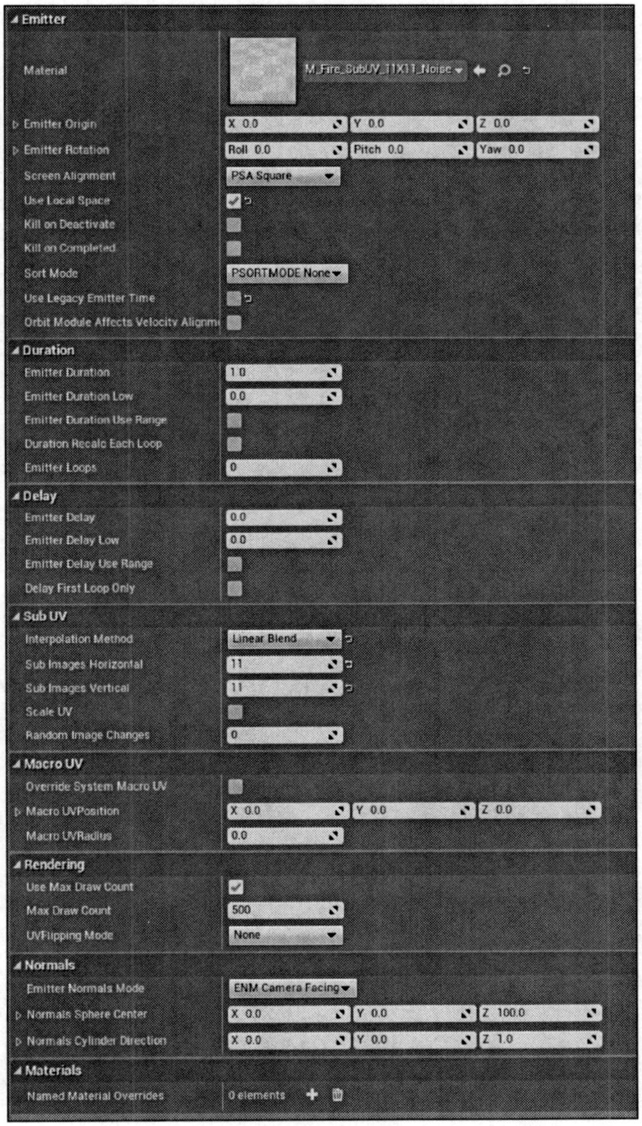
Emitter
Material
M_Fire_SubUV_11X11_Noise
Emitter Origin
X 0.0
Y 0.0
Z 0.0
Emitter Rotation
Roll 0.0
Pitch 0.0
Yaw 0.0
Screen Alignment
PSA Square
Use Local Space
Kill on Deactivate
Kill on Completed
Sort Mode
PSORTMODE None
Use Legacy Emitter Time
Orbit Module Affects Velocity Alignm
Duration
Emitter Duration
1.0
Emitter Duration Low
0.0
Emitter Duration Use Range
Duration Recalc Each Loop
Emitter Loops
0
Delay
Emitter Delay
0.0
Emitter Delay Low
0.0
Emitter Delay Use Range
Delay First Loop Only
Sub UV
Interpolation Method
Linear Blend
Sub Images Horizontal
11
Sub Images Vertical
11
Scale UV
Random Image Changes
0
Macro UV
Override System Macro UV
Macro UVPosition
X 0.0
Y 0.0
Z 0.0
Macro UVRadius
0.0
Rendering
Use Max Draw Count
Max Draw Count
500
UVFlipping Mode
None
Normals
Emitter Normals Mode
ENM Camera Facing
Normals Sphere Center
X 0.0
Y 0.0
Z 100.0
Normals Cylinder Direction
X 0.0
Y 0.0
Z 1.0
Materials
Named Material Overrides
0 elements

- **Spawn**: This module controls how quickly the particles will spawn from the emitter:

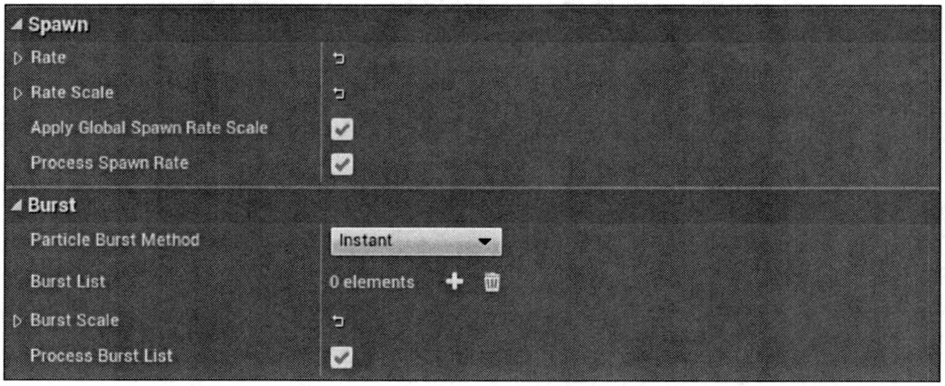

- **Lifetime**: This controls how long each particle will live once it is spawned. You can remove this module if you want the particles to live indefinitely:

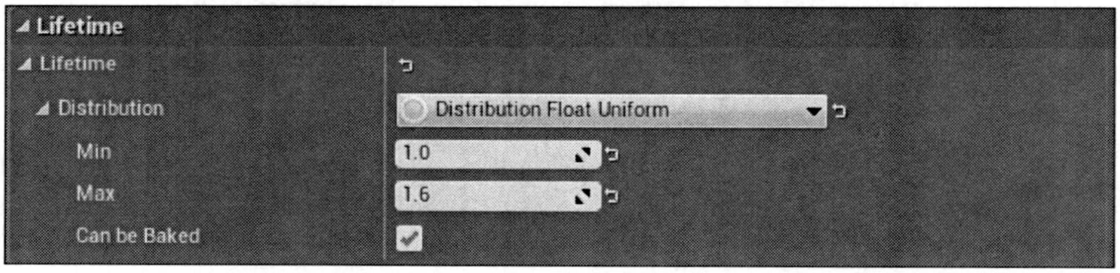

- **Size**: This module controls the scale of a particle at the moment of its spawning:

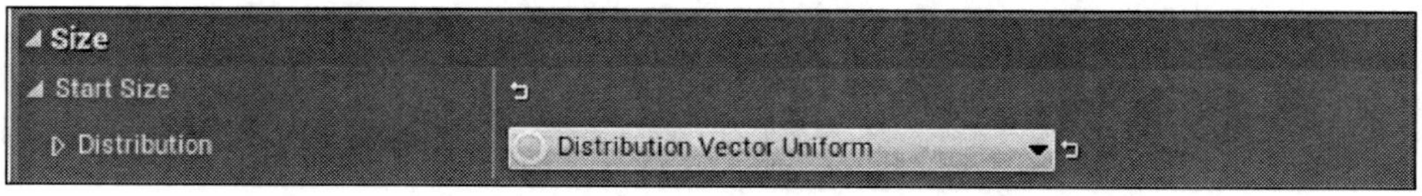

- **Velocity**: This module controls the movement of a particle at spawn time:

- **Color Over Life**: This module controls how the color of each particle will shift throughout its lifespan:

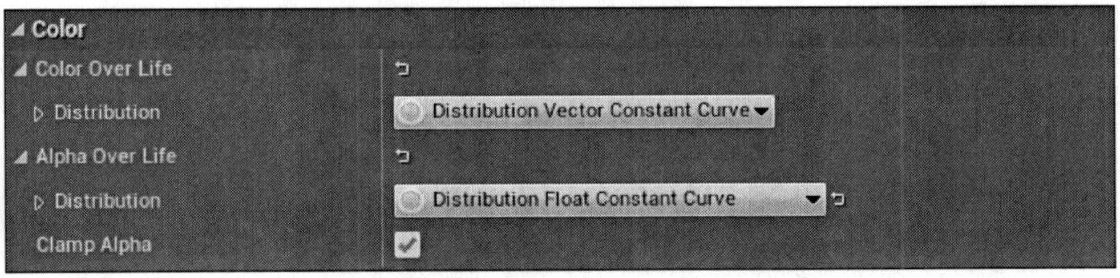

Spawning Particle Systems

After creating an outstanding Particle System, now comes the time to use it and start seeing it in action. There are two ways to use the Particle System:

- **Dragging and Dropping**: This can be done by selecting the Particle System's blueprint from the Content Browser and directly dropping it in the level. This will help you see the particles directly once the level is launched.
- **Spawn at Runtime**: The majority of the Particle Systems we use in games are to be used at runtime. For example, an officer shoots with a shotgun; you can't add the shotgun smoke to the scene, you have to spawn it on demand. In order to do this, the Unreal editor gives you an easy-to-use interface for this.

  While there are some calls you can make to instance actors in general, there are two specific calls that are built for the Particle System's spawning purpose only:

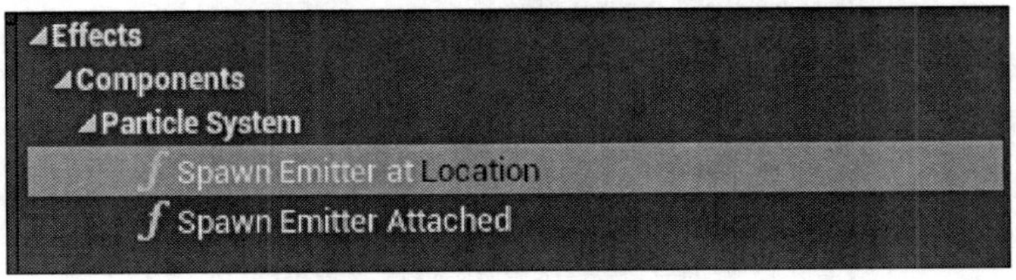

- **Spawn Emitter at Location**: By selecting the correct Particle System, you can directly choose its spawn point, and it will either be destroyed automatically or not:

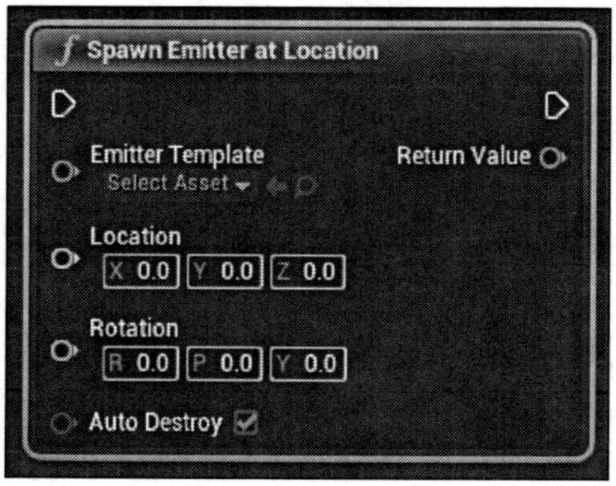

- **Spawn Emitter Attached**: This is a more advanced spawning emitter functionality, where you not only choose the emitter and the spawn point, but you can also attach it to a component or a point. With this, you'll make sure that the the newly created Particle System will keep moving with its attacher. Think about it as some smoky air infront of a torch while the character moves, and the smoke emitter should be attached to his head at the cigarette tip as an attach point:

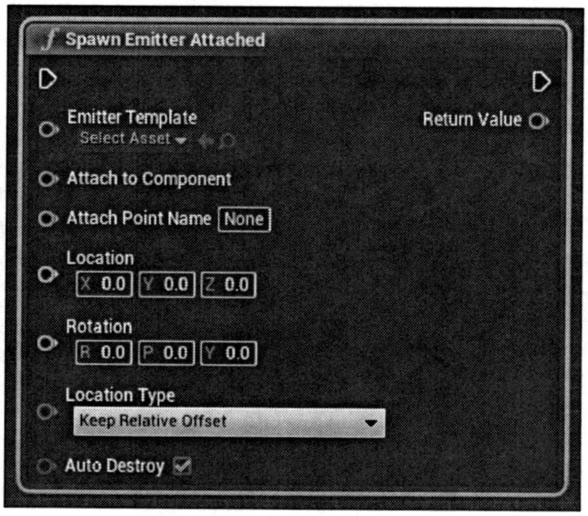

Regardless of the method you decide to use, or whether the usage condition forces you to use it, don't forget to make sure you select the correct particle emitter to be used, and whether it is going to self-destruct or not. Setting one of these to the wrong value will end up with unwanted results.

Applying the Particle System's optimizations

Once you get your game running with a lot of particles, you might start facing some performance issues. These issues might be related to the Particle Systems you made and or it might not be tied to them at all. To learn how to define the reason, you might have to take a look at *Chapter 7, Render Performance Debugging*, where we will discuss the performance debugging. Let's assume that the problem is in the Particle Systems, so what exactly needs to be changed in order to get the game running, and at the same time, contain all the eye candy?

Well, as I've worked on optimizing tons of games, I have found it is easier to have a kind of checklist that I follow; the check list varies based on the game type, the target platform, or the debugging results, or even varies based on the engine! However, assuming that we are using Unreal Engine (which in fact is the truth) and the problem came from the Particle Systems, it is better to do the following:

- Reduce the particle emission count per emitter if there are lots of emitters in the scene.
- Reduce the total number of Particle Systems in the level.
- Reducing the lifetime per emitter is a good way to get less particles drawn per frame while keeping the same result.
- If a collision is not required, don't check it. If it is necessary, then reduce the amount of particles that collide, while adding others that do not collide.
- Set fixed bounds on the Particle Systems. This way guarantees that you will not calculate them in every frame.
- Set up LODs if you are not already using them.
- Increase the LOD distance check time in order to check the LOD less.
- Replace the game thread calculated particle effects with static mesh effects. For example, replace the fire with a projected flame texture on a cylinder.
- Using materials with less complexity will help you reduce the expense on the GPU.
- Reduce the particle size and amount in the case of high overdraw on the screen (smoke).
- Disable the lit particles.
- Replace sprite emitters with the GPU ones if they output a lot of particles.

Creating your own particle is the best way to make sure that everything is tied together. So, let's start building a Particle System, and once we speak about the Particle Systems, there is nothing better than a fire:

1. Start by adding a Particle System blueprint in the content browser. Right-click on an empty space in the Content Browser, and select Particle System. Then, feel free to name it whatever you want:

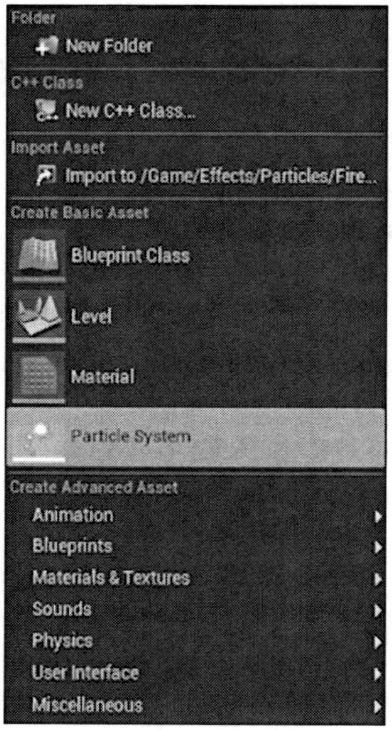

2. Once you are done, double-click on it to launch the Cascade editor. You'll find that it contains one emitter by default, which has the small points moving upwards:

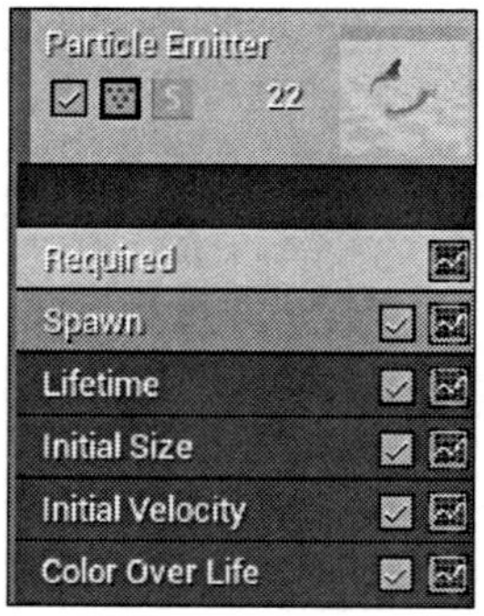

3. Add a second emitter, as the fire Particle System will contain the fire itself and the embers. Then, start adding some modules to it based on the look you are seeking. I've added some modules to move the fire faster, change the sprites, do some rotations and some drag:

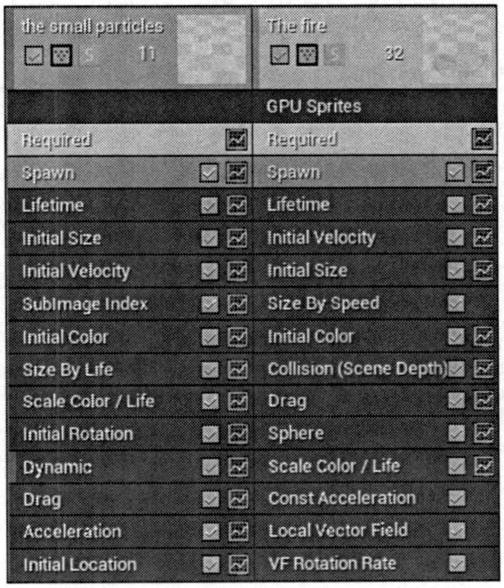

4. Get a sprites animated atlas (the one I got from the Unreal samples), and use it to build a material (refer to *Chapter 2, Understanding the Working of Materials*) that will be used with the Particle System:

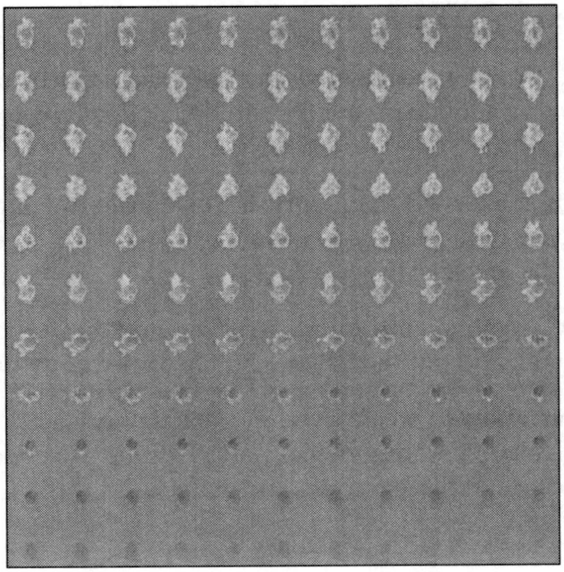

5. Keep tweaking and changing the added modules' values (a value between **5** and **9** was working fine with me with all the modules) until you reach the point that you are satisfied:

Summary

Now, you have learned the Unreal Engine's powerful Cascade editor in detail and started building Particle Systems.

Learning the concept behind the Cascade editor was a good step toward the proficiency for building Particle Systems, knowing the underlying core is always a good way to get in depth quickly.

Understanding the different module types is a skill itself. Once you know the power and limits of your tool, then you'll be able to define how to go about it with each module.

What comes after making a particle blueprint? You can start using it in the game. Using a couple of nodes, you are able to instance the particles on demand, or even use them directly at the level.

Now, with all this still fresh in your mind, go ahead and make some smoke, fire, trails, explosions, blood, and perhaps, water but be aware of getting yourself wet.

Now that we have seen how to create dynamic visual effects at runtime, let's take a step back and look into generating precomputed lighting to create efficient and visually appealing scenes to place our dynamic effects.

4
Precomputed Lights

Nowadays, with the innovations in gaming hardware and software, games are characterized and defined by both their gameplay and visual quality. When developing games with increasingly complex scenes, it becomes equally important for them to not only look good but also run efficiently.

A huge part of these optimizations is left to the rendering team, as they take the final decision on shading an object (let's say a character) using one light source, two lights sources, or even without any light sources. It is their decision to use their rendering tools in order to reduce the amount of rendered triangles over the GPU.

One major technique that has been invented over the years is the precomputed lights technique (lightmaps or lightmass). This technique will make sure that the game's lighting will be close to zero over the GPU performance. Well, not 100 percent zero, but I want to show you how much the precomputed lights technique is going to save you. It will be drastically reduced as dynamic lighting is another important tool that can be used in real-time games.

By the end of this chapter, you will be able to:

- Understand the concept of the precomputed lightmass in Unreal Engine
- Understand when it is not possible to use the lightmass and that this should be replaced with something else
- Understand the AO (Ambient Occlusion) and its settings
- Know how to set up the lightmass volume
- Understand all the lightmass settings and the usage of each parameter

- Set different settings per light source to control its effect over the lightmass
- Cache the indirect lighting
- Capture the reflection all over the map using the Reflection Capture volumes

With all our goals defined, and as you are already so eager, let's get started!

Understanding lightmass

Have you ever heard of the term "lightmaps"?

Well, it is one of the innovations that has arrived in the past few years. It is basically textures (or maps) that have the light data. This means that textures are applied to the entire scene with the light and dark areas.

Unreal Engine provides its rendering toolset the ability to bake the light data into a lightmap that will be used later at runtime to light the level. The lightmass builds the lightmaps for the stationary light sources and the static light sources only. It is obviously clear why it does not support the Dynamic (Moveable) lights, as these types of lights can't be precomputed with any means.

The Swarm agent

Building lightmaps for large and complex levels could cost you time and performance to produce them. As Unreal Engine is full of surprises and hidden tools, there is a small C# tool that is connected to the Unreal editor, which plays the role of the manager to handle the communication between the lightmass and the editor. This manager is called the Swarm agent. The Swarm agent runs on a Windows platform only (there is still a Mac copy of it, but Epic is still planning to convert it to a C++ tool to make it more efficient and more cross-platform). It distributes the workload for computation across multiple machines (build farm).

Swarm is auto fired in order to perform its job and stay minimized, which means that you don't have to manually run it from somewhere else. It was written to know the time it takes to start, finish its job, and then shut down.

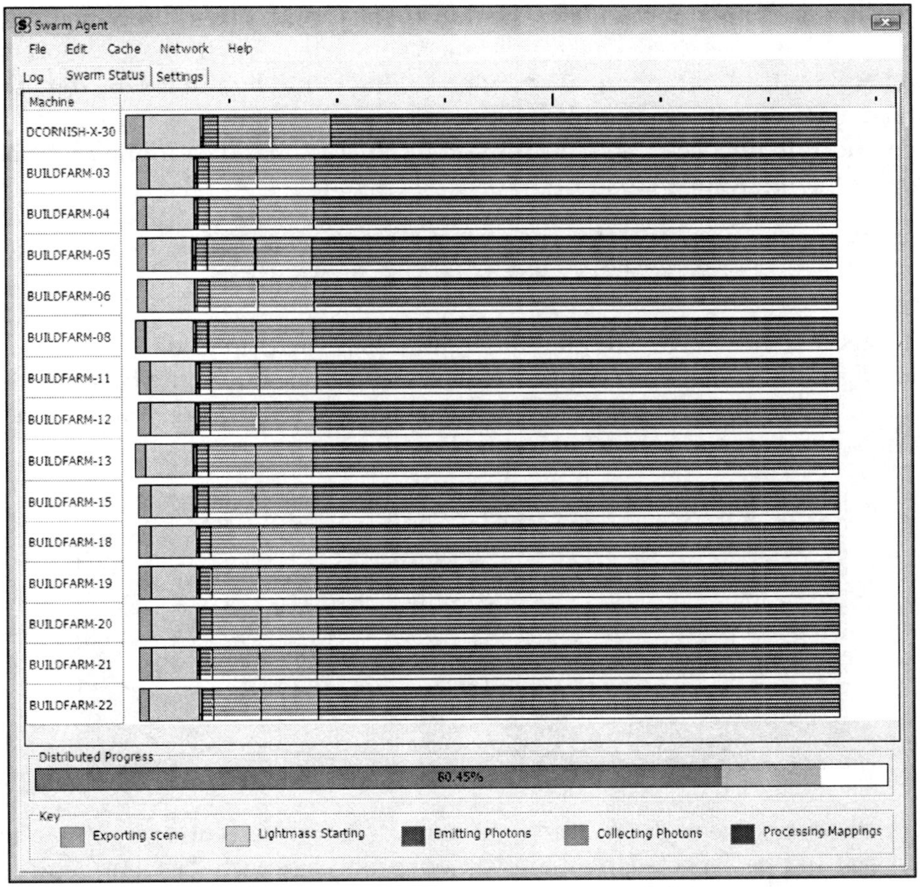

For more information on the Swarm agent, you can check out the Unreal Engine 3 UDN documentation site at `http://udn.epicgames.com/Three/Swarm.html`, as Swarm is still not covered in Unreal Engine 4 at the time of writing.

The Ambient Occlusion

The Ambient Occlusion term is a shading and rendering technique used to calculate how exposed each point in a scene is to ambient lighting.

When lightmass is built, it calculates the indirect shadows; this indirect shadowing is called **Ambient Occlusion** (**AO**). Lightmass supports calculating AO, applying it to direct and indirect illumination, and then baking it into lightmaps. By default, AO is enabled, but you still can disable it for your own artist goals. Disabling it is very easy; you need to uncheck the **Use Ambient Occlusion** checkbox in the **Lightmass Settings** of the **Lightmass** tab under **World Settings**.

Don't forget that you have to rebuild the lightmass in order to update it to the latest configurations that you changed. You can check the difference between the two images. While the first image has AO disabled, the second one has it enabled (check out the edges and corners of indirect shadowing):

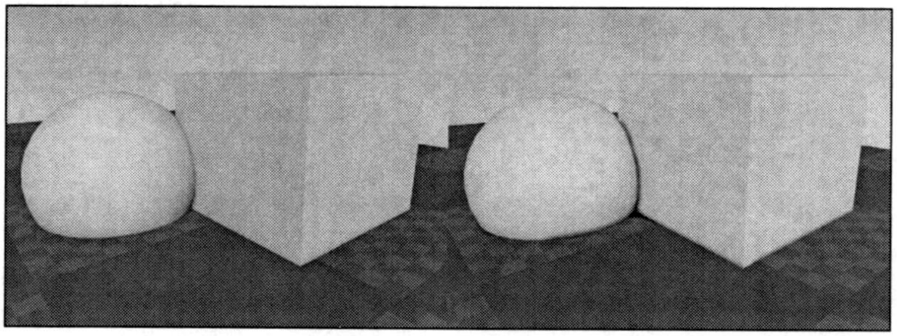

The only disadvantage of the AO is that it requires a high resolution lightmap in order to look like as expected, and it never looks like as expected as long as the quality setting is set to the **Preview** quality.

The Ambient Occlusion settings

In the **Lightmass** option, there are a lot of parameters that can be tweaked, but only five parameters out of them are responsible for the AO settings.

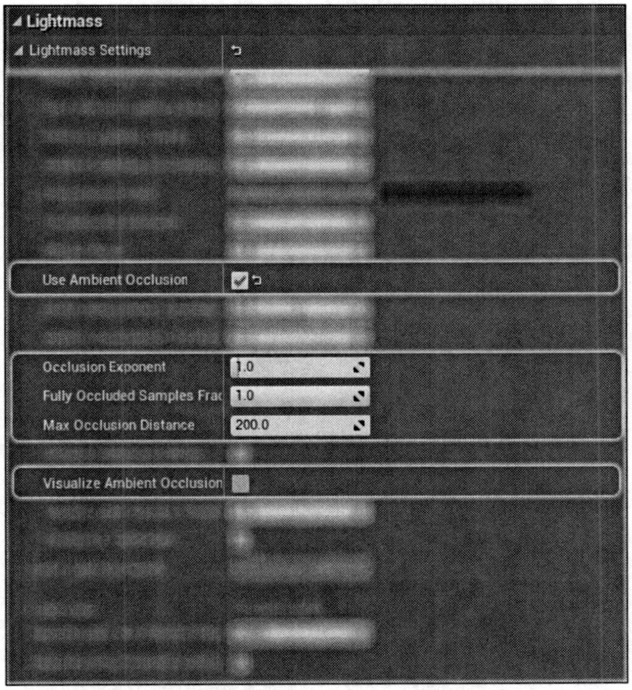

- **Use Ambient Occlusion**: This enables and disables the feature.
- **Occlusion Exponent**: Higher exponents increase the contrast.
- **Fully Occluded Samples Fraction**: Higher values cause the indirect lighting to be more smooth.
- **Max Occlusion Distance**: This is the maximum distance for an object to cause occlusion on another object.
- **Visualize Ambient Occlusion**: This is useful to see the occlusion changes you have made and to compare the effects of the different settings, as it works on overriding the lightmaps.

The Lightmass Settings option

In order to get control over the lightmass' final results, Epic has given you a lot of attributes to be adjusted. Unfortunately, not all of them are in one place, which means that there isn't a panel where you can adjust all the parameters related to the lightmass. The reason for this is the wide modularity of the engine. So if you are going to use lightmass (which is what everyone does nowadays), you will need to adjust the settings for the levels, meshes, brushes, materials, light sources, and finally, the **Lightmass Importance Volume**.

- **Lightmass Settings**: The global **Lightmass Settings** can be found under the **World Settings** window in the **Lightmass** section.

> When adjusting the settings to render quality, it is dangerous to change the numbers very quickly. These settings should be adjusted in small increments in order to find the perfect balance of quality and performance, unless you want to crash the game.

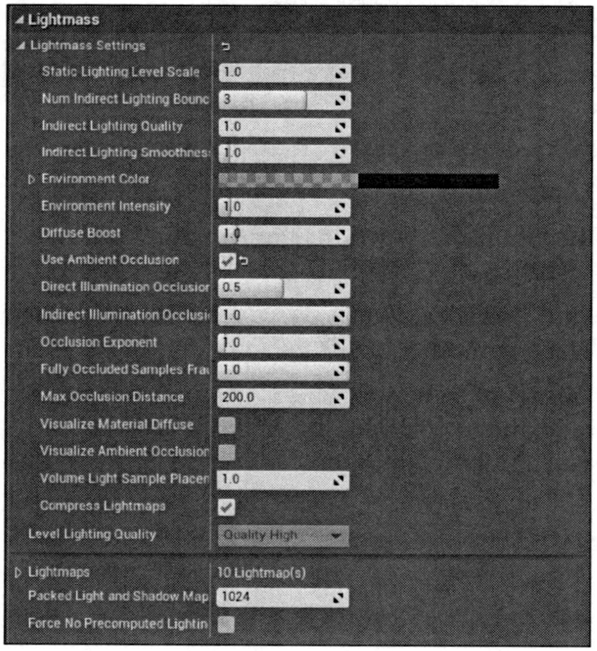

  - **Static Lighting Level Scale**: While 1 Unreal unit is equal to 1 cm, this value represents the scale of the level relative to the scale of the engine. This is usually used to decide how much detail to calculate in the lighting. Logically, the smaller scales will increase build times.

- **Num Indirect Lighting Bounces**: This is the number of times light is allowed to bounce off surfaces, starting from the light source. 0 is direct lighting only, 1 is one bounce.
- **Indirect Lighting Quality:** This scales the sample counts used by the Lightmass GI solver. Higher settings result in fewer solver artifacts but longer build times.
- **Indirect Lighting Smoothness**: Higher values cause the indirect lighting to be more smooth, which can hide the solver noise, but this also causes detailed indirect shadows and Ambient Occlusion to be lost. It is useful if you are looking for a more dramatic effect. It's best to keep the smoothness lower as it then gives a sharper and more dramatic edge to the end of the light radius.
- **Environment Color**: This is the color that rays that miss the scene will pick up.
- **Environment Intensity**: This scales the previous value to allow an HDR environment color.
- **Diffuse Boost**: The value here will be used as a multiplier (or scaling factor) for all the diffuse used with all the level materials. Increasing this value will increase the intensity of the scene's indirect lighting.
- **Use Ambient Occlusion**: This enables the static AO.
- **Direct Illumination Occlusion Fraction**: This shows how much of the AO to apply to direct lighting.
- **Indirect Illumination Occlusion Fraction**: This shows how much of the AO to apply to indirect lighting.
- **Occlusion Exponent**: Higher exponents increase the contrast.
- **Fully Occluded Samples Fraction**: In order to reach the full occlusion, this defined amount of samples must be occluded.
- **Max Occlusion Distance**: This is the maximum distance for an object to cause occlusion on another object.
- **Visualize Material Diffuse**: This is a toggle value that overrides the direct and indirect lighting with the exported lightmass diffuse. It is useful when you want to verify that the exported material diffuse matches with the actual scene diffuse because the end result will look a lot brighter.
- **Visualize Ambient Occlusion**: As discussed earlier, this toggle value should only be used for visualization purposes, as it isolates the Ambient Occlusion only by overriding the direct and the indirect lighting with the Ambient Occlusion.

  - **Volume Light Sample Placement Scale**: While the volume light samples are computed via the lightmass, this value will scale the distances where the volume lighting samples area is placed. Using the larger scales will result in less sample memory usage and will reduce the indirect lighting cache's update time.
  - **Compress Lightmaps**: This enables or disables the texture's compression. Disabling it will result in an increase in the memory size and the disk size, but it also produces more tidy textures with less artifacts.
  - **Level Lighting Quality**: This reflects the current level lighting build quality settings.
  - **Lightmaps**: This is a list of the lightmaps textures.
  - **Packed Light and Shadow Map Texture Size**: This is the maximum size for the packed light textures and the shadow maps.
  - **Force No Precomputed Lighting**: A true or false value will force the lightmaps not to be created at the time when the engine wants to auto compute them. It is a good choice if you are looking for a fully dynamic lighting at your level.

- **Importance Volume Settings**: At a big level, there are a lot of level parts that are mostly there for the sake of having them.

  Some parts are not visible to the player at all, while other parts are visible but are neither reachable (such as far mountains) nor playable elements, and they do not have any interaction with the player.

  Only the actual playable area needs high-quality lighting, while the lightmass emits photons based on the size of the level. These background unused objects and meshes will be there to just increase the number of photons that need to be emitted. This will end up with a higher lighting build time.

  Here comes one of the most outstanding tools in Unreal Engine, the **Lightmass Importance Volume**, which is used to control the area that lightmass emits photons from, and allows you to concentrate on the lightmass' efforts. But the scene meshes that are outside the importance volume will end up with a lower quality, and only one bounce of the indirect lighting.

As you can see, this is a map of a racing game. In the first image, you will see the size of the full map, but actually what the player needs is the central part, which is in the second image.

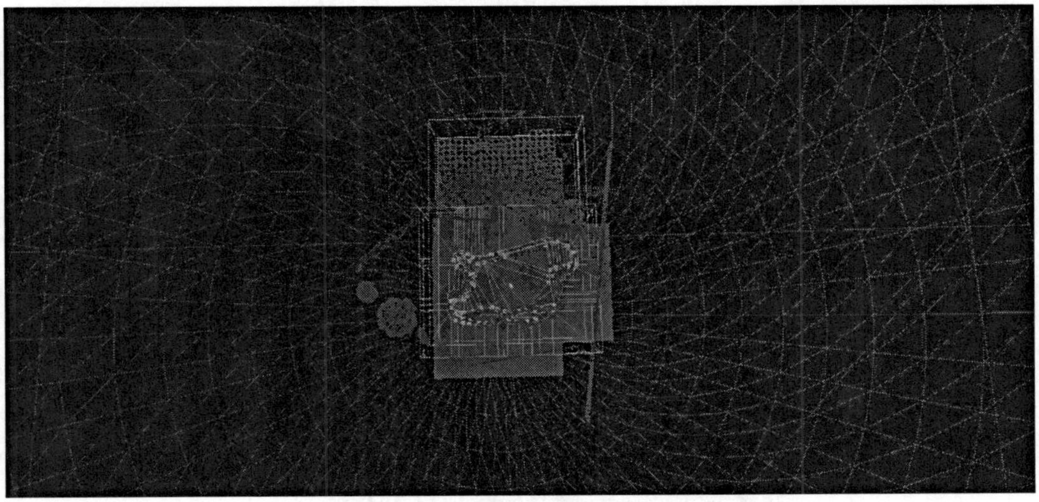

In the preceding screenshot, it looks big and giant size, but it is zoomed too far away to display the map of a racing game. While there are lots of elements that are far away from the gameplay area, these elements are excluded from the importance volume. The volume only contains what is necessary to the player.

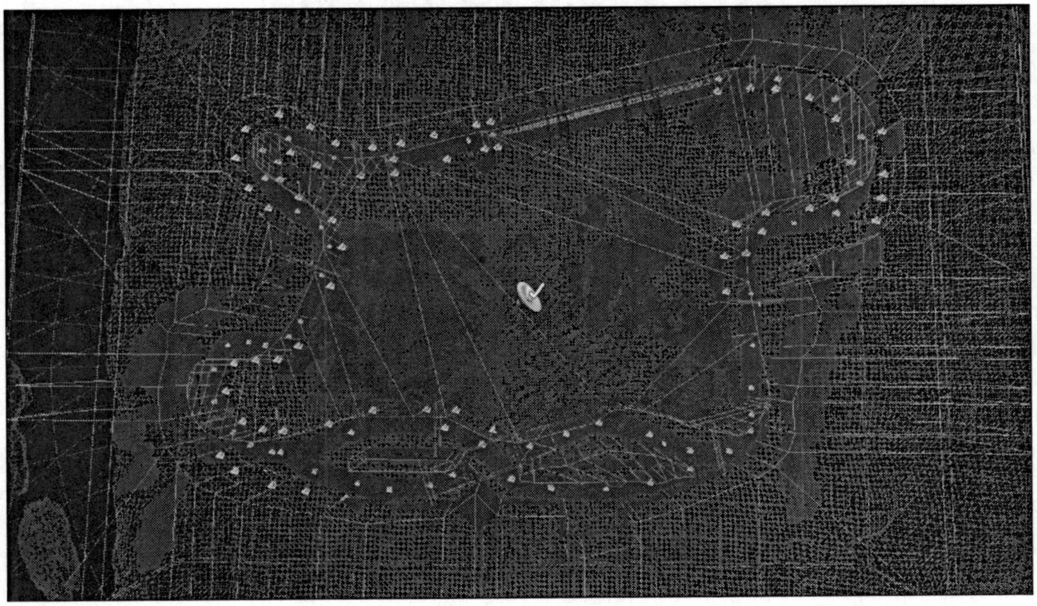

Lightmass Importance Volume is added to the level in the same way you can add any other volumes by just dragging and dropping them into the level. You just need to know where to find them in the **Modes** panel.

Here, not only the volume can be used, but any brush shape in Unreal Engine can be used as the importance volume. You just need to convert the brush into the **Lightmass Importance Volume** by selecting the actor and choosing the **Convert** actor.

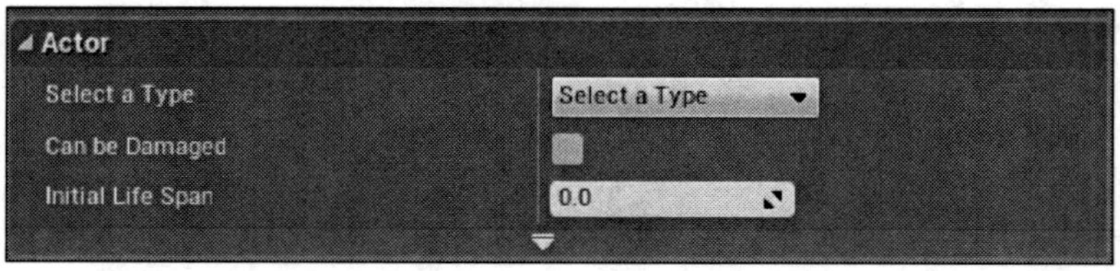

Then, select the proper type from the list. This method is not only used to convert brushes into a **Lightmass Importance Volume**, but it can be used to convert a brush into any of the types listed in the drop-down list.

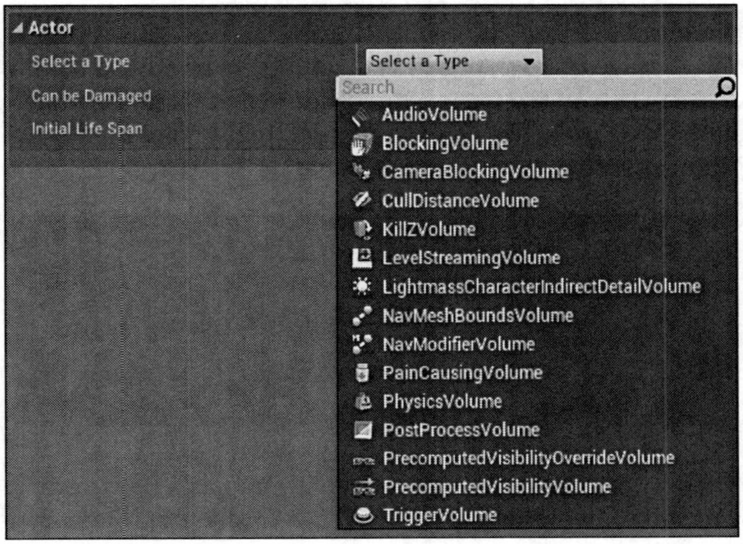

The light shape settings

Any light source that can be found in the Unreal editor has some lightmass parameters that are listed in the **Lightmass** section in its **Details** panel.

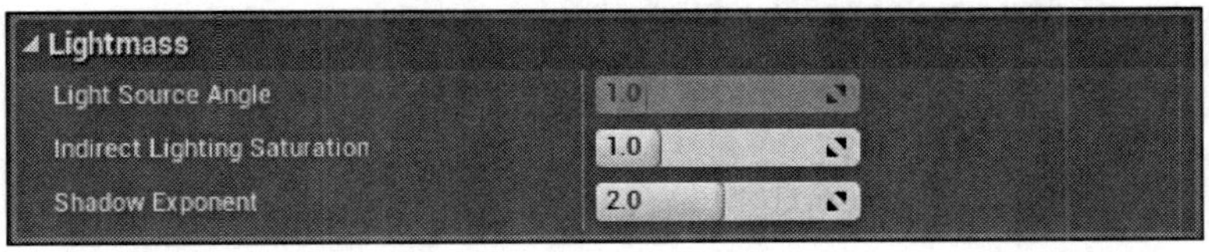

- **Light Source Angle**: This determines the angle that the light's emissive surface extends in relation to a receiver (but only for Directional Light sources)
- **Indirect Lighting Saturation**: 0 will result in indirect lighting being completely desaturated, 1 will be unchanged
- **Shadow Exponent**: This controls how fast areas change from fully lit to fully shadowed, or in a more technical manner, it controls the shadow penumbras' falloff value

The materials settings

Even a material asset has its own **Lightmass** settings to be adjusted. To access them, you have to double-click on the material in order to open it in the Material Editor, and then select the base node of the material, and finally, find the **Lightmass** settings under the **Lightmass** section of the **Details** panel.

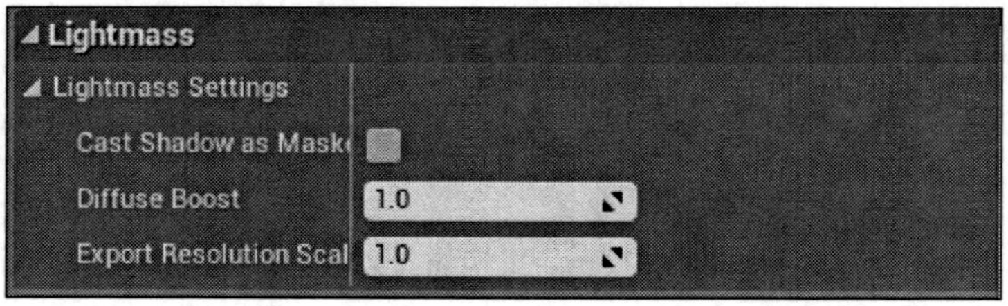

- **Cast Shadow as Masked**: This works with translucent materials, as it is meant to treat the material as if it is masked for the purpose of shadow casting
- **Diffuse Boost**: This scales up the diffuse contribution of this material to the static lighting
- **Export Resolution Scale**: If you need more details of a surface using this material, then scaling up this value will scale up the resolution that this material's attributes are exported at

The brush settings

After adding a brush, you might need to apply some changes to it in order to be able to see its **Lightmass** settings in the **Details** panel.

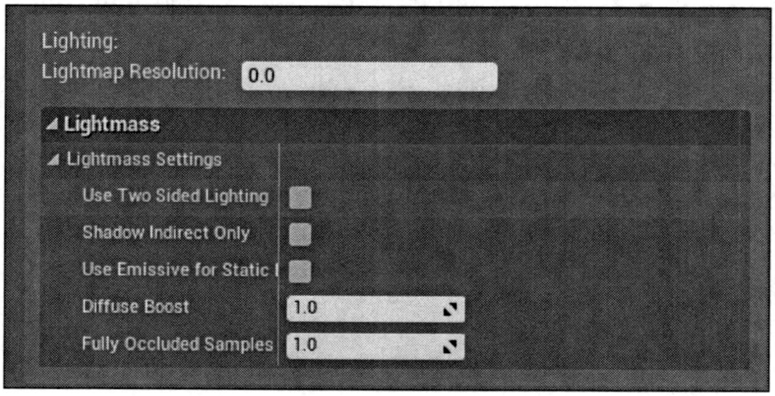

- **Lightmap Resolution**: This is the resolution of the lightmap
- **Use Two Sided Lighting**: Setting this to true makes this object light up as if it receives light from both sides of its polygons
- **Shadow Indirect Only**: A true or false value indicates if the object is going to only be shadowed with the indirect lighting
- **Use Emissive for Static Lighting**: Setting this to true will allow you to use emissive for static lighting
- **Diffuse Boost**: This scales the diffuse contribution of all the materials applied to this brush
- **Fully Occluded Samples Fraction**: This value allows you to control how much occlusion an object causes on other objects

Building the lightmaps

If you have made some changes to the lightmaps' options, don't expect to see them at runtime. It makes no sense!

As lightmaps are a precomputed solution, you have to build/rebuild the current lightmaps or even make new ones.

In order to rebuild the lightmaps, you can navigate to the famous **Build** button in the top bar. Don't hit the button yet.

The **Build** button is not only there for the lightmaps, but this is a general **Build** option that triggers all the build processes, which include building the navigation meshes, geometries, reflections, lightmaps, and so on.

In order to trigger a specific job, you have to press the down arrow next to the button to open the long list of wonders and pick **Build Lighting Only**.

This will trigger a building process, which will display a small window in the lower-right corner of your screen, where you can see the progress or even cancel the job. Once it is done, it will notify you with that it is complete, as shown in the following screenshot:

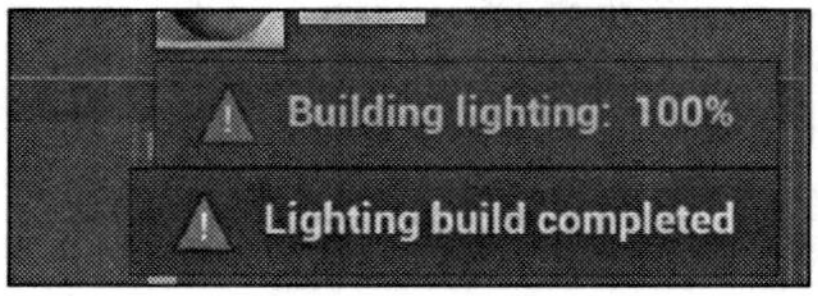

The Indirect Lighting Cache

I've mentioned earlier that the lightmass works on generating lightmaps for the indirect lighting on static (non-moveable) objects. What about dynamic objects?

In your game, you mostly have static objects, such as the environmental elements, such as trees or buildings. However, you can also have dynamic/moveable objects, such as the player characters, enemies, or NPCs. These dynamic objects can still receive indirect lighting too. But not via lightmass lightmaps.

In order to get indirect lighting on the dynamic objects, we can use Epic's Indirect Lighting Cache, which uses samples generated by the lightmass at build time (in the editor or edit mode) to calculate the indirect lighting for dynamic objects at runtime (during the gameplay). If you come from a Unity 3D background like a lot of my students, I like to say, "*It is just the equivalent of the light probes*".

The image to the left shows the dynamic object without the indirect lighting cache, while the image to the right shows the effect of the dynamic light cache. It is very clear that the mesh is not lit at all as it is dynamic and the normal lightmaps are not going to include it.

While the lightmass is building, it places the lighting samples on the static surfaces. The lightmass places these samples in the **Lightmass Importance Volume** and on top of the upward-facing surfaces with high density, and everywhere else with low density.

In order to be able to visualize the lighting samples generated by the lightmass, you can easily do this by navigating to the **Show** button at the top of the viewport. Then, from the **Visualize** section, choose the **Volume Lighting Samples** option:

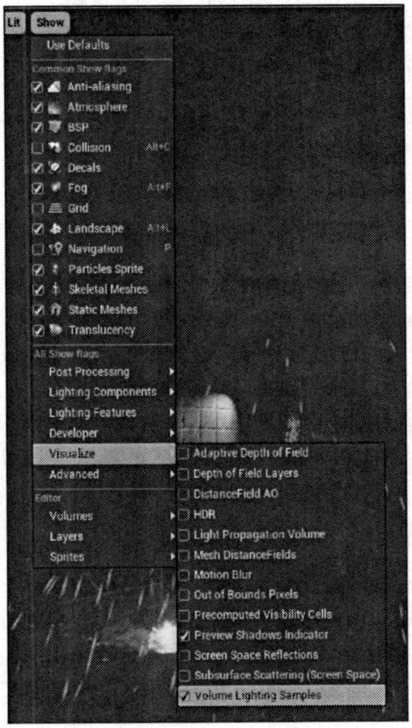

What is a dynamic object then?

Similar to lights, objects can also be defined as static or dynamic to determine how they interact with lights. The same method is used to set objects to either static or dynamic. The Dynamic/Movable object is just any object or component (mostly the Static Mesh component) with **Mobility** set to **Movable**.

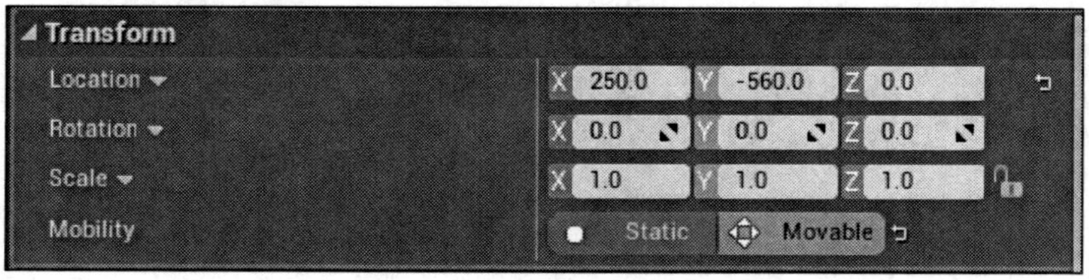

Do static meshes use the Indirect Lighting Cache?

Well, in real-time simulations (games), no. However, technically, yes! This is where the intelligence of Unreal Engine comes in. The Indirect Lighting Cache allows you to preview Static Meshes with unbuilt lighting. This means that when you move a Static Mesh that has lighting built (already has part of the lightmap, and as it is a Static Mesh, it should not be moved and it makes sense), it will automatically switch to the Indirect Lighting Cache rather than displaying it in complete darkness, until the next lighting build, and then it will switch back to use the lightmap data. So neat! It is worth mentioning that the Indirect Lighting Cache is great for conceptualizing the look of a level without having to constantly recompile and build lighting. Still neat!

You can see this behavior tons of times in the editor while building a level; if you already have a lightmap working fine, and you have decided to duplicate one of the static meshes for the sake of level design, then you will see that the object is wrongly lit until you rebuild the lightmaps again.

While working on building the lightmaps, lightmass places the lighting samples throughout the level and computes the indirect lighting for them during a lighting build. Then, when it's time to render a dynamic object at runtime, the Indirect Lighting Cache first checks to see if it already has the lighting available for that object. If it doesn't, then the Indirect Lighting Cache will interpolate lighting from the precomputed lighting samples that already exist. Which means at runtime, the Indirect Lighting Cache will interpolate the lighting samples to the positions around the movable object.

Using the **LightmassCharacterIndirectDetailVolumes** around the scene at the spots where it is expected that the dynamic object will pass through in order to get more details because the auto placement of the samples is not always going to give the expected results.

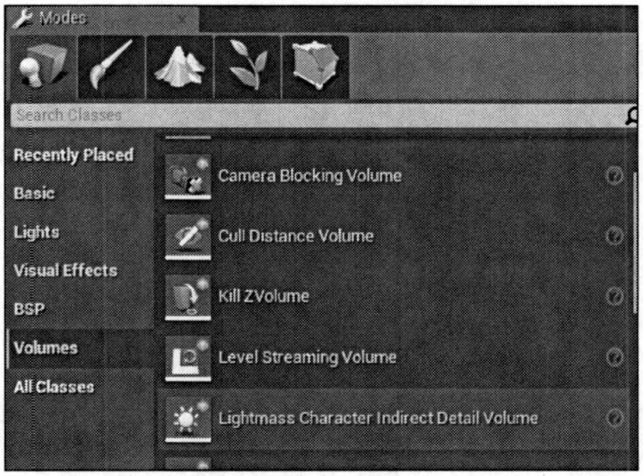

The Reflection Captures and the Reflection Environment

The Reflection Capture is not only a volume name but also the functionality name. Have you ever thought how much it costs to render the real-time reflections? Is it possible to reduce this cost?

So, with the same concept of the lightmaps, here is another different (but similar to its core goals) feature that Unreal Engine has in its toolset called the Reflection Environment via the Reflection Captures.

The Reflection Environment provides efficient reflections in all the directions of the scene, such as metal surfaces (the idea is to have objects that have materials with high and noticeable specular, and low roughness values, so it is not only metals!). While this sounds like an awesome feature, this includes dynamic objects, but they are not sharp reflections, which can be achieved using other Unreal methods such as the Screen Space Reflections.

By setting up some light sources and building the lightmass once, you are ready to start setting up the Reflection Environment. You will never be able to build it without having a prebuilt lightmap, as its calculations are based on having indirect diffuse lighting around the scene.

As with anything in the world, if there are pros, then there are some cons, or a mixture of disadvantages and limitations.

The cubemaps that are used to capture the scene are all 128 on each side. Due to DX11 hardware limitations, the world can have at most 341 reflection captures enabled at one time.

Reflections this way are approximate. Because of the projection into multiple simple shapes and creating multiple versions of that object in reflections, the reflection of an object will not match up to 100 percent with the object in the scene.

The capturers only capture the scene's diffuse in order to reduce the errors and artifacts. Also, the dynamic objects cannot be reflected at runtime due to the performance capturing needs.

Setting up the Reflection Environment is super simple. It is done usually by inserting the **Sphere Reflection Capture** actor into the scene (this is usually the sphere shape but there is still one cube, and we will discuss the differences later).

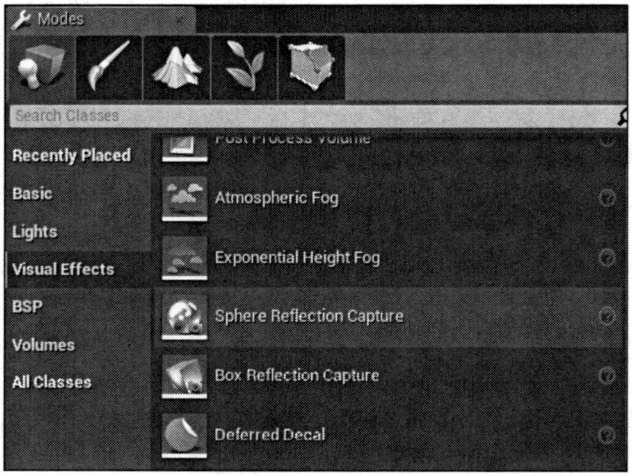

You've got to keep in mind that the reflections captured are not always kept up to date. This means that if you add a new object to the scene, move an object, or even make any changes to the scene, these changes will not be captured.

Only loading a map or building lighting will update the reflection captures. So anytime you've made a change, and you want it to be included and captured, you have to select a capture and click on **Update Captures** in order to capture the latest changes.

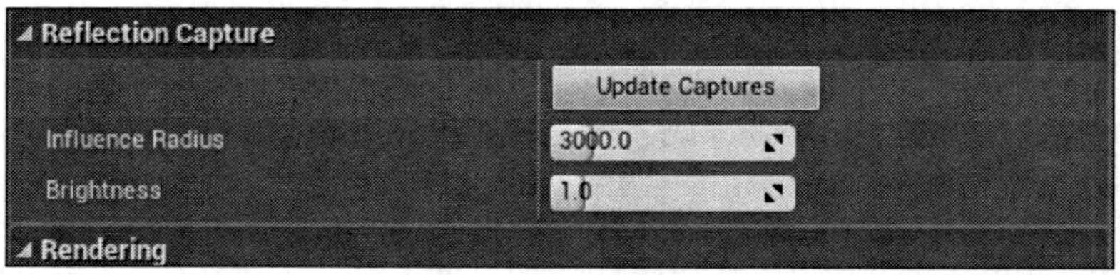

As with all the other optimizations you are going to make with Unreal, there is always a way to visualize and review the changes you make. While you are able to display the Indirect Light Cache, you are able to display what is being captured by the **Sphere Reflection Capture** by enabling the **Reflection Override** view mode.

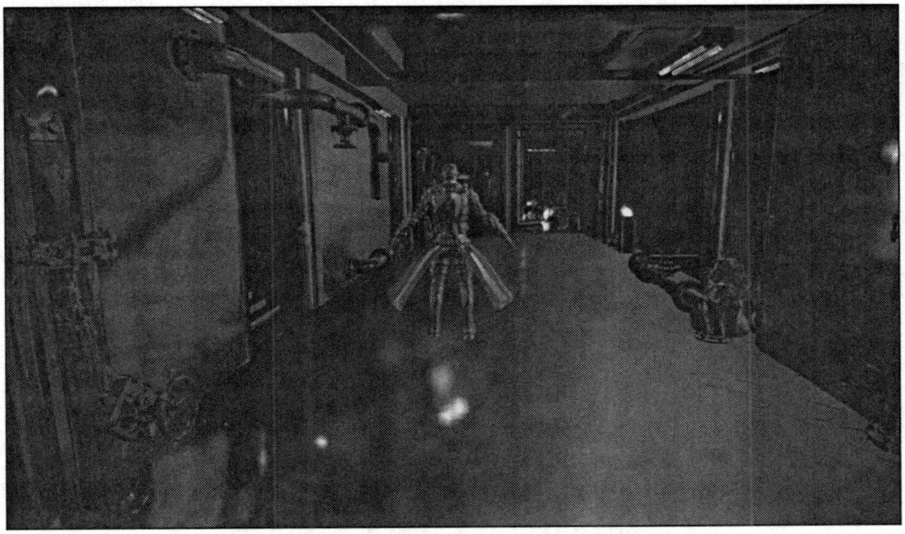

The Reflection Environment mechanic is simple. It works on capturing the static objects of the scene at different capturing spots, and then projecting them as reflections onto simple surfaces such as spheres. This is the reason behind the spherical shape of the capturer actor.

You can manually select the capturing spots by just placing the Reflection Capture actors and you can ask Unreal to define this area as a Reflection Capturing area. As long as you are in the editor and build your levels in edit mode, the reflections on the spherical shape will keep them updated in real time during the editing process. Once you hit play or package your project into a game, the reflections will be static during runtime.

The Reflection Capture actors

There are two Reflection Capture actors supported by Unreal Engine. You can find both of them listed in the **Modes** panel.

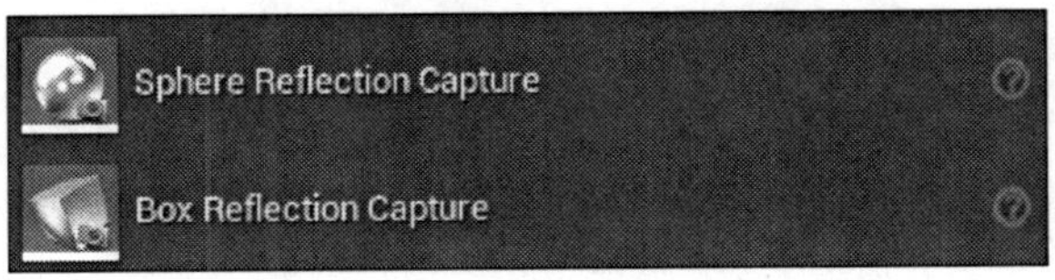

The main difference between them is the shape of the capturer itself, as the shape of it is the most important element of this process. The shape works on defining which parts of the scene are captured in the cubemap, and then which parts of the scene can receive reflections from that cubemap. The two supported shapes are discussed in the later section.

The sphere shape

The sphere shape is the most useful one. As it has no corners (discontinuities), it is hard to match the reflected object.

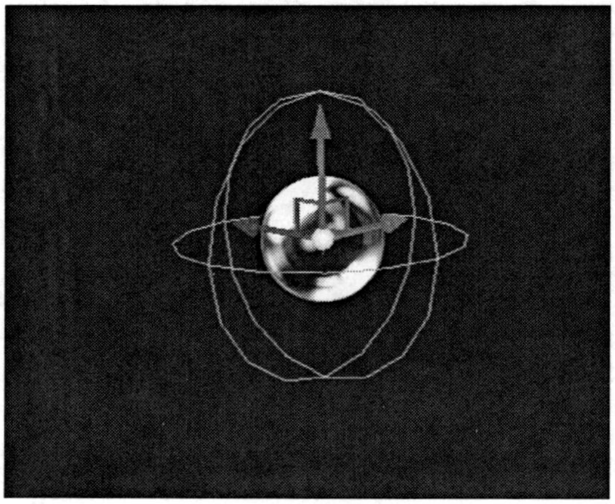

As you can control the radius of the effect, smaller captures will override larger ones, so you can provide refinement by placing smaller captures around the scene. If you have a room, putting a large one in the middle, while putting smaller ones in the corners will be your best solution to get all perfectly done.

Using the orange gizmo surrounding the sphere shape, which visualizes the radius, you can control which pixels can be affected by the cubemap.

The box shape

It is easier to call it the useless shape or the limited one, as it only works well when it is used with rectangular rooms, but a lot of people still use the sphere shape for that case too! Lots of people do not trust it for the sake of being a cube as it produces lots of artifacts due to the projection onto a box shape.

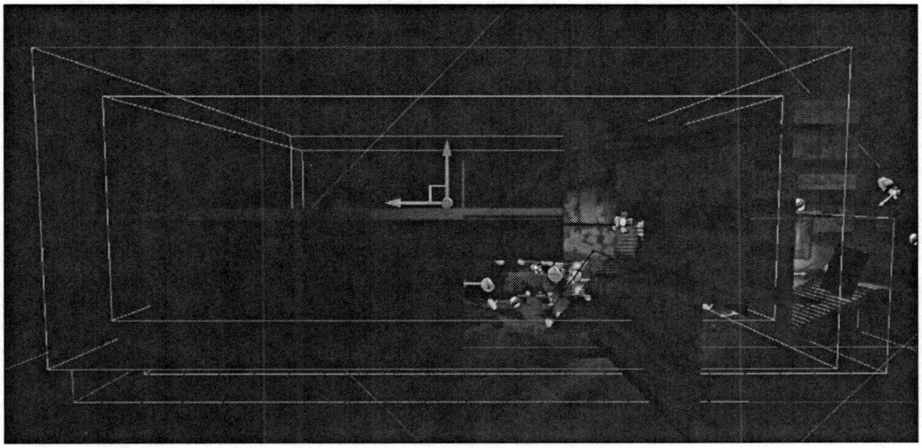

As is the case with the sphere, the box has a gizmo that displays its range too (this is also colored orange).

Summary

Now you have learned all about precomputed lights, and how to make them in order to help you game perform better without the real-time lights (which is not a bad thing by the way, but you have to take a look at the balance between the quality and the performance regarding your game and platform requirements).

You now have your hands on the lightmass and global illumination, and how to manage all its settings in order to set up the best lightmass.

Also, you have learned how to cache the indirect light samples in order to use them for the global illumination of the moveable objects.

The Reflection Environment is essential in order to get acceptable levels. This is because it keeps the performance cost as low as possible, while giving you lots of heavy reflection details for free frame rate dropping. Now you know how, why, and when to use the Reflection Capture actors to capture reflections and reuse them at runtime.

Now with all this fresh in mind, I would suggest you directly go and read the next chapter, to learn even more about the performance and the other type of lights. In the next chapter, we will discuss the other party of light types, which are the Dynamic lights. If you are ready, then let's go!

5
Dynamic Lights Versus Performance

In the previous chapter, we discussed the precomputed lights and the performance that is going to save to you. Now comes the time to speak more about what might cost you some performance, but it is absolutely worth it!

Dynamic lights are lights that are computed at runtime, unlike precomputed lights, which are prebuilt before running the game. Dynamic lights are live! This means that the lighting can change as the game changes. Since dynamic lights are not precomputed, they will affect the performance of your game.

Unreal Engine 4.x has a lot of techniques and methods for the Dynamic lights, starting with the simple moveable light. While there are almost five techniques related to the Dynamic Lights, I decided to pick up the most popular, optimized, and regularly needed ones.

By the end of this chapter, you will be able to:

- Correctly set up a Movable light
- Use Distance Field Ambient Occlusion
- Use Ray Traced Distance Field Soft shadows
- Properly use a mix of both in the game to get a high quality real-time rendering but still have the lowest possible performance cost
- Understand the pros and cons of each feature, and how to get around some of them

With all our goals defined, and you already so eager, let's get started!

Movable Lights

Have you ever thought of moving a light? I guess you must have done it before! Moving a light will not just change its position in space, but as long as that light emits photons and light's surfaces, its light will be affected too. This is the core concept behind calling these Dynamic Lights type by the name "Moveable lights", as they can not only move at runtime, but also rotate and update any of their attributes. This means that they can not only affect the overall lighting of the scene, but they can also change the rotation of some of the attributes, including the color and brightness.

Keep in mind that while the Movable lights emit the most accurate and intensive dynamic lights and/or shadows, this was enough for Epic to exclude them from the light maps. This means that if you are baking a scene with different light types, the affect of all the Moveable Lights will be ignored and not baked into the final lightmap.

As discussed in *Chapter 1, An Introduction to Lighting and Rendering*, each light has something called the **Mobility Option**, which defines its state. Regardless of the light source type (spot, directional, point, and so on), you can find its mobility state close to its transform values. By setting it to Moveable, the following will happen:

- The light will be considered as Moveable (hmmm, makes sense, hah!)
- The gizmo in the scene view will be changed to the moveable light icon, so you can recognize the light types directly without the need to select them first.

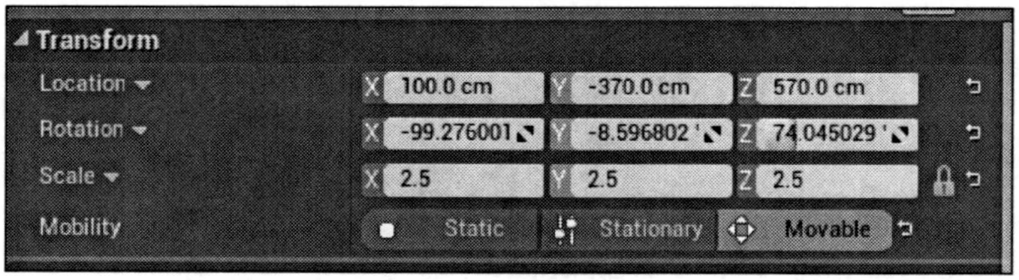

The most important benefit of having a moveable light is having a real-time shadow that is up to date in each single frame. Can you imagine lighting a city in real time and emitting shadows out of each single item in the scene that has a huge performance cost, which sometimes leads to overheating your graphics card (never been lucky enough to bet my cards broken because of an engine or game yet!)? This performance cost comes from the amount of meshes affected by the light and the number of triangles for each mesh. So, try to use it wisely, or not use it at all!

Anyway, the Moveable Light is still the most raw and basic method of having a real-time dynamic light in your game.

Distance Field Ambient Occlusion

Have you seen *The Kite* demo, also known as *Set it Free* by Epic games? If you haven't, I would recommend that you watch it. It is perfect from all aspects, such as the technical side and story side. There is no normal way to light such a massive environment in real time with a dynamic light and good performance (currently, on NVidia Titan X), without using Unreal's **Distance Field Ambient Occlusion** (let's call it **DFAO** for short).

With such a big environment shadowing a Movable Sky Light, while it supports dynamic scene changes can be made possible by this new feature presented in GDC 2015.

This feature will generate a medium-scale Ambient Occlusion from the Distance Field Volumes precomputed around each rigid object.

While this sounds like a cool and well-optimized dynamic lighting solution, it has its own advantages and disadvantages, which are as follows:

- It does not support all the mesh types; for now, it only supports Static/Instanced Static Mesh Components, landscape, and foliage.
- Sometimes the large meshes produce poor quality results.
- It does not support high nonuniform scaling. However, slight changes are fine.

The Kite demo - GDC 2015

Setting it up

As a rule of thumb, any **Distance field shadows-based** feature will require the **Project** setting **Generate Mesh Distance Fields** in the **Rendering** tab. If you can't see any changes, you need to restart your editor:

1. Enable the **Project** setting (under **Rendering**) **Generate Mesh Distance Fields** and restart the editor.
2. Reload the map or scene in order to generate distance fields.
3. Set the **Engine Scalability Settings** to **Epic** for **Shadows**:

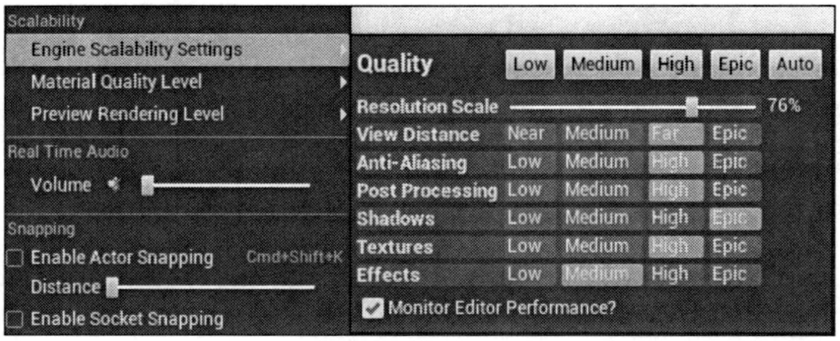

4. Place a **Skylight** in your scene view.
5. Set the **Mobility** of the **Skylight** to **Movable**.
6. While it is working, you just need to tweak some options to get the look you want. Mainly, you might need to set the level and AO from **Static Meshes** to avoid the splotchy lighting.

> **Two things to keep in mind**
>
> - Generating the distance fields takes place in the background while loading the level. This process is multithreaded, which means that the more cores you have, the less generation time it takes.
> - The rigid meshes can be moved or disabled and it will affect the occlusion. Unlike Screen Space Ambient Occlusion, the occlusion is computed from the world space occludes, so there are no artifacts from the missing data off the screen.

Limitations

While the Distance Field Ambient Occlusion looks solid the first time you read about it (you might have already said the same thing as I did the first time I knew about it, "I'll always be using only this feature; it is enough for me"), there are some limitations that I've figured out, and you have to know that it cannot suit all cases:

- Only Static Mesh Components, Instanced Static Mesh Components, foliage, and landscape are supported
- In order to make foliage work, foliage must enable **bAffectDistanceFieldLighting** on its settings
- Its support is limited to DX11 only
- The high values of nonuniform scaling can cause artifacts
- It casts shadows only from the rigid meshes
- It provides only the Ambient Occlusion
- The materials with a vertex shader that deforms the world position offset of the mesh, or even the displacement, will cause artifacts
- Large objects have a poor AO quality due to the low distance field resolution
- Foliage that has LODs enabled will probably have artifacts

Performance

As it is a feature heavily based on DX11, all the work is done on the GPU side and in its video memory. According to the Epic team's calculations:

> *In a fairly large Fortnite level, with the camera still, it costs 3.5ms on a Radeon 7870 at 1080p resolution. And the worst case when the camera is rotating rapidly is ~6ms. For reference, SSAO costs 1ms with this setup. ~150mb of distance field volume textures were used.*

It requires more time if the camera moves quickly. The shading is done adaptively, so the flat surfaces and static surfaces (not moveable) have the lowest cost. Even the small objects and the ones that are not moving cause performance spikes, as the main cost comes from the density, which means that you should be careful with the large open areas, as each object will be considered as a separate object for the occlusion.

This doesn't mean that it is impossible to get the best quality with a lower performance cost. In game development, it can get tricky, and you can go around the techniques in order to get better results. Once I read an article about how to make a DFAO in UE 4 with the lowest performance cost possible. It was basically done by disabling the **Lower Hemisphere Is Black** option in the sky light (as discussed later in the *Settings* section), then painting some color to the ground of the cube map. Finally, playing and enjoying the results!

Settings

As the Distance Field is not just a feature that can be checked to see whether it is active or not, it has a lot of settings scattered between different places. In order to start getting the correct results, you have to set some settings to various aspects of the editor.

The Sky Light

By selecting a Sky Light from the scene, and navigating to the **Details** panel, you'll be able to access the **Distance Field Ambient Occlusion** settings that are related to the Sky Light:

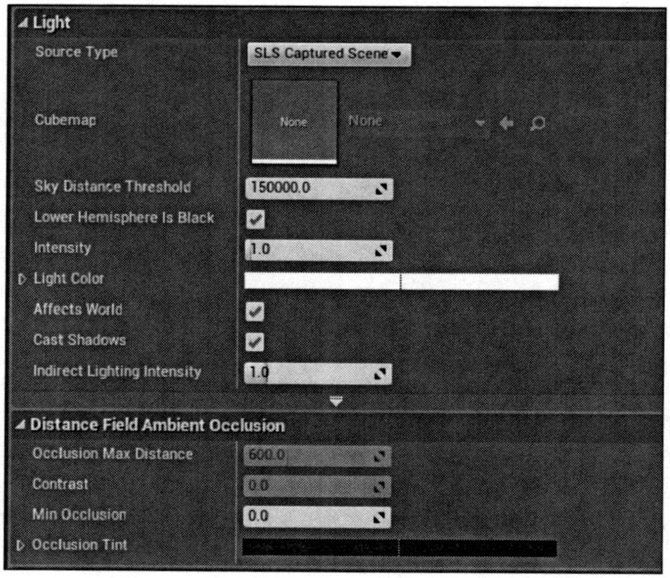

Some of the options available for this are as follows:

- **Affects World**: This shows whether the light can affect the world, or whether it can be disabled.

- **Cast Shadow**: This forces DFAO to only be computed if the light is set to cast shadows.
- **Indirect Lighting Intensity**: This scales the indirect light contribution from this light. A value of 0 means that it can disable any Global Illumination from this light source. It is 1 by default.
- **Occlusion Max Distance**: This is the maximum distance from an occlude for computing occlusion.
- **Contrast**: This controls the contrast of the computed occlusion.
- **Min Occlusion**: This is the minimum value of occlusion. It is very useful for preventing the occlusion from going fully black when desired.
- **Occlusion Tint**: This is used to color the occlusion with that color, and the color black should be the default color, but you might need to change it for some artistic reasons.

The primitive components

By selecting any of your actors, you'll have direct access to its components. Some of the actor's components will have a list of light options and settings, while others will not. What is the most important part of the mesh components? By selecting a mesh component and navigating to the details panel, you can activate them under the **Lighting** section. The **Affect Distance Field Lighting** option will enable or disable the primitive's influence on the DFAO:

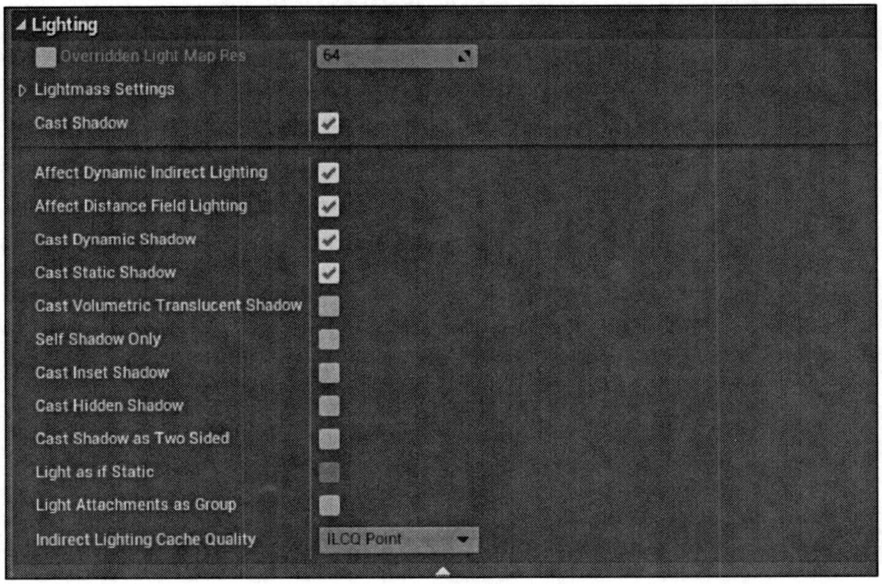

The Mesh Build settings

When you import any of the 3D meshes into Unreal Engine, you can open the mesh in the mesh editor by double-clicking on it from the content browser.

In the Mesh Editor, you can simply open the section named **Build Settings**, and there you will find a lot of settings. The most important ones are those related to the **Distance Field Ambient Occlusion**:

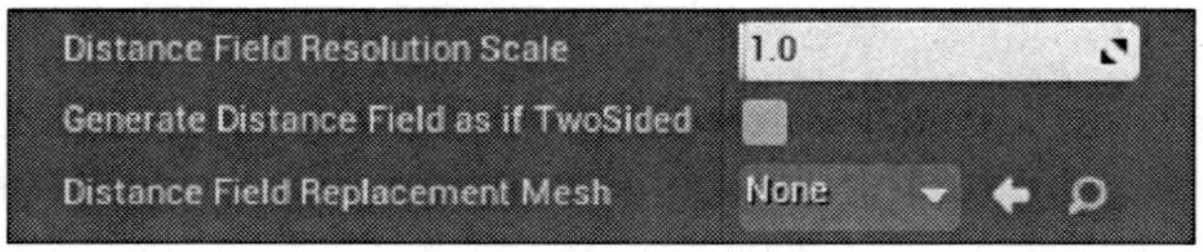

The three most important settings are as follows:

- **Distance Field Resolution Scale**: In the way that DFAO works, it assumes that every static mesh will be placed in the world with a uniform scale of 1, and then a space is allocated to it. If there are objects with different scales, let's say doubled or so, this value will work on compensating those static meshes' allocation on texture. It works on improving their quality, and it makes sense to increase the resolution of an object once it increases its scale beyond the normal value.
- **Generate Distance Field As If Two Sided**: This enables or disables the DFAO for objects if both the sides are needed. Imagine a ribbon or sheet of cloth, or even a leaf on the foliage mesh.
- **Distance Field Replacement Mesh**: This is one of the neatest options in DFAO. Imagine that you have a mesh that will have some world position offsets at runtime. By changing the mesh from how it looks, the DFAO will generate results that make no sense. By enabling this option (enable it by just assigning a static mesh), the DFAO will use the alternate static mesh to light the distance field AO of it.

Debugging

In fact, the word "*debugging*" might not be the best fit for the feature, but I guess you get the point. It might be better to say "*visualize*", but I picked debugging because the only time you might need to visualize such a feature is when the results are not as expected, and then you visualize them in order to debug them to look good.

There are three main view options you can use in order to display the exact result of the DFAO in the scene view. The visualize options are as follows:

- From the **Show** menu (the **View** menu in some older Unreal versions), select **Lighting Features**, and finally, set the **Distance Field AO** show flag in order to toggle the DFAO in the scene view:

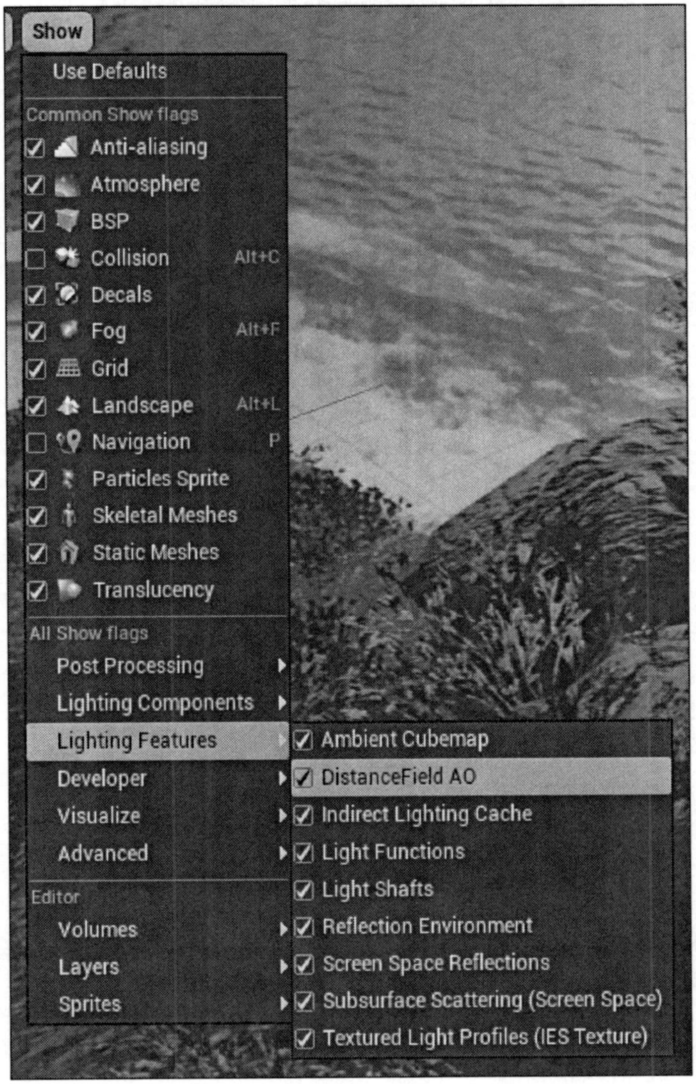

- From the **Show** menu (the **View** menu in some older Unreal versions), select **Visualize**, then set the **Distance Field AO** show flag. This will result in isolating only the Ambient Occlusion from the DFAO:

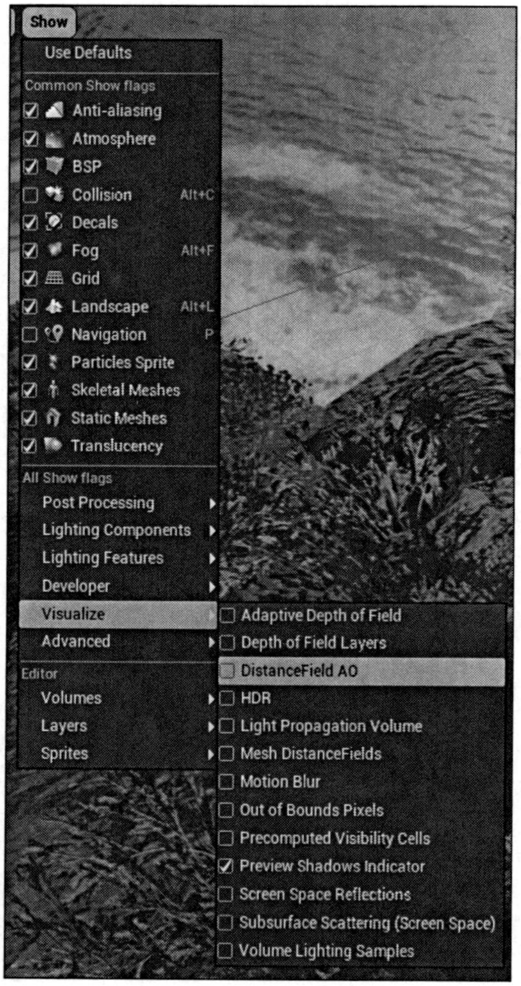

- From the **Show** menu (the **View** menu in some older Unreal versions), select **Visualize**, then set the **Mesh Distance Fields** show flag. This will display the distance field representation for the level. Don't get panicked, as your level will look extremely ugly in the negative black and white level:

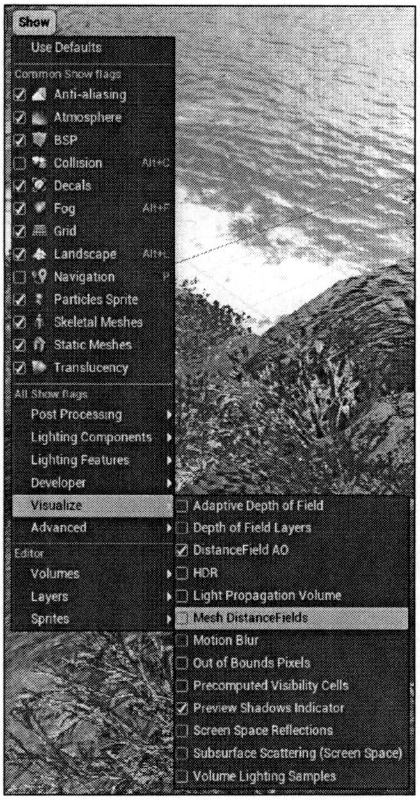

The effects

As discussed earlier, the **Distance Field Ambient Occlusion** has some limitations. This means that it has no complete effect over the scene, which means that not all the level elements *will* be affected:

- **The foliage occlusion**: As mentioned earlier, I saw this feature the first time in the popular Kite demo with this massive landscape environment in the demo. You can tell that the DFAO was used with foliage. In order to get the best results, you just need to enable the **Generate Distance Field As If Two Sided** option in the build settings in the Mesh Editor (as discussed earlier in the *The Mesh Build settings* section) in the foliage meshes as discussed in the earlier mentioned *Settings* section. Enabling it will soften the computed occlusion DFAO mostly working on surfaces, but it still can handle foliage.

  Also, as mentioned in the *Limitations* section, the foliage with LODs enabled will probably have some artifacts with **Distance Field AO**. It is quite common and gets worse when you get more from the foliage itself. The reason for this is that the distance field is still accurate at the X distance while the triangle mesh LOD is not accurate at the same distance.

- **The diffuse occlusion**: DFAO produces a *Bent Normal* that is used to modify the skylight diffuse calculation, and its updates in real time look a lot more natural and acceptable to human eyes.
- **The specular occlusion**: DFAO also provides approximate specular occlusion on skylights. It is computed by intersecting the directional occlusion cone with the reflection cone.

Ray Traced Distance Field Soft Shadows

Ray Traced Distance Field shadows fills its properties from a distance field representation of the scene (same as DFAO). This uses the same data as DFAO and allows both of them to share some pros and cons.

Calculating shadowing is a fairly straightforward process, where the point being shaded in a surface will trace a ray through the scene's signed distance fields toward all the lights.

Limitations

As always, there are some limitations that bound any new feature; some of them back the feature itself, while others back the implementation, and the last ones are going to be fixed very soon. As I've mentioned before, this technique shares a lot with DFAO; it mostly shares the bad side, so it means that it shares some limitations too. The limitations are as follows:

- Only Static Mesh components, Instanced Static Mesh components, and foliage generate distance fields can cast shadows.

- Only tiny nonuniform scaling of meshes are supported.
- Ray Traced Distance Field Soft Shadows have some self-intersection issues.
- Deformation through World Position Offset or Tessellation cannot be represented and may cause self-shadowing artifacts. It can be useful to use CSM to cover areas near the viewer to support vertex animation while using Ray Traced shadows in the distance.

Directional Lights

With this light source type, the value of **Light Source Angle** is the one used to determine how large shadow penumbras can be.

As mentioned before, in the limitations section, the Ray Traced shadows have some self-intersection problems that lead to avoid leaking and over biasing problems in the distance that the traditional shadow mapping has:

The **Cascaded Shadow Maps** (**CSMs**) are the typical solutions used in order to provide us with a dynamic shadowing of the directional light source. The way it works is that it helps you fix the aliasing problem (the aliasing problem comes with the shadow maps) by providing a higher resolution of the depth texture near the viewer, and a lower resolution further away.

However, the problem with CSM is that it requires you to render meshes in the scene in several cascade shadow maps. This is not the best solution ever, as the cost of the shadowing process will insanely increase with the large distances due to the amount of meshes that are rendered in the shadow maps. It is going to render all the triangles per mesh, regardless of how big the visible pieces of that mesh are.

On the other hand, the Ray Traced Distance Field shadows work more efficiently and wisely with the large distances, as it allows the shadowing to work only for visible pixels, so if half of the object is outside the screen, only the visible half what will be taken cared of.

So, this doesn't mean that Ray Traced Shadows are the best and the CSM are the evil here! Each method can be used under some circumstances, and it is wise to use CSMs to cover areas near the camera so that we can enjoy the details of the close distances, and use the Ray Traced Shadows to cover areas that are far away.

Point and Spot Lights

You can change the size of the shadow penumbras by changing the **Source Radius** value in this light type. Try not to intersect the light source sphere (the yellow or orange gizmo) with the scene elements just to avoid any artifacts:

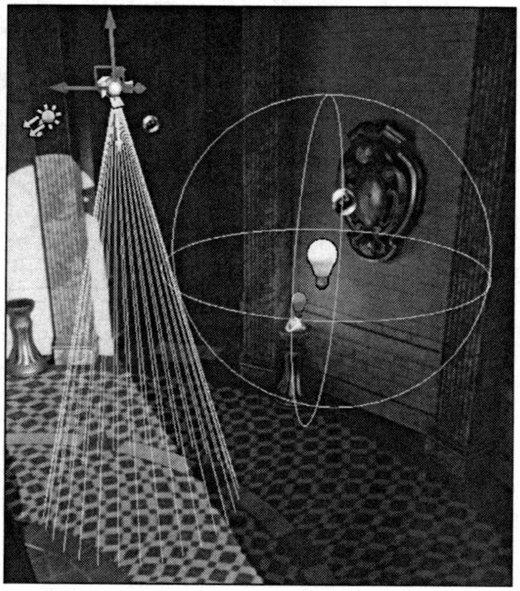

Performance

The larger **Light Source Angle** used with the directional light will increase the GPU cost for your scene and more objects will be affected by the light, and they have to be considered for each point being shadowed.

To measure the cost would be impossible with our normal tools, so I decided to quote the exact values Epic was able to capture with their in-house GPU debugging tool:

> *These GPU timings were done on a Radeon 7870 at 1920x1080 in a full game scene:*
>
> *Directional light with distance 10k, 3 cascades:*
>
> *Cascaded shadow maps 3.1ms*
>
> *Distance Field shadows 2.3ms (25% faster)*
>
> *Directional light with distance 30k, 6 cascades:*
>
> *Cascaded shadow maps 4.9ms*
>
> *Distance Field shadows 2.8ms (43% faster)*
>
> *One large point light:*
>
> *Cubemap shadow map 1.8ms*
>
> *Distance Field shadows 1.3ms (30% faster)*
>
> *Five small point lights:*
>
> *Cube-map shadow maps 3.2ms*
>
> *Distance Field shadows 1.8ms (45% faster)*

Settings

There are a few settings that you can tweak in order to adjust the final results. While some of these attributes are shared between the different light sources, there are others related to each light source type.

Light

While **Use RayTraced DistanceField Shadows** looks like as an enable or disable toggle button, it is a switch option because while you are not using **RayTraced DistanceField Shadows**, it will flip back to using shadow mapping:

Point and Spot Lights

Source Radius is the size of the light source sphere which reflects the size of the penumbras at the same time:

Directional Lights

After selecting a directional light, you will find a **Distance Field Shadows** in the Settings section. It is not unique to find a section in the directional light. If you've selected any other light source type, you will find that it has fewer options in that section.

After picking your directional light from the scene, you can find these options available for the DFS:

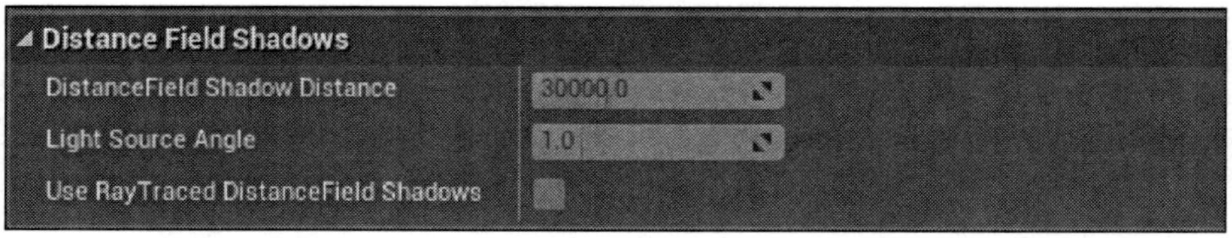

The options available in DFS are as follows:

- **Distance Field Shadow Distance**: This is the distance that needs to be covered by the ray traced shadows. As discussed before, it needs to represent an area, which is the one covered by the **Dynamic Shadow Distance** by CSMs.
- **Light Source Angle**: This is the half angle that the directional light source covers from a receiver's perspective. Try to avoid the large angles in order to get a low performance, as these large angles will cause huge penumbras.

Summary

Now you have learned all about the Dynamic Lights and how to make them in order to get a better game quality. But we are still fighting against the performance cost.

You have your hands on the basic setup of a Movable light, which is the most easy way to get real-time lighting. While it is not a 100 percent optimized method, it still works in some cases. Like I said before, the game type, genre, art, and so on is what is going to decide whether that method works well or not. In general, with simple 3D games, the moveable lights are not costly at all.

You also learned the amazing DFAO (Distance Field AO), which in short is a great choice for an open environment, such as the one Epic made for *The Kite* demo. You learned its pros and cons, how to set it up, and its performance cost. You also learned where to find its artifacts, how to debug and visualize them, and how to avoid them.

You learned about Ray Traced Distance Field Soft Shadows, their major goals, and what type of environments are the best for them. You are now aware of their limitations, how to set them up correctly, and how to work with the Distance Field AO.

Now with all this fresh in mind, I would suggest that you stop for a while and don't even touch the next chapter, as we are going to take a different turn in the rendering pipeline, and start looking more into the post-processing effects, and how to make your games and experiences different, climatic, or even prettier with less effort.

I strongly suggest that you either purchase some assets (environments assets) or download samples for free from Epic's market place. The goal is to get some environments and then start training on them.

Try to use just moveable lights, test them, check their performance, compare them in editor with a full executable build of the map. Do the same for the Distance Field AO, try them, change the different options, check how they work with foliage, and switch to the Ray Traced Distance Field Soft Shadows. Try to mix both as recommended. Rendering is not about reading and understanding only, but it is all about trying the values yourself. This way, you will be able to light different game types, level types, and landscape types. A few tweaks in numbers might turn the look and performance 180 degrees, but by learning them by trial, you are the one who decides that this 180 degree will be the best or the worst performance.

6

Post Processing Effects

Since its first release, Unreal Engine has been widely known for its Post Processing Effects. Post processing is a final screen space pass that alters the final result of a scene. I sometimes like to call it the last tweaks over the frame, as the game is just a series of rendered frames, and these post processing effects are just the final layers of processing for each rendered frame of the game.

With all the different post processing types, Unreal Engine gives the artists and designers the opportunity to tweak the overall look of the scene/level. This includes tweaks over the final color tone, **Depth of Field (DoF)**, different camera different blur types, and camera distortions, or even per material post effect. By the end of this chapter, you will be able to:

- Control the project setting's overall Post Processing Effects options
- Set up a post processing volume
- Check whether a post processing volume is local or global one
- Use more than one Post Processing Volume in the scene
- Understand the usage of each post processing effect and the look of its final result
- Understand all the attributes related to the different post process effects supported by Unreal Engine
- How to make and use lookup tables

With all the targets upfront, let's get our hands dirty!

The Post Process Project Settings

The rendering pipeline for Unreal Engine 4 is designed to be visually stunning, so, by default, some post processing effects are enabled, and you will be able to get their results in your editor window while working every day. These effects are there to give you a nice looking scene, but they are not a mandatory thing; for example, if you are building a 2D game in Unreal that does not require some of the heavy bloom effects, you still can disable or enable any of them at your request.

You can access them from the **Rendering** section under the **Project Settings** window from the **Edit** menu. Drag them all the way down to the **Default Postprocessing Settings**, and then, you can pick what you want and leave the rest.

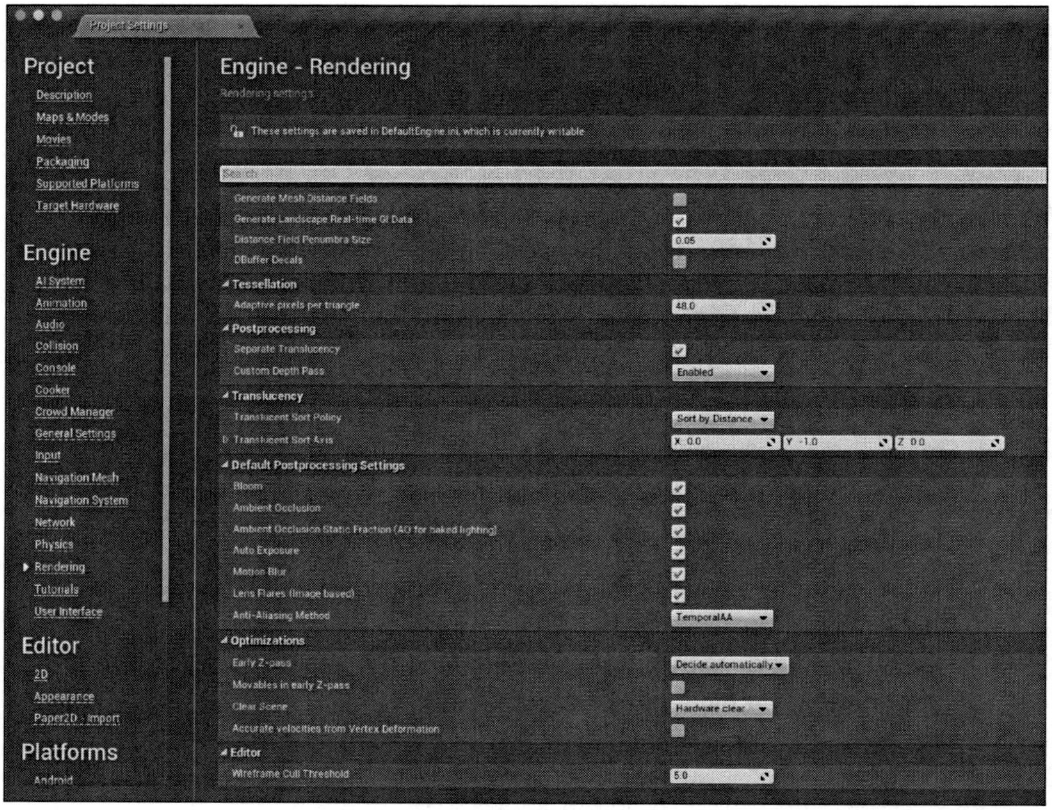

The Post Processing Volume

Just like any other volume bounded feature in Unreal Engine, the **Post Process Volume** is another volume cube that can be added to a level and can get its own position and size, which might be a reason for getting different results.

These types of volumes are the only possible way to manipulate post processing parameters. While the other engines handle the post processing by connecting them to the camera as components or something else, Epic decided a long time ago to go for it in through volume. Why?

Simply because a volume can be considered to be global, which will act as a constant effect; volumes can also be added spatially to represent an area of a scene.

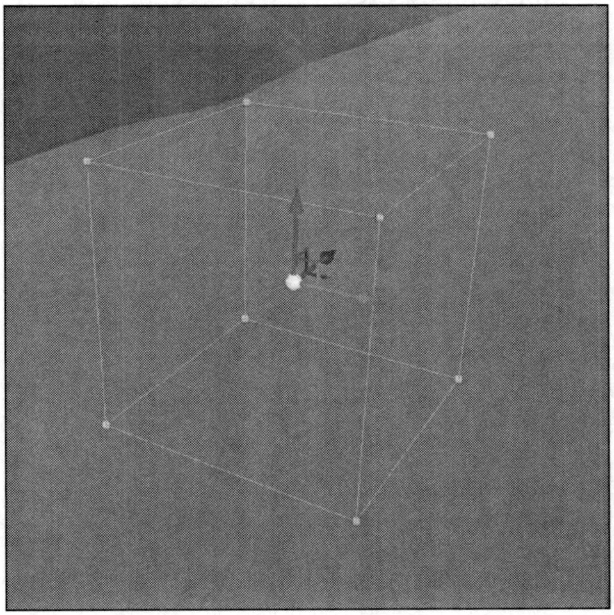

This may look like a typical volume, but it is exceptional!

Well, no one can explain the exact reason except the people at Epic, but after years of experience with the engine, I can say that the reason behind this was to really give you a control over the look of the scene.

Let me be more specific - if the volume works as an attachable component or attribute to the camera, it will always affect the overall look of the camera, but the volumes in Unreal are different; they mostly affect the camera as long as they exist in that volume. Brilliant!

This means that you can have different blur types in the scene just based on the spread of your volume. For example, you can have a character underwater, and he gets outside. So, you can put two different volumes: one in the water area and the other outside. Both have different blur values and different color corrections. Unreal will do the transition while your character/player navigates between the both. Brilliant, isn't it?

After all, Unreal still adds a default Postprocessing class/struct to each camera, so you can set up the different post processing effects per camera too.

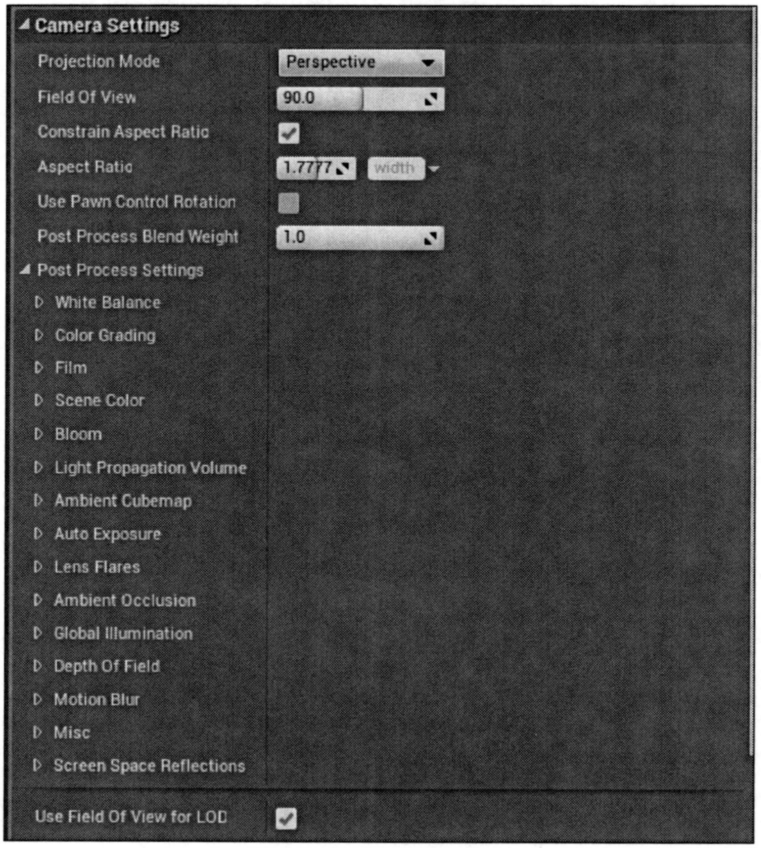

Each **Post Process Volume** in Unreal Engine works as a blend layer, whereas the other blend layers might be the results of something else - another post process volume, or results from various places in the game engine, such as the game code, the camera itself, the Matinee editor, or even the UI code. Each layer can have a weight, so you can blend between the different effects with a Linear Interpolation curve (Lerp). As mentioned earlier, the reason behind having volumes is that the Post Processing Volume will only be applied and blended when the camera is in its bounding box, unless the Unbound property is checked (check the next paragraph, don't just wonder!).

The Epic's team was very smart while designing this system in the rendering toolset. What if the designer wants to give one color tone, one mood, and one bloom value for the whole level? Does it make sense to have a giant Post Processing Volume to affect the whole level and just scale it up? Or does it make sense to just keep putting volumes all over the level?

What they found made sense was actually what I really feel makes sense. They put a property in the Post Processing Volume, which is set to either true or false. This attribute is called **Unbound**. If that value was checked, it means that the Post Processing Volume will affect the entire scene, regardless of its size and the camera position from it.

What really makes perfect sense is that it fits the concept of the level blueprint. While there is a normal blueprint per object or per actor, there is a global blueprint for the entire level. If you just set this small property, then the volume will be a global effector to the level.

The properties

Here is a list of the normal properties found in the **Post Process Volume,** regardless of which effect you are going to use. These are the normal minimum requirements needed for a **Post Process Volume**.

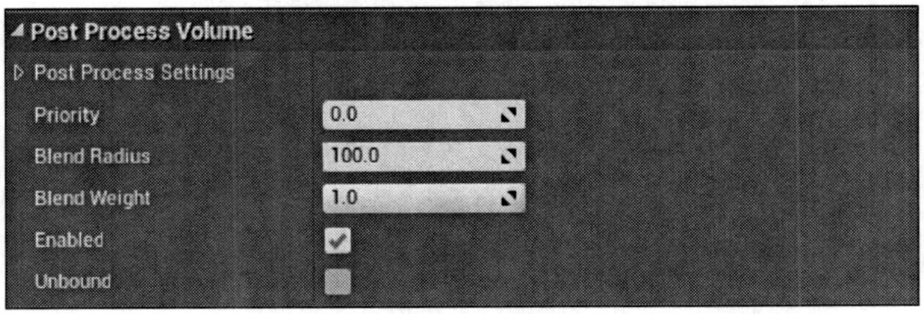

- **Post Process Settings**: This is an expandable list that contains the **Post Process Settings** for all the effects for that volume.

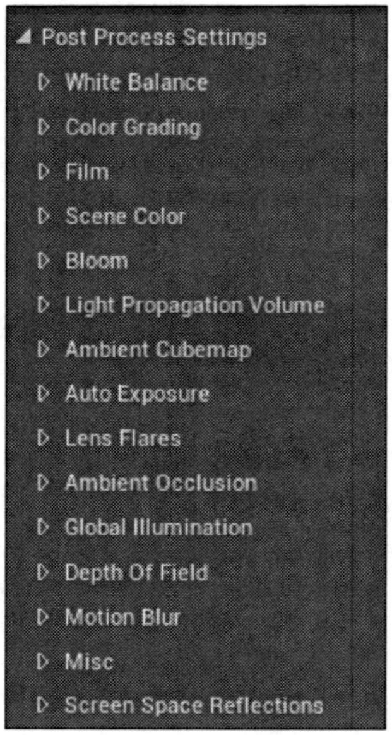

- **Priority**: This is the order when it comes to multiple volumes blending. The volume with the highest priority value will take precedence over all the other volumes overlapping with it.
- **Blend Radius**: This is the distance measured in Unreal units around the volume at which blending with the volume's settings takes place.
- **Blend Weight**: This is the amount of influence the volume's properties have. The value of 1 means that it is a full effect, while the value of 0 means that there is no effect.
- **Enabled**: This checks whether it is working or not.
- **Unbound**: Remember that this is the local VS global option. It defines whether the bounds of the volume are taken into consideration or not. If the value is true, the volume affects the entire level, regardless of its bounds or portions from the camera. If it is set to false, the volume only has effect in its bounds and camera inside those bounds.
- One thing to mention here is that if the volume is going to be unbound, the **Blend Radius** value will be disabled as it make no sense to use it anymore.

The available effects

As we discussed earlier, Unreal Engine has a lot of different post processing effects in order to guarantee your full control over the final look. So, as it is not the only effect or parameter, here is a list of all the supported post processing effects for each one of them in detail. Just keep in mind that they are not ordered with a priority or with a certain rendering order, but they are just ordered here with the order found on a **Post Processing Volume Details** panel.

While the effects used can be arranged in the settings panel in a different order, as long as the engine keeps upgrading, Epic keeps adding new effects and arranges the whole menu in a different way. The available effects include the following:

- White Balance
- Film Tints
- Anti-aliasing (AA)
- Bloom
- Color Grading
- Depth of Field (DOF)
- Auto Exposure (eye adaptation)
- Lens Flares
- Post Process Material
- Scene Fringe
- Vignette
- Grain
- Screen Space Reflection
- Light Propagation
- AO and GI
- Motion Blur
- Screen Percentage

Perhaps there are some more tweaks that could not be listed, or can be classified as color corrections (there is no an actual list or tab named color correction). I decided to put a list of the available post processing effects as the menu is not overly clear. For example, anti-aliasing is a world standard post processing effect nowadays, but there is no actual menu or tab with that name, and the AA options are listed below a **Misc** menu.

This is the same case for the popular Fringe, Vignette, and Grain, as the three of them are super popular and famous effects, but the three of them are under one menu named **Scene Color**. So, this is just for your reference to let you know what you have and can achieve with Post Processing Volumes.

White Balance

This all boils down to the concept of color temperature. The color temperature is a way of measuring the quality of a light source. It is based on the ratio of the amount of blue light to the amount of red light, and the green light is ignored. The **White Balance** is the process of removing unrealistic color casts so that objects that appear white in person are rendered white in your photo. A proper camera white balance has to take into account the *color temperature* of a light source, which refers to the relative warmth or coolness of the white light, and as it is all about the temperature; the unit for measuring this ratio is usually in degree Kelvin.

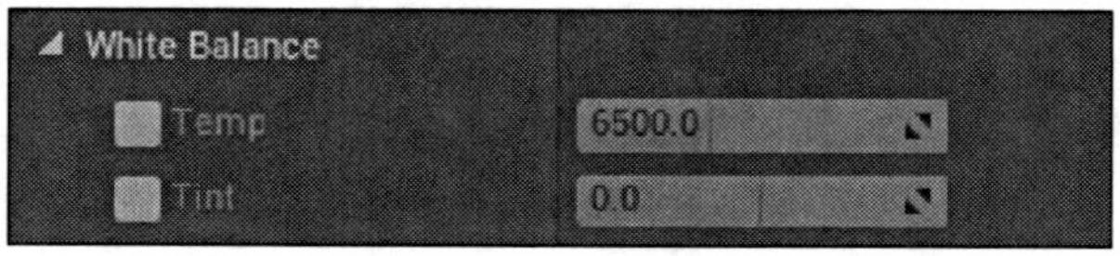

- **Temp**: This is the temperature of the white color. Higher values result in a bluer light, while lower values result in a redder light.
- **Tint**: This is an overall tint for the white color.

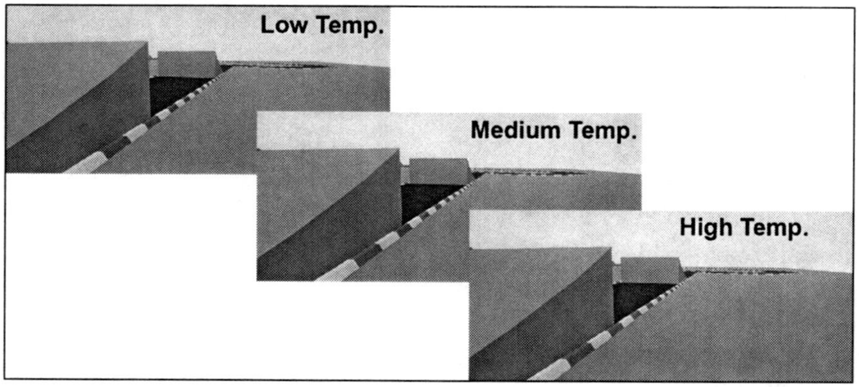

Color Grading

This is the part where I really would like to call it color correction, or at least color adjustments, as it looks pretty much like the typical color processes you find in Photoshop, or in video edit software, such as **After Effects** or **Nuke**.

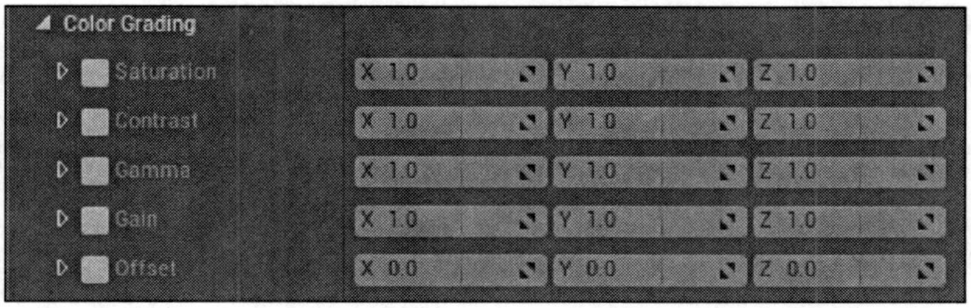

- **Saturation**: This is the basic color saturation
- **Contrast**: This is the basic color contrast
- **Gamma**: This is the basic color gamma
- **Gain**: This is the basic color gain
- **Offset**: This is the basic color offset

Film

The **Film** section contains another part of the color correction methods. Some of the parameters here are duplicates of the previous section (color grading) but work in a different way.

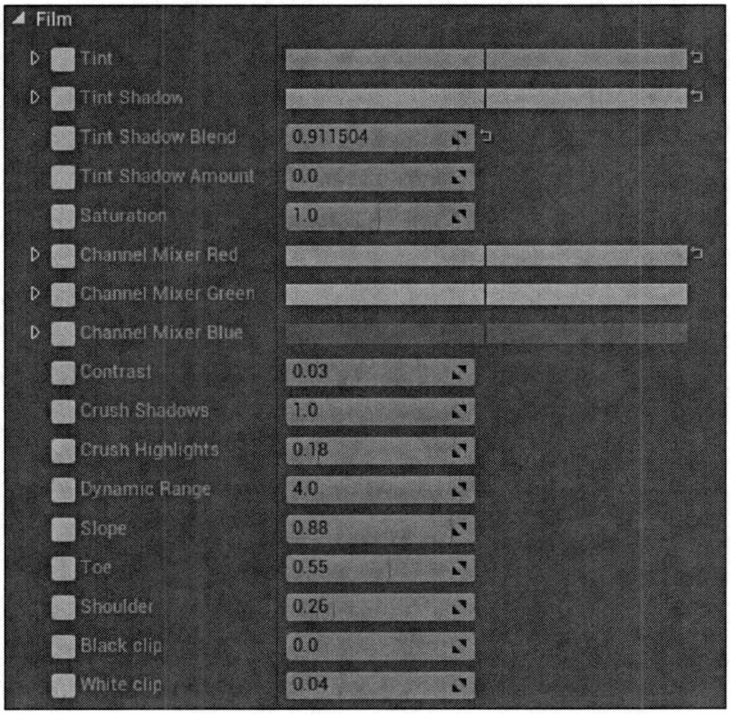

- **Tint**: This is an overall color tint for the scene.
- **Tint Shadow**: This is the color for shadow tinting. Don't get confused and think that it will change the shadow colors. It will just adjust the overall shading color of the surfaces. Shadow colors can be changed from different places, as discussed in the dynamic lights and baked lights.
- **Tint Shadow Blend**: This is a blend value used with the shadow tinting color. A value of 0 will use the shadow tint directly, while a value of 1 will do a very long blend.
- **Tint Shadow Amount**: This is the amount of shadow tinting. A tint shadow color with this value set to 0 will not change anything in the scene.
- **Saturation**: This is the saturation for the rendered image. It is a good way to get a black and white render type with the lowest values.
- **Channel Mixer Red**: This changes the overall red color in the scene.
- **Channel Mixer Green**: This changes the overall green color in the scene.
- **Channel Mixer Blue**: This changes the overall blue color in the scene.
- **Contrast**: This is a contrast of the colors. Higher values always give me nice results—perhaps because I'm a color blind.
- **Crush Shadows**: This is the film toe amount, which means the lower the value, the brighter the image you get, and the higher the value, the darker image the you get. The light and dark here is just an expression, as the amount of light or darkness is not that vast.
- **Crush Highlights**: This is the film heel amount, which means the higher the value, the higher the contrast of colors you will get for the final image.
- **Dynamic Range**: This is the film dynamic range.
- **Slope**: This is the film slope, and it is not one of the more effective values. It's very hard to see its result.
- **Toe**: This is the film toe, and it is not one of the more effective values. It's very hard to see its result.
- **Shoulder**: This is the film shoulder, and it is not one of the more effective values. It's very hard to see its result.
- **Black clip**: This is the film black clip, and it is not one of the more effective values. It's very hard to see its result.
- **White clip**: This is the film white clip, and it is not one of the more effective values. It's very hard to see its result.

Scene Color

The **Scene Color** section includes things that are not 100 percent related to the scene color. I guess the name came for some reason! While this section's name seems disappointing, I think it actually contains three of the most beloved Post Processing Effects.

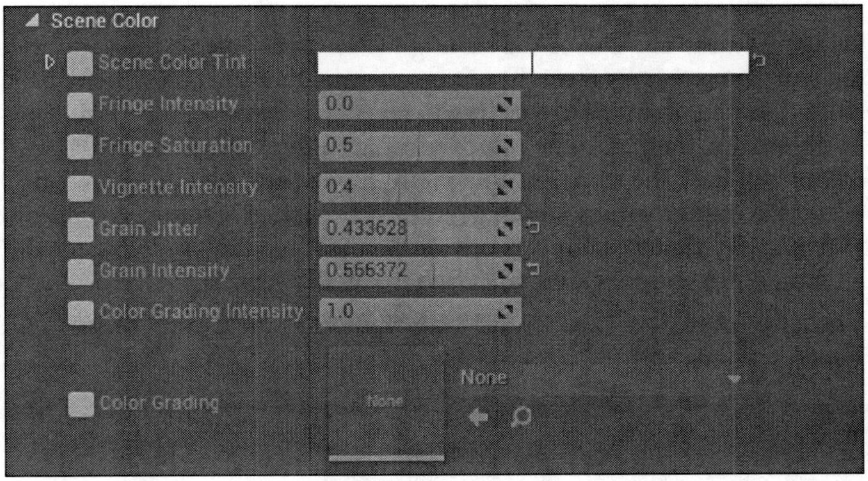

- **Scene Color Tint**: This is an overall color tint for the scene, just like the one in the **Film** section.
- **Fringe Intensity**: This is the scaling factor that controls how much the colors shifts.

- **Scene Fringe** (chromatic aberration in other engines): This is super popular nowadays in video games and must be implemented one way or another in any modern game engine, particularly the engines used for shooters and AAA smi-life games. It is basically a chromatic aberration effect that simulates the color shifts (reds, greens, and blues are so obvious with this effect) in real-world camera lenses. The closer to the edge, the clearer that effect.
- **Fringe Saturation**: This is the scaling factor that controls the saturation of the shifted colors. As it might not be obvious that the colors have been shifted, for some human eyes due to some eye disease; here, you can saturate or desaturate them. Lower values produce a more blurred result as all the colors will look the same (so this might make the effect used blur too), while the higher values just make the chromatic aberration crystal clear. I have to say that this effect is one of the most wanted, and I've used it with all my games since it came out, even in my 2D games!
- **Vignette Intensity**: This controls the amount of darkening of the screen corners.

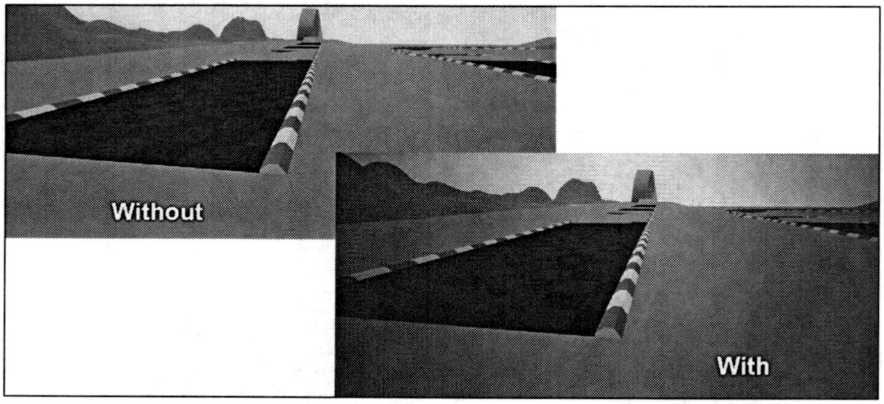

Vignette is super popular nowadays in video games and must be implemented in one way or another in any modern game engine (just like **Scene Fringe** or chromatic aberration), as it is an effect that simulates the darkening in real-world camera lenses. This effect takes place near the edges of the image, and due to some performance reasons, this is not going to affect bloom wherever it was.

- **Grain Jitter**: You can consider this as the grain speed.
- **Grain Intensity**: This is the amount of the grain and controls how clear and how obvious it is on the screen.

- **Color Grading Intensity**: In the Unreal Engine, the term Color Grading covers the Tone Mapping function (HDR to LDR transformation) and the Color Correction (LDR color to screen color transformation). This value controls the intensity of the color grading.
- **Color Grading**: A **Lookup Texture (LUT)** is used in order to color grade the scene. If you are interested in how to make a LUT, check it as a bonus by the end of this chapter. It is marked as a bonus as it is something that is done in Photoshop, not Unreal Engine.

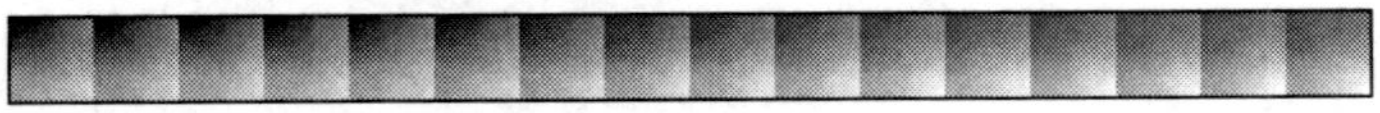

Bloom

Bloom is a computer graphics effect used in video games to reproduce an imaging artifact of real-world cameras. The effect produces fringes (or feathers) of light extending from the borders of the bright areas in an image, contributing to the illusion of an extremely bright light overwhelming the camera or eye capturing the scene. This can be seen by the human eye when looking at very bright objects that are on a darker background—a lot darker.

So, it is a real-world light phenomena that adds to the perceived realism of a rendered image at a moderate render performance cost. If you are interested to know the secret behind the cool bloom implementation in Unreal, which is widely known for its great look and best performance across all the known engines in the market, here is a quote from Epic:

> *"Bloom can be implemented with a single Gaussian blur. For better quality, we combine multiple Gaussian blurs with different radius. For better performance, we do the very wide blurs in much lower resolution. In UE3, we had 3 Gaussian blurs in the resolution 1/4, 1/8, and 1/16. We now have multiple blurs name Blur1 to 5 in the resolution 1/2 (Blur1) to 1/32 (Blur5). We might add Blur 0 for full resolution blur if ever needed."*

Bear in mind that this is an easy filter to overdo. Many beginners have a habit of over-using bloom, and the colors become too bright and bleed into each other when the scene contains a bright light.

So, it means that they combine the blurs differently to get more control and higher quality with the lowest performance possible.

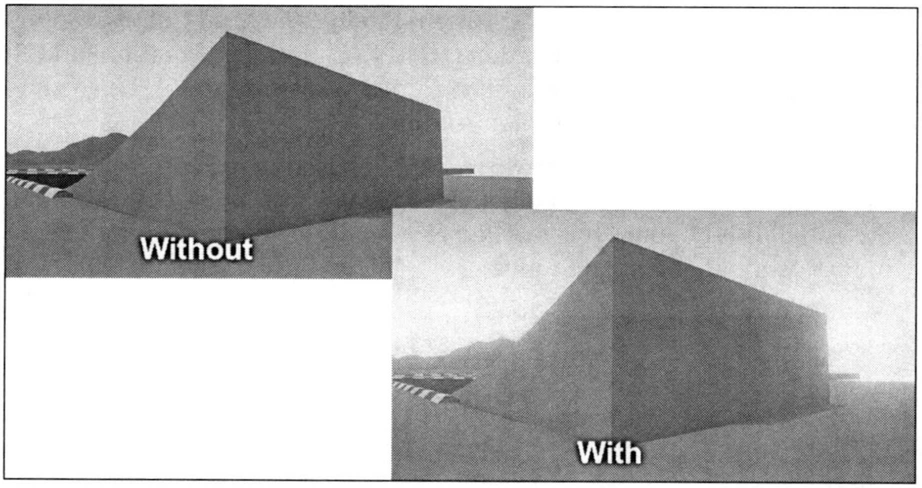

While bloom used to be a couple of parameters that could be tweaked in order to control the final look, now, with the huge evolution of the graphic cades' capabilities, you'll find a huge list of parameters that give you detailed control over all the bloom bits and pieces.

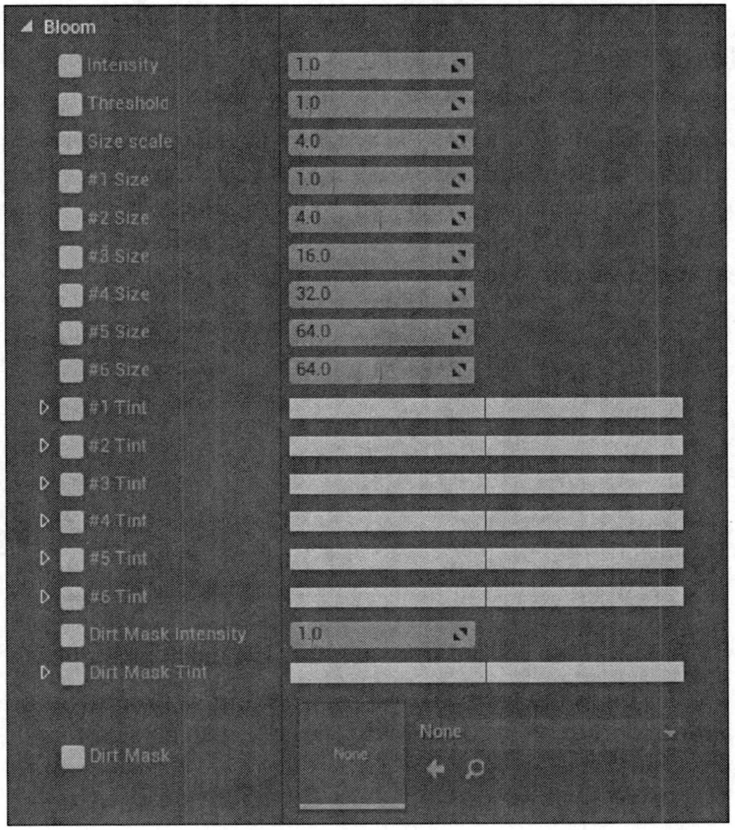

- **Intensity**: This is the scale factor of the color of the bloom effect.
- **Threshold**: This defines how many luminance units a color needs to have to affect bloom.
- **Size scale**: This is the scalar for the bloom size.
- **#1** to **#6 Size**: This is the size of a screen width in percent. Depending on the size index, the screen resolution will be different:
    - **#1**: 1/2 resolution
    - **#2**: 1/4 resolution
    - **#3**: 1/8 resolution
    - **#4**: 1/16 resolution
    - **#5**: 1/32 resolution

- **#1** to **#6 Tint**: This changes the brightness and color of the bloom.
- **Dirt Mask Intensity**: This is used to tweak the dirt mask brightness by scaling the color of the bloom dirt mask effects.

  The Bloom Dirt Mask is a process where you can use a texture to brighten up the bloom in some defined screen areas based on that texture. This feature is used to make even more interesting bloom effects. It can be used to build more impressive HDR effects or camera imperfections, which maximize the reality of your final look.

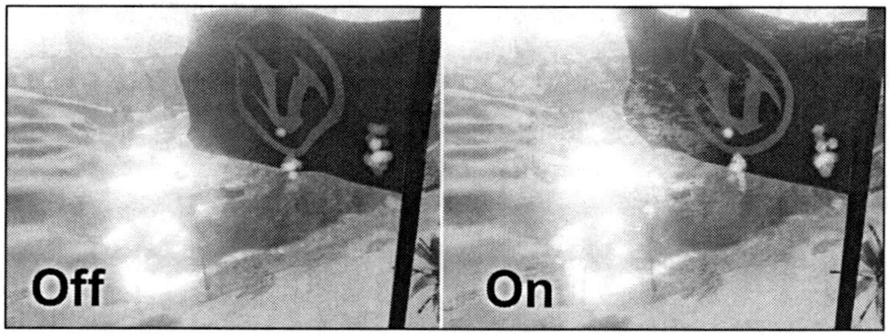

- **Dirt Mask Tint**: This is used to tweak the dirt mask brightness and color tint.
- **Dirt Mask**: This is the texture used for masking. A nonpower of two textures is recommended to be used as it will fit the screen size better and will avoid mip-maps creation.

Light Propagation Volume

The **Light Propagation Volume** (the **LPV** for short) is an implementation of a technique to approximately achieve global illumination at real time.

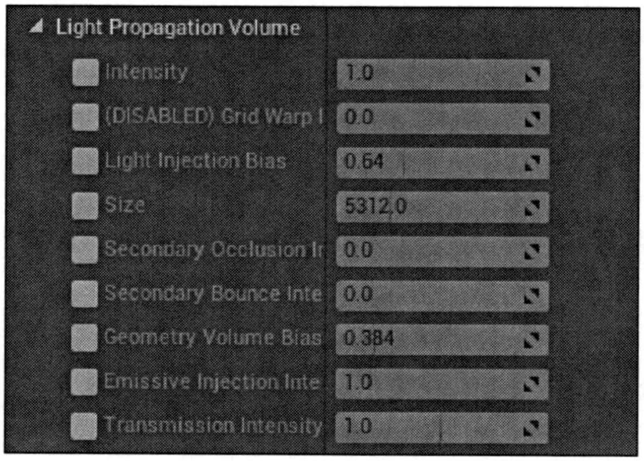

- **Intensity**: This defines how strong the dynamic global illumination from the LPV should be. A value of 0 means it is off, while a value of 1 is the normal value. A higher value can be used to boost the effect.
- **(DISABLED) Grid Wrap Intensity**: It is currently the disabled feature, and it represents the strength of the warp offset used to reduce the light bleeding. A value of 0 means it is off, while a value of 1 is the normal value. Also, a higher value can be used to boost the effect.
- **Light Injection Bias**: This is the bias applied to the light injected into the LPV in cell units. Increase this to reduce the bleeding through the thin walls.
- **Size**: This is the size of the LPV volume in Unreal units.
- **Secondary Occlusion Intensity**: This is the secondary occlusion strength (bounce light shadows). A value of 0 means that it is disabled.
- **Secondary Bounce Intensity**: This is the secondary bounce light strength (bounce light shadows). A value of 0 means that it is disabled.
- **Geometry Volume Bias**: This is the bias applied to the geometry volume in cell units. Increase it to reduce the darkening due to secondary occlusion.
- **Emissive Injection Intensity**: This is the LPV emissive injection intensity.
- **Transmission Intensity**: This defines how strong the light transmission from the LPV should be. A value of 0 means that it is disabled, while a value of 1 is the normal value. A higher value can be used to boost the effect.

Ambient Cubemap

The **Ambient Cubemap** lights the scene from an image, as the selected image will be mapped into a spherical shape.

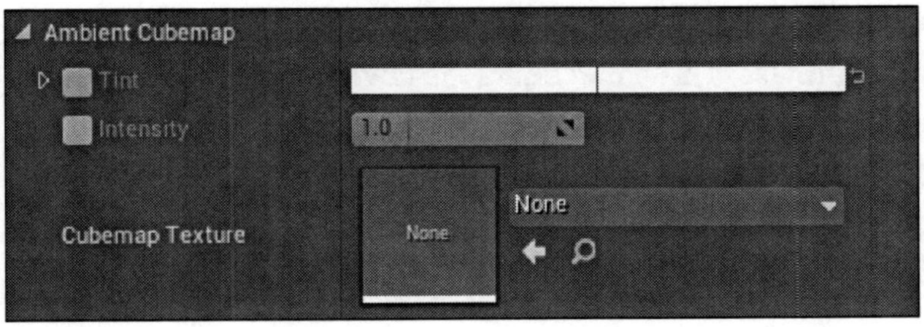

- **Tint**: This is the overall tint color of the **Ambient Cubemap**.
- **Intensity**: This is used to scale the ambient cubemap's brightness. A value of 0 means that it is off, while a value of one means that it is the default value. If the value is more than 1, then it will give brighter results.

- **Cubemap Texture**: The **Ambient Cubemap** (affects diffuse and specular shading) blends additively, which is different from all the other settings here.

Auto Exposure

This is also known as **Eye Adaptation**, as it causes the exposure of the scene to automatically adjust in order to recreate the same effect as when human eyes adjust when going from a high contrast light environment into a darker environment or vice versa.

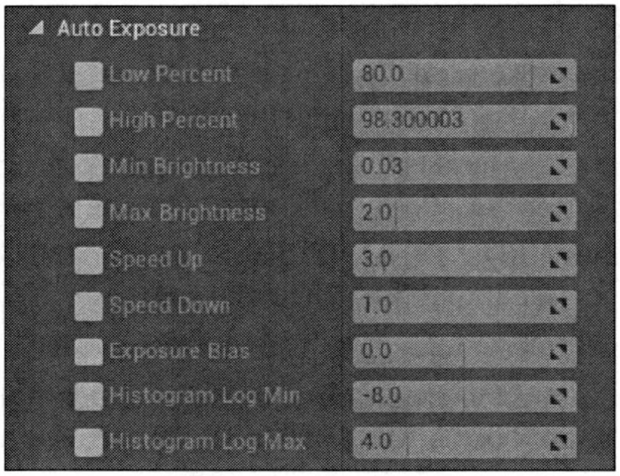

- **Low Percent**: This value defines the lower percentage of the histogram that is used to find the average scene luminance. The eye adaptation will adapt to a value extracted from the luminance histogram of the scene color.
- **High Percent**: This value defines the higher percentage of the histogram that is used to find the average scene luminance. The eye adaptation will adapt to a value extracted from the luminance histogram of the scene color.
- **Min Brightness**: This value limits the lower limit for the brightness that the eye adapts within.
- **Max Brightness**: This value limits the higher limit for the brightness that the eye adapts within.
- **Speed Up**: This is the speed at which the adaptation occurs from a dark environment to a bright environment.
- **Speed Down**: This is the speed at which the adaptation occurs from a bright environment to a dark environment.

- **Exposure Bias**: This is the logarithmic adjustment for the exposure. It is only used if a tone mapper is specified. The value of 0 means that there is no adjustment, while -1 is two times darker, and -2 is four times darker. 1 is two times brighter, and of course, 2 is four times brighter.
- **Histogram Log Min**: This is a temporary exposed value from the Epic's team until they find values. This parameter is to be hidden and auto set self. -8 means 1/256 while -10 means 1/1024.
- **Histogram Log Max**: This is another temporary exposed value from the Epic's team until they find values. This parameter used to be hidden and auto set self 4 means 16 while 8 means 256.

Lens Flares

This is the light scattered in the lens systems through unwanted image formation mechanisms. It is an image-based technique that simulates the scattered light when viewing bright objects due to imperfections in camera lenses.

As you can see from the previous image, there is a punch of hexagonal shapes that have different colors. Lens flares in Unreal Engine is not just a feature used to toggle; you have a chance to change every single detail of how it looks.

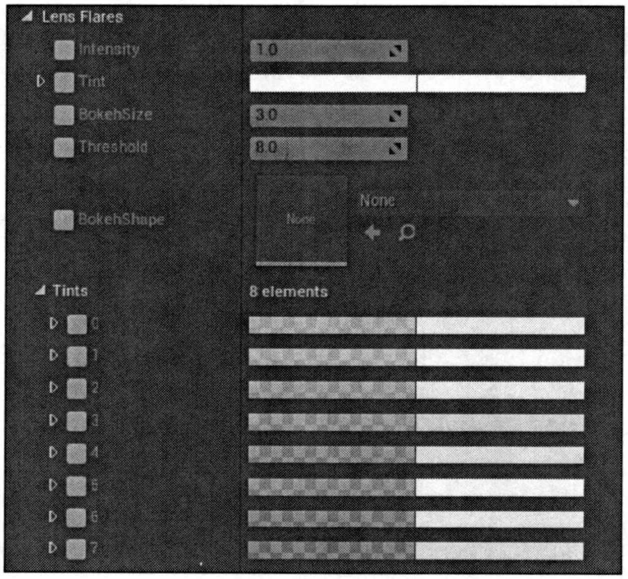

- **Intensity**: This is a brightness scaler.
- **Tint**: This tints the color of the lens flare post effect.
- **BokehSize**: This scales the radius of the bokeh shape.
- **Threshold**: This defines the minimum brightness of pixels that are included in the lens flare.
- **BokehShape**: This texture is used to define the shape of the lens flares. You can use the shape you want, but normally, it is either a hexagonal or spherical shape that matches the real-life lens bokeh shape. A black and white texture is enough to define it.

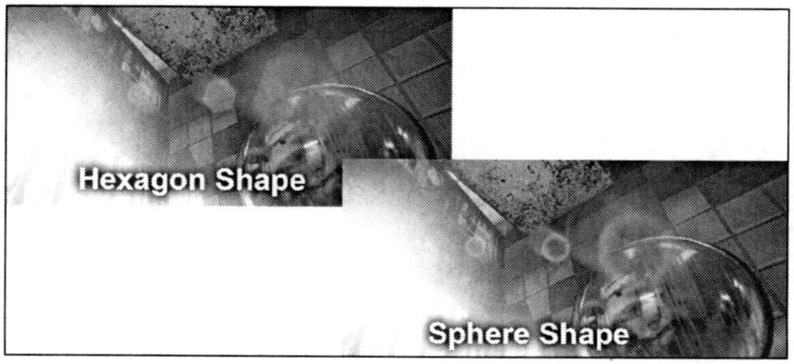

- **Lens Flare Tints 0** to **7**: This controls the color tint of each individual lens flare.

Ambient Occlusion

While **Ambient Occlusion** is a rendering feature that can be enabled or disabled in the light sources and lightmap settings, there is also an implementation for AO as a post processing effect too.

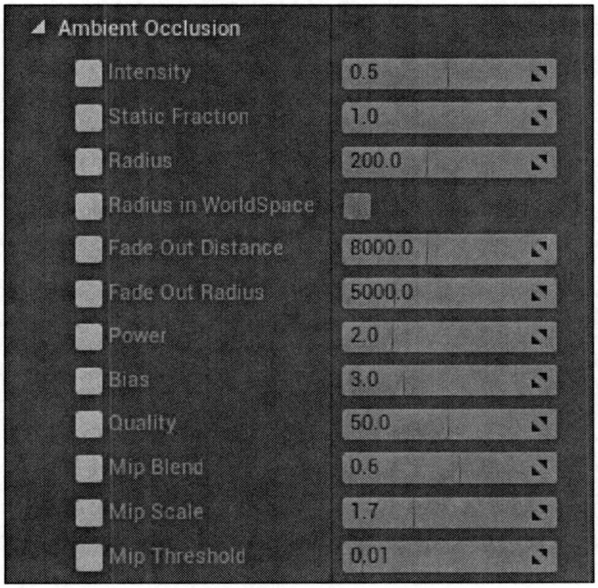

- **Intensity**: This is the intensity of the ambient occlusion. A value of 0 means that it is off, while a value of 1 means that it is a strong ambient occlusion. This value will define how much it affects the non direct lighting after the base pass.
- **Static Fraction**: This affects the static lighting. The value of 0 means that it is off, which means there are no extra rendering passes. While the value of 1 means that the Ambient Occlusion affects the static lighting.
- **Radius**: This value should be greater than 0 in Unreal units in order to work. The bigger values mean that even distant surfaces affect the Ambient Occlusion.
- **Radius in WorldSpace**: When this is set to false, it means that the ambient occlusion has locked the view space in 400 Unreal units. If set to true, it means that the Ambient Occlusion radius is in world space units.

- **Fade Out Distance**: This is the distance calculated in Unreal units too. It represents at which distance the Ambient Occlusion effect disappears in the distance.
- **Fade Out Radius**: This is the distance calculated in Unreal units too. It represents how many units before the Ambient Occlusion fade out distance it stars to fade out.
- **Power**: The higher values means that even distant surfaces affect the Ambient Occlusion.
- **Bias**: The bias default value is 3.0 and it works well for flat surfaces, but it can reduce the details.
- **Quality**: This represents the quality level. The value 0 represents the lowest quality while the value 100 represents the maximum quality.
- **Mip Blend**: This affects the blend over the multiple mips. A value of 0 means that it is fully use full resolution, while a value of 1 means fully use the low resolution.
- **Mip Scale**: This value affects the radius of the Ambient Occlusion radius scale over the multiple mip maps.
- **Mip Threshold**: This value is meant to tweak the bilateral up-sampling when using multiple mip maps.

Global Illumination

As the AO, the GI can not only be a rendering **feature** for your game, but it can be a post processing effect that is bounded to a specific area of your game or level.

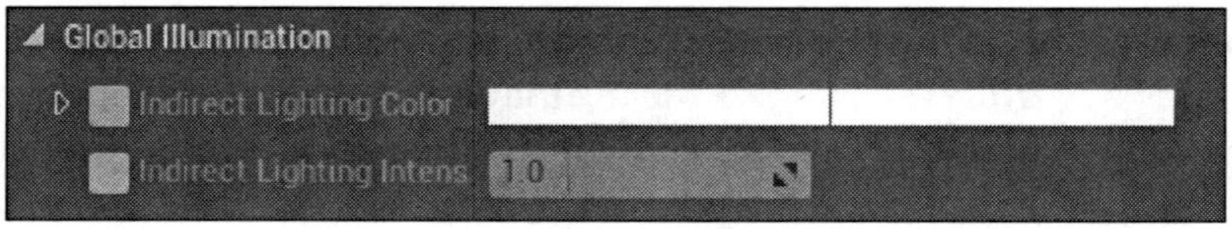

- **Indirect Lighting Color**: This adjusts the indirect lighting color value. The show flag global illumination must be enabled in order to use this post processor effect.
- **Indirect Lighting Intensity**: This scales the indirect lighting contribution. A value of 0 disables the global illumination. The show flag global illumination must be enabled in order to use this Post Processor Effect.

Depth of Field

Depth of Field (DoF) simulates what happens in real-world cameras or a human eye regarding the focus on a certain object. It applies a blur to the scene based on the distance in front of or behind a focal point. Keep in mind that, as always, all the distances are measured in Unreal units.

As you can see from the previous image, while Pac-Man is in the front and is super clear, the ghosts in the background seem blurry and are barely visible. Will I be able to reverse the effect?

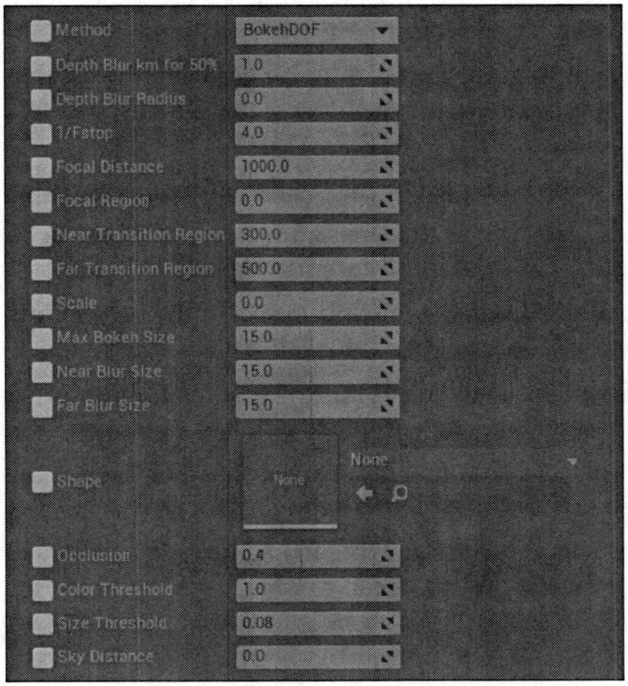

- **Method**: Choose the method for DoF. Try both, and you will be able to figure out the difference in the visual look:
    - **BokehDOF**: This is the performance expensive type where a textured quad is going to be rendered for each pixel using a texture (take a look at the **Shape** property) to define the shape of the resulted depth.
    - **Gaussian**: This type will blur the scene using the typical Guassian blur (just like Photoshop, but in real time). Because it is not that special, it renders faster.
- **Depth Blur km for 50%**: This is the depth blur in km for 50 percent and it works with the Circle DOF type only.
- **Depth Blur Radius**: This is the depth blur radius in pixels at 1920 x, and it works with the Circle DOF type only.
- **1/Fstop**: Fstop number (1/Fstop), and it works with the Circle DOF type only.
- **Focal Distance**: This represents the distance of the camera that acts as the center of the region where the scene should be focused.
- **Focal Region**: This represents the distance beyond the focal distance where the scene is focused.
- **Near Transition Region**: This is the distance from the focal region on the side nearer to the camera at which the scene is focused to blurred when using Gaussian-based DoF.
- **Far Transition Region**: This is the distance from the focal region on the side farther from the camera at which the scene is focused to blurred when using Gaussian-based DoF.
- **Scale**: This is the scalar factor for the Bokeh-based blurring.
- **Max Bokeh Size**: This is the maximum size of the blur in percent for Bokeh-based. Higher values of it has a performance cost.
- **Near Blur Size**: This is the maximum size of the near blur in percent for Gaussian-based DoF. Higher values of it has a performance cost.
- **Far Blur Size**: This is the maximum size of the far blur in percent for Gaussian-based DoF. Higher values of it has a performance cost.
- **Shape**: This is a texture that defines the shape of the Bokeh with the Bokeh-based DOF when objects get out of focus.
- **Occlusion**: This controls how much the blurred geometry extends beyond its usual silhouette and its opacity.

- **Color Threshold**: This controls the threshold where adaptive DoF switches to using full-resolution based on color. Smaller values cause most of the scenes to use full-resolution processing.
- **Size Threshold**: This controls the threshold where adaptive DoF switches to using full-resolution based on size. Larger values cause most of the scenes to use full-resolution processing.
- **Sky Distance**: While the DoF is a Gaussian DOF type, this value represents the distance to allow the skybox to be in focus. A value of 0 means that the feature is turned off.

Motion Blur

This applies a noticeable blur effect to the dynamic objects. This effect can only be seen at runtime.

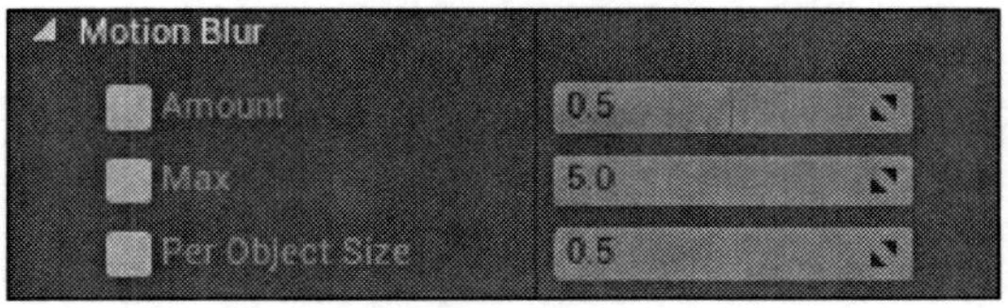

- **Amount**: This is the strength of the motion blur. A value of 0 means it is off.
- **Max**: This is the maximum distortion caused by the motion blur. It is calculated in percent of the screen width. A value of 0 means the effect will be turned off.
- **Per Object Size**: This represents the minimum projected screen radius for a primitive to be drawn in the velocity pass. It is calculated in a percentage of the screen width as well. The smaller values will create more draw calls and that leads to more performance costing.

- **Misc**: This is one of the most important post-processing sections as it describes the process of custom post processing effects.

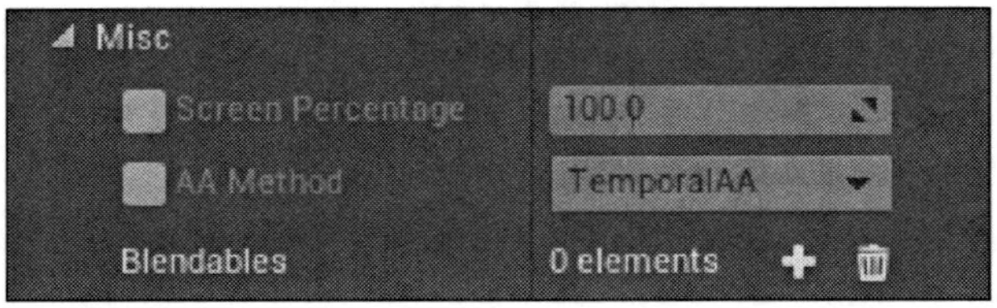

  - **Screen Percentage**: Use this value to define if you want to render the game in higher of lower resolution than the default one. A value of 100 means that it uses the default resolution, while a value less than 100 means that the rendered image will be up-sampled and results in a lower performance. Clearly, a value higher than 100 means super sampling the final image, which will have some performance cost.
  - **AA Method**: It is the anti-aliasing method, which was used to be called **AA**, and it refer to the smoothing of aliased lines when displayed on the screen.

    Anti-aliasing in Unreal Engine is performed as a post processing effect, which is under the hood, using the famous Fast Approximate Anti-aliasing (FXAA implementation), which is an efficient GPU MLAA anti-aliasing algorithm created by Timothy Lottes under NVIDIA.

    This method solves most causes of aliasing artifacts, but cannot fully prevent temporal aliasing as its smoothing is applied as a per-pixel effect. That is, there is no explicit representation of the edges.

    You can simply enable or disable the AA Post Processing Effect by changing the show flag Post Process Anti-aliasing.

    As usual, if not everything goes well, or only 95 percent goes well, with AA (FXAA), there is one disadvantage that you should be aware of, just in case you hit any of them, don't think that there is a problem with your project or editor version, it is something with the implementation itself. The textures may not appear as sharp if they are included in the edge detection.

    There are still other techniques used by Unreal Engine to handle the AA, such as MSAA (multisample anti-aliasing), which was implemented only to affect the editor 3D gizmos.

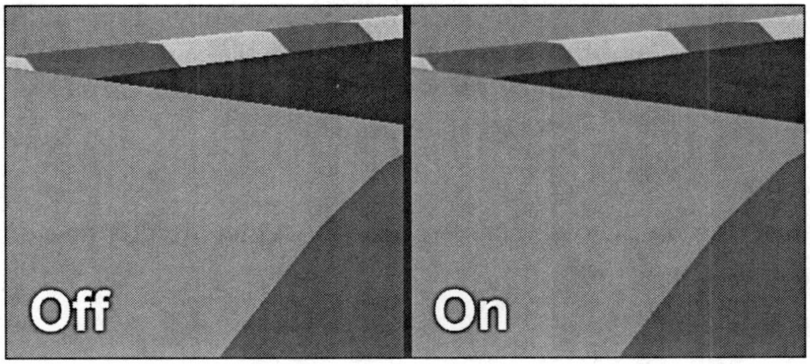

Screen Space Reflections

This is one of those Post Processing Effects where you can find it enabled by default; this effect alters the appearance of objects on the surface of materials.

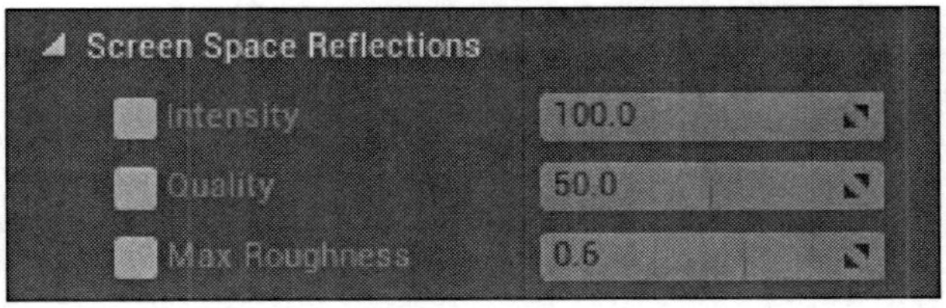

- **Intensity**: This enables, disables, or fades the **Screen Space Reflection** effect by a certain percentage.
- **Quality**: This is the quality of the resulted reflections; a value of 0 means it is the lowest quality, while a value of a 100 is the maximum quality. The higher the value is, the more performance it requires to do the calculations.
- **Max Roughness**: This determines the roughness where a fade happens to the **Screen Space Reflections**. This value also increases the required performance when it gets increased.

Creating a Lookup Table Texture (LUT)

Creating a Lookup Texture in order to use it with the color grading might be tricky, but it is a very simple way to get a really artistic look.

While Unreal doesn't have the same tools as image processing applications, such as Photoshop, Epic implemented this technique to allow artists to do whatever they want, and they used to do it in Photoshop (or similar applications) and switch the Unreal scene into that look within a few clicks.

You have to keep in mind that not every single filter or image effect in Photoshop can be used in the LUT, and this is the only limitation it has. As far as I know, and until this moment, the only color correction processes that you can use and transfer from PS to Unreal via the LUT are as follows:

- Saturation
- Contrast (the simple contrast effect and the higher quality one)
- Color curves
- Brightness

Regarding the process of creating one, you just need to follow a few simple steps:

1. Take a screenshot from your editor (it is better if you could hit the *G* button before that in order to hide the gizmos).
2. Load the sample LUT 256.X.16, which comes by default with Unreal Engine, into Photoshop.

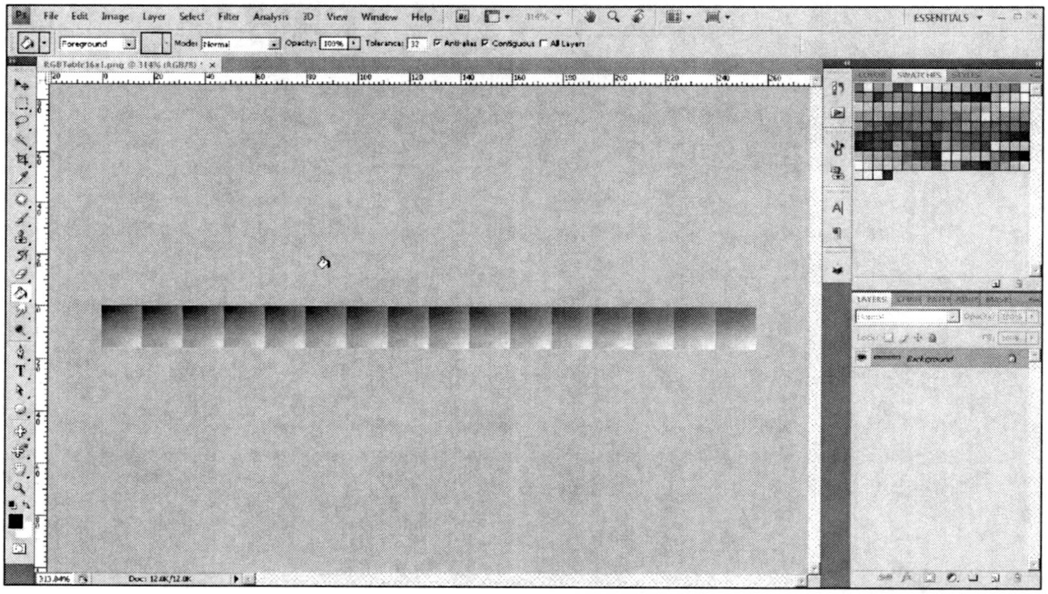

3. Copy the whole thing from the LUT document in Photoshop, and paste it into the **Screenshot** tab in Photoshop as well.

4. Apply any color effects and calculations you want.
5. Select the **LUT** layer.
6. Copy and merge the content of the LUT using the **Copy Merged** option from the **Edit** menu.

7. Paste it and save the 256 X 16 texture in a new uncompressed file format (`.png` is awesome).
8. Drag and drop this newly created texture into the Unreal Editor. Set it to the **ColorLookupTable** texture group and disable the **MipMaps**.

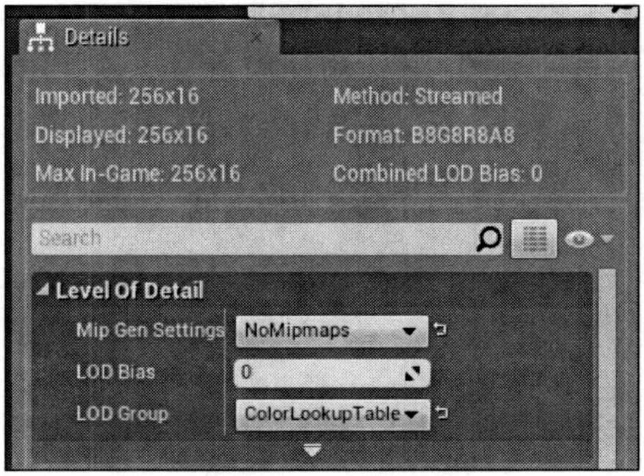

9. Assign it to the color grading texture.

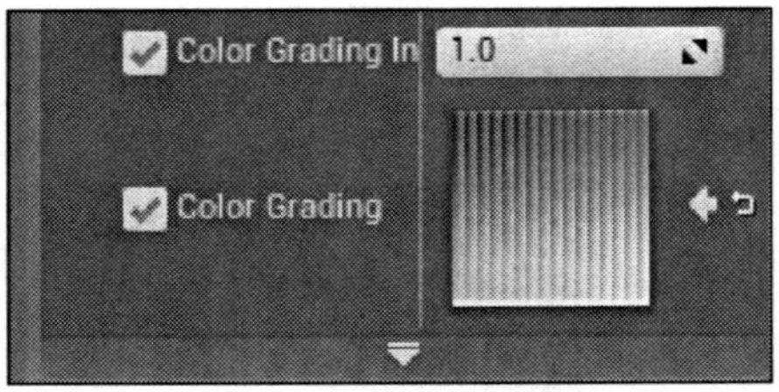

Summary

Now, you know what Post Processing Effects mean, how Epic was smart in implementing them, and the way they work. Enabling the Post Processing Effects via the project render settings might be good in some cases, but let's be honest, we all like to do those small tweaks per level or even per meter.

You now know how to enable or disable Post Processing Effects for the entire project. Using the Post Processing Volumes is essential in order to get a control over every Unreal Unity in your world using a volume or different volume's approach; now you know how to achieve both the approaches.

You have mastered all the different parameters for the different Post Processing Effects, and you can easily get the visual look you had in mind.

Editing, creating, and using the Lookup tables from Photoshop in your Unreal project became an easy and friendly trick, which you also mastered throughout this chapter.

Remember that it is very easy to put in too many over powering post processing effects. The effects are very powerful and visually appealing, and it's easy to get lost in throwing in different effects and overdoing them. You have to find a happy medium between lighting and post processing effects. This helps both for memory constraints and for the overall look of the scene.

Now, after having the visual look you want, have you met some performance issues, some lagging, or even crashes? Don't panic because the next chapter will cover all this.

If you are ready, flip the page, and jump into the world of rendering debugging methods in Unreal Engine. See you in the next chapter, go ahead—I'm waiting for you there. Well, I'm partly there!

7
Render Performance Debugging

In the previous chapters, we focused on adding stuff that contributes to the visual quality of the project. As you know, every feature has its own performance overhead. The combination of these features will have an impact on the performance of the game.

In this chapter, we will go together on another little journey that will help you measure your performance and understand what might be the source of your problems and how to avoid them.

While working on a real-time application, the performance is a high-priority topic that you have to consider in your list. A beautiful experience with a lack of performance would be pointless. This has prompted developers to be mindful about the amount of frames displayed each second, which is widely known as the frame rate or **frames per second** (**FPS**).

You need at least a frame rate of 30 frames per second in order to be able to show something that is kind of acceptable (but still not the expected result from your players and users). In general, with the different platforms and their configurations, the game should run at 30 or 60 FPS, or even higher frame rates can be achieved with more optimization on powerful platforms.

Unreal Engine 4 features tons of different tools and methods that take a long time to be implemented for you in the easiest way. To make your life easier when it comes to profiling the rendering performance and your willingness is to optimize them into a targeted frame rate.

By the end of this chapter, you will be able to:

- Understand how to use the console to toggle the view modes
- Use the console to generate the FPS charts

- Use the view modes in the editor and game
- Understand the difference between the view modes and the visualizers
- Switch between the different visualizers for more rendering details
- Understand the importance of the GPU Visualizer and how to run it

Let's go and dive deep into these topics and start optimizing your content based on what we going to learn here!

The to-do list

I used to be a gameplay programmer and mostly focus on gameplay, and sometimes I used to write tools to support the game design and the level designers. In the past few years, I found out that all companies put the performance optimization into the gameplay's tasks section, and then I found out that it is part of my day-to-day work to make sure that the game is as optimized as possible.

Of course, in the olden days, the gameplay engineers were taking care of the performance, from the code logic, by writing a well-optimized code. Nowadays with the already packaged engine, the gameplay engineers have to do tons of optimization outside the gameplay code.

After trying several techniques with different game types and various platforms, I ended up with a to do list (this is for rendering related points only), regardless of the method or technique you are going to use:

- Try to make all the content optimized from the first step. For example, all the precomputed lightmaps should be built with ready optimized parameters in order to get a good quality but a lower map size. Why would you put 2048 as the resolution for an Android port?
- Profile as soon as possible in the target platform. Created production builds are becoming faster and easy to create so there are no excuses to not test them often. Just try to test them as much as possible in the builds.
- Profile a build multiple times to make sure that the data is concise and accurate.
- If possible, write your own frame rate counter in milliseconds. Unreal Engine gives you stats with frames per second, but accurate profiling should be done in **milliseconds** (**ms**).

- Don't profile the game while the VSync is enabled as it will prevent you from getting accurate profiling results.
- Specifically, define where the bound comes from. As you know, a lot of calculations were done on the GPU side, but are still part of the game, and probably, rendering calculations are related to the CPU. So, you have to check whether the issue came from the CPU or the GPU as optimizing in the wrong direction will just waste your time and will produce new problems.

One quote from Epic that really helps is as follows:

> *First you should check if your frame rate is limited by CPU or the GPU cost. As always you either can vary the workload (e.g. change the resolution) and see what has effect. Here it is easier to look at the engine build in feature stat unit.*

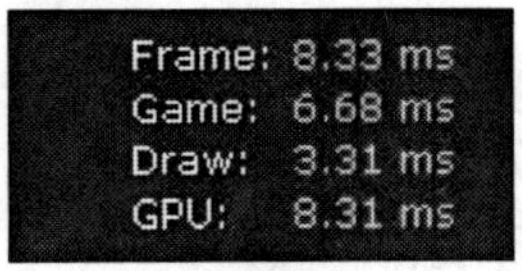

> *The actual frame time is limited by one of the three: Game (CPU game thread), Draw (CPU render thread) or GPU (GPU). Here we can see the GPU is the limiting factor (the largest of the three). In order to get a smaller Frame time, we have to optimize the GPU workload there.*

Console show flags versus view modes and rendering visualizers

The most important thing to know about the three features is that all of them do the same job, which is turning on and off some rendering features. It is more about where and how to use each of them. While the console show flags are more about using written console commands, they can be found in the game and editor. The view modes and the rendering visualizers are solutions with a UI display and they exist in the editor only.

If you don't know how to display the console, it is usually done using the input key "~", but you can change it in the **Input Settings** of the **Project Settings**.

Understanding console show flags

Unreal Engine provides a lot of console variables, which can be used at runtime in order to debug the game. Some of these console variables are called the **show flags**, which were implemented in order to allow you to toggle a lot of rendering features at runtime. This is only in the executable builds; however, in the edit time (in the editor), it is even easier, as the editor is a convenient place to have lots of menus and buttons. The Epic team puts them in the one of these menus, which will be discussed in the next section, *View modes and rendering visualizers*.

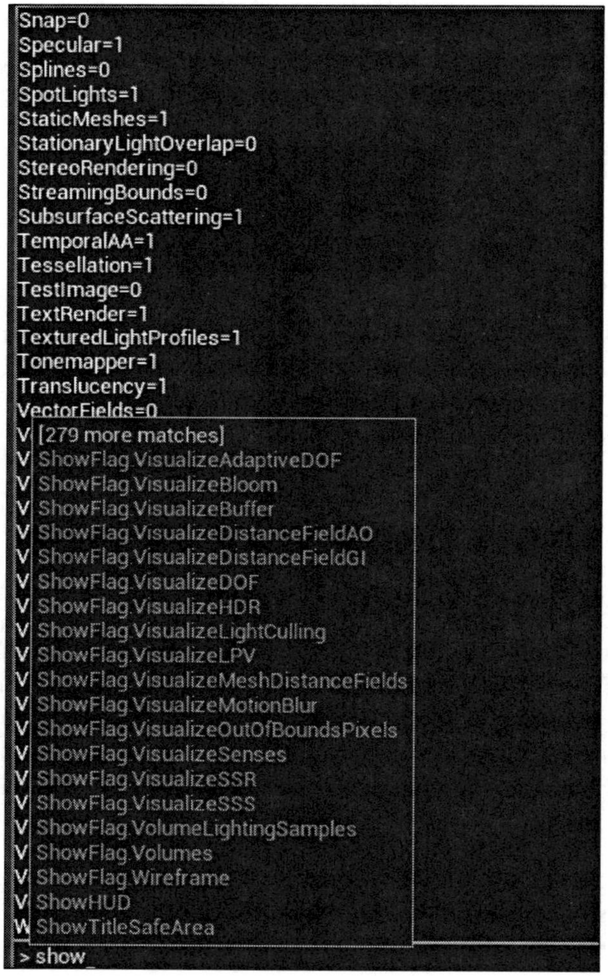

In the game, you can use the `show` command. Use the `show` command to get a list of all the show flags and their states. Use `show showflagname` to toggle a feature.

All the show flags are exposed as console variables, for example, `console show Bloom`, `showflag.Bloom 0`, or `showflag.Bloom = 0` in the configuration `*.ini` files.

Everything related to the configurations is stored in the configs directory in your Unreal project source or Unreal game build in a set of `*.ini` files, as shown in the following screenshot:

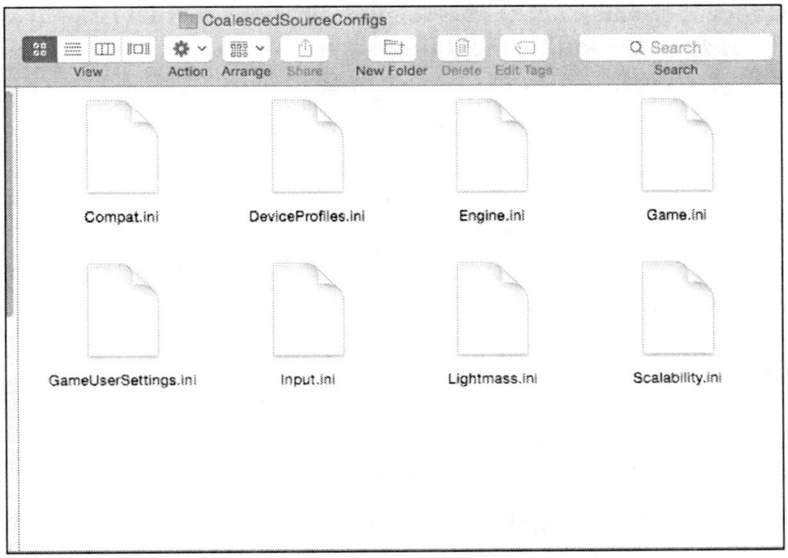

Keep in mind that some features will consume the performance even if the features are not enabled and do not render any more. Yes, I know that it sounds silly, but for example, by disabling the show flag, the show particles will hide the particles, but the simulation time is still required to support them in order to re-enable them later. So, they are not rendered, but there is still a possibility of enabling them again.

This is not the only example, but there are tons of other things that can be disabled, but unfortunately they are still running underground.

Now, here is a list of the most useful show flags used to profile the rendering pipeline:

- `AmbientOcclusion`: This toggles the **Screen Space Ambient Occlusion (SSAO)**
- `AntiAliasing`: This toggles any anti-aliasing type (Temporal AA or FXAA)
- `Bloom`: This affects the image-based lens flares and the bloom
- `Bounds`: This toggles the bounding volume of the selected objects (in the editor)
- `DeferredLighting`: This toggles all the deferred lighting passes

- `DirectionalLights`, `PointLights`, `SpotLights`: This toggles the different types of supported lights
- `Decals`: This toggles the decal rendering
- `DynamicShadows`: This toggles all dynamic shadows (which includes the Shadow Map rendering and the shadow projection)
- `GlobalIllumination`: This toggles baked and dynamic indirect lighting
- `IndirectLightingCache`: This toggles if the objects that have invalidated lightmaps use the Indirect Lighting Cache
- `Landscape Brushes`, `StaticMeshes`, `SkeletalMeshes`, `Landscape`: This toggles the rendering of the different geometry types
- `LightFunctions`: This toggles the light functions rendering
- `PostProcessing`: This toggles all the post-processing passes
- `ReflectionEnvironment`: This toggles the reflection environment passes
- `Rendering`: This toggles the whole rendering
- `Refraction`: This toggles the refraction passes
- `ScreenSpaceReflections`: This toggles the screen space reflections
- `Tessellation`: This toggles the tessellation (the tessellation shaders will keep running anyway but will be spawning more triangles)
- `Translucency`: This toggles the translucency rendering
- `Visualize SSR`: This renders the pixels affected by the screen space reflections in a bright orange color

The view modes and rendering visualizers

The view modes is one of the easiest ways in the Unreal Engine that you can use to isolate some behaviors. They look like just a combination of show flags in the editor UI, but they hold a lot of Unreal's power. They are almost the same as the show flags we discussed previously, that can use the view mode console command to switch between them (check the previous paragraph, if you have already forgotten). However, their job is limited to display some of the aspects of the final picture, or even the full final picture.

As you know, the final result that you see on the screen is basically a combination of different kinds of layers, and here, you can separate them.

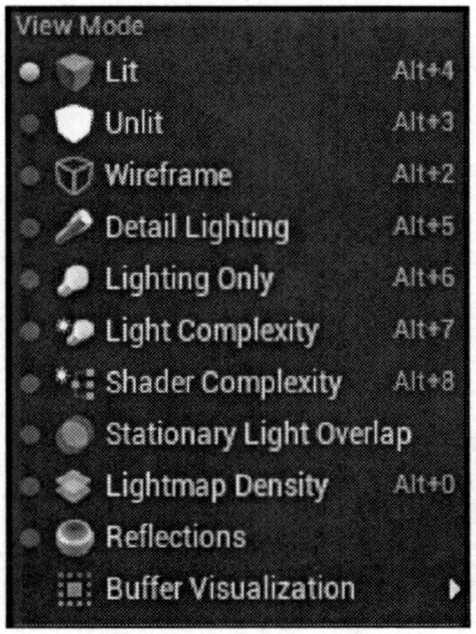

As you can see, their names imply what exactly you should expect on switching to one of these. For example, the reflections view mode will help you easily see and focus on the reflections only.

Another benefit is that you can use the shortcuts defined to make your workflow even faster. Just hold the *Alt* key and keep swapping between the numbers to have an overall view of them all quickly. I do it this way:

- **Lit**: This mode is used to display the final result the player will see in the final game.

- **Unlit**: This mode displays the diffuse passes only without any lighting or shadowing passes. It is a good mode for checking the textures and clearance of your levels.

- **Wireframe**: As the name implies, this displays the wireframe of the rendered scene. While this is totally useless for the game itself, for developers it is essential to learn more about meshes overlapping, transparent objects, or any other issues that cannot be shown in the lit mode.

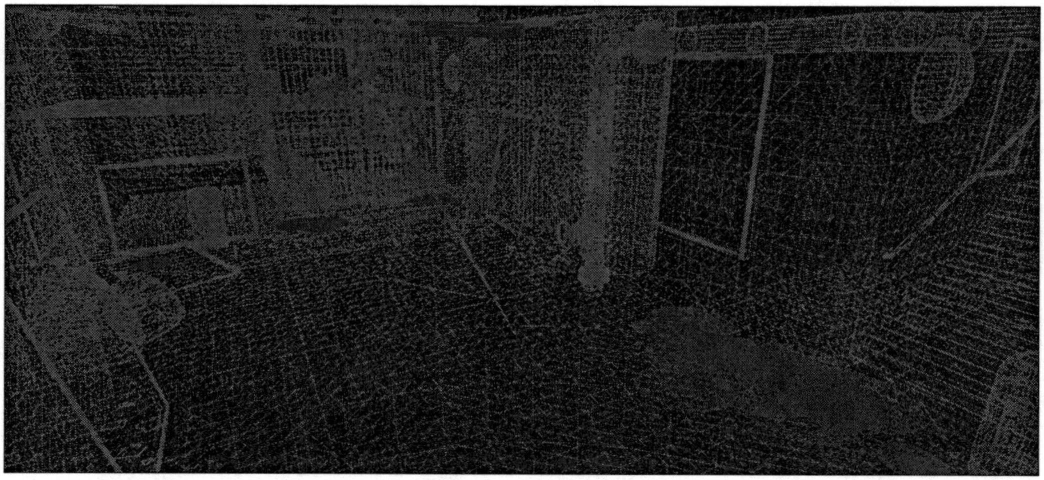

- **Detail Lighting**: As mentioned earlier, the unlit mode displays the color and texture without the light and shadow data. Here it is vice versa, the detail lighting mode displays the light and shadow information and ignores the color and texturing data.

- **Light Only**: The **Light Only** setting is almost the same as the detail lighting, but this mode is less complex as it ignores some of the secondary lighting features, such as the reflections and normal mapping.

- **Light Complexity**: This mode represents the light distribution over the scene. The darker the area, the less light is reaching those areas, while the brighter the areas, more the more light photons are reaching it it.

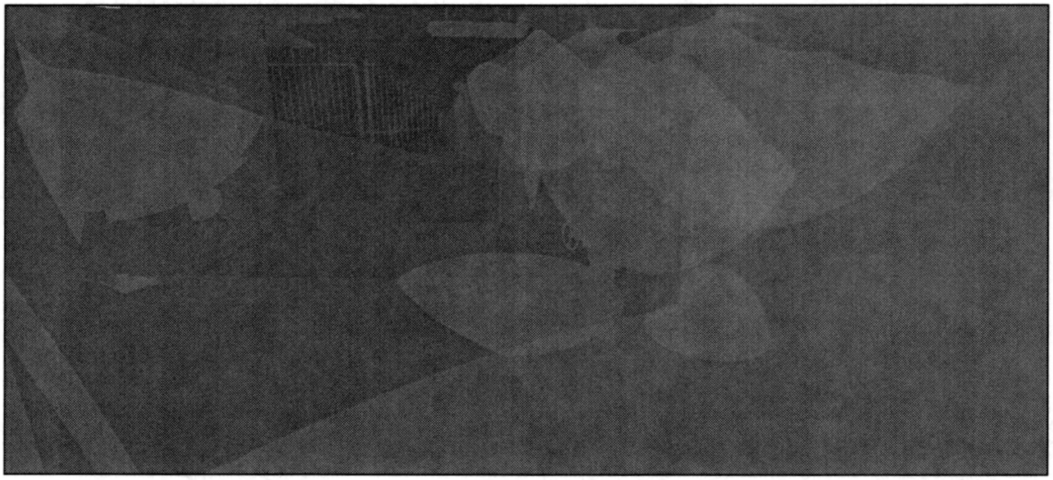

- **Shader Complexity**: This mode visualizes the number of shader instructions used to calculate each pixel of the scene. As long as you see a lot of green, it means that it a good indication of inexpensive shaders.

- **Stationary Light Overlap**: This view mode displays the overlap between lights over the scene objects. The areas with more green, means that there is more light sources overlapping there. And the darker green you find, it means that areas represents less lights overlapping around.

- **Lightmap Density**: This mode displays the lightmap's density of the scene objects. While the blue color is good, the red color indicates a very high texel density. The green color is in between.

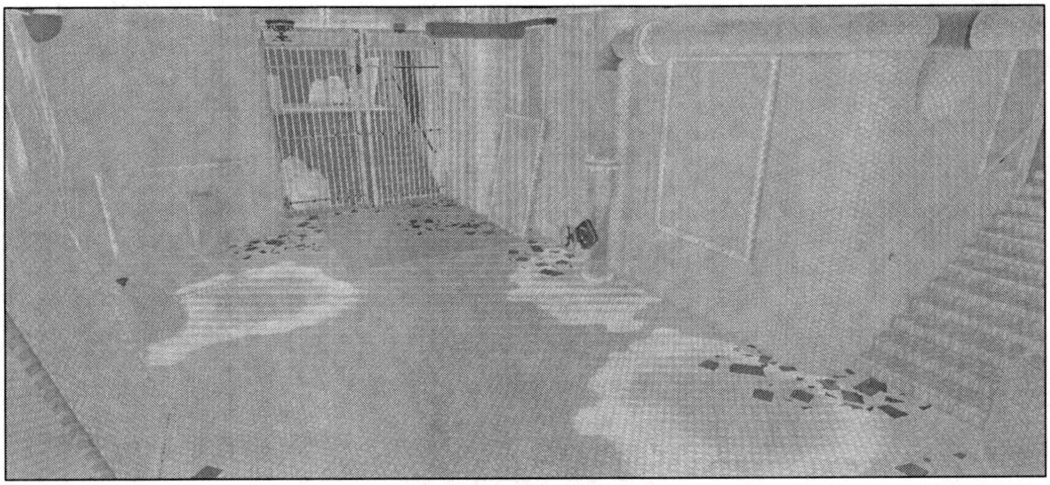

- **Reflections**: This view mode will apply a reflective material to all the scene surfaces. This way, you can understand the details of the reflections around the scene while placing the reflection capturers.

- **Buffer Visualization**: Here, you can find more and more to visualize. However, keep in mind that it is still a different menu than the rendering visualizers. Feel free to keep investigating all of them, but in general, this is what you are going to find in the menu.

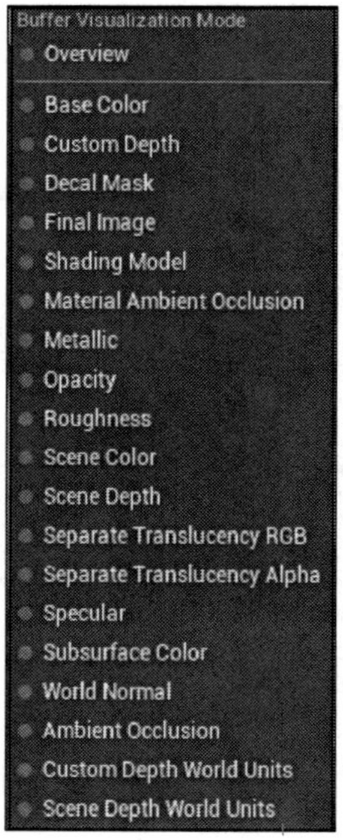

Using the overview choice has always been my favorite in order to get an overview of the most important buffers and compare the results in real time.

At the same time, there are the visualizers that are almost the same as the view modes, but serve different purposes and display different results. The visualizers are there in order to enable you to debug or view what Unreal does behind the scenes.

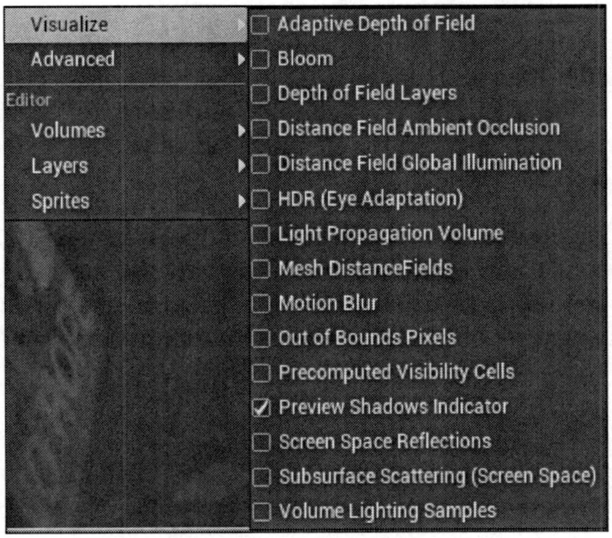

The visualized modes can be the rendering steps or paths, such as the depth pass, or the specialized views, such as the motion blur vector visualizer. While the view modes allow you to display one at a time, the visualizers allow you to display different amount of options at the same time. The view modes' UIs are built based on the toggle buttons, while the visualizers' UIs are built using checkboxes.

While some of the visualizers display only a result for you, the others will display a lot of useful statistics too. For example, the **Depth of Field (DoF)** visualizer.

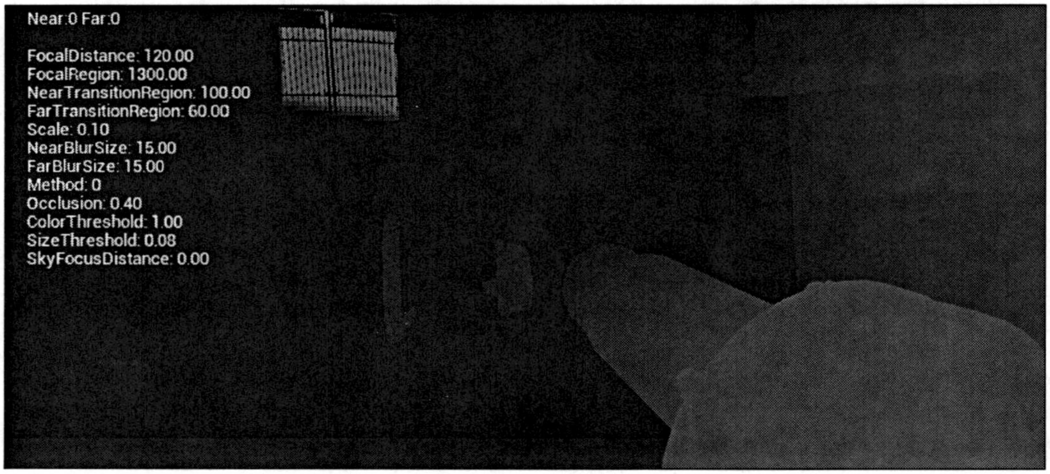

One last thing, in order to make you really understand the difference between both, you can consider the view modes used to toggle the steps or the different components of building the frame you see, such as diffuse, reflections, lights, and so on. The visualizers will help you toggle the features you are using, such as DoF, bloom, blur, and so on.

I've to say that, regardless of any other tools available in the engine, the console show flags, view modes, and rendering visualizers are the most important methods for debugging the rendering pipeline, and this is because of their ease of access. Now let's move on to the next set of tools, which are frequently used while debugging.

Console charts

Console charts are not only made for immediate toggles or displays, or even an immediate value change. Using console commands, such as `StartFPSChart` and `StopFPSChart`, will allow you to generate a performance chart over a period of time.

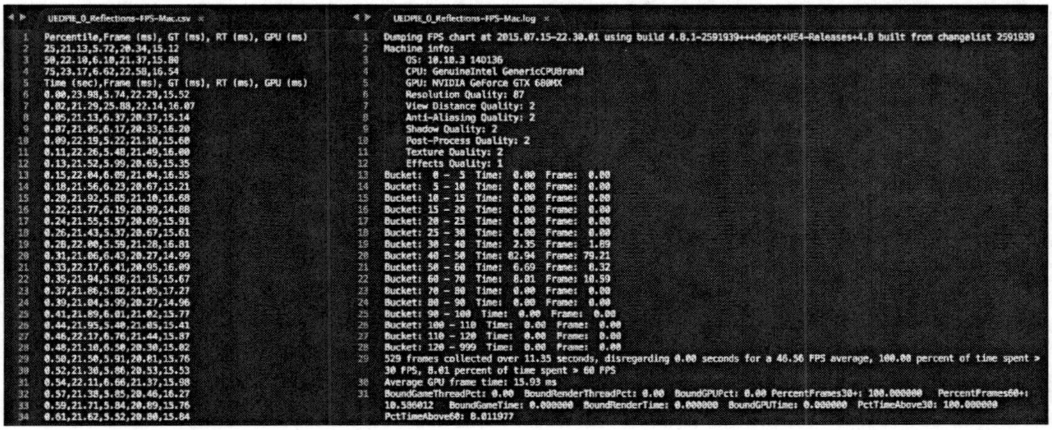

Using such a command will generate a spreadsheet file (with the extension `*.cvs`) in the profiling folder (which is located in the `ProjectFolder]\Saved\Profiling\SubwayPatrol\FPSChartStats`) \ `[Date of today]` \ folder.

You can easily load the `*.csv` file with Excel or any similar application. Then, you can check the values you want. It might be a very useful step to get the stat unit times over a period of time where you suspect some performance issues.

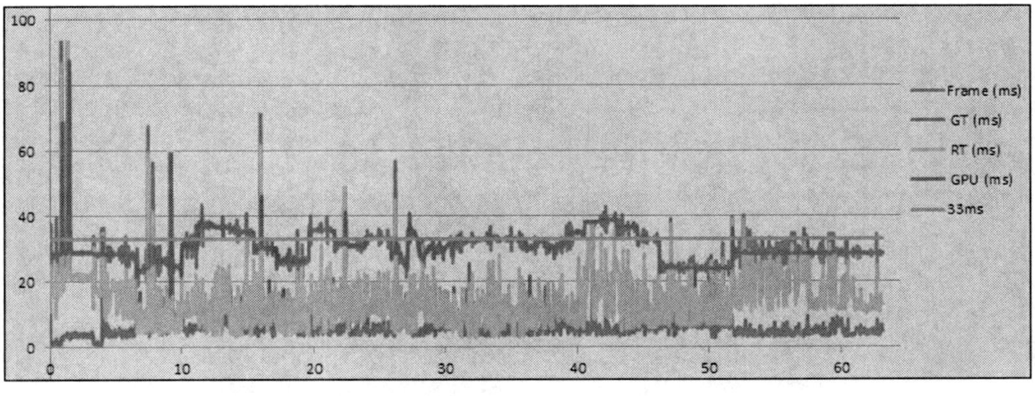

Though `*.csv` is the most important one, it is not the only one that you get. You also get a `*.log` file, which contains a lot of useful information (almost related to the device configurations, setup, and overall performance) alongside two tables of HTML files that hold some more information about the frames. Everything is named with the map/level name.

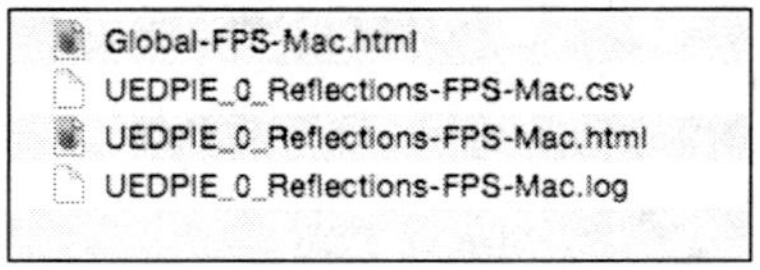

The GPU Visualizer

The GPU Visualizer is a place where you can see the visualization of each unit's performance in the GPU. As you might know that the GPU has many different units that work in parallel to do all the requested calculations. Sometimes, some of these units hit their bounds and can't process any faster, and that's when you get the lag and performance issues based on the rendering pipeline. It is common by the way, and this doesn't mean that your content is bad, but to be bound by different units for different parts of the frame happens everyday with the most complex projects, and at the same time, with the most simple projects.

Using the GPU Visualizer will allow you to take a look at the parts where there is a bottleneck, and then you will know exactly what needs fixing.

As the visualizer is not embedded in the editor UI by default, we have to launch it through the console (the same way you did earlier for the show flags), but this time, you need to display the editor console and not the game console.

This is the same way as using the console shortcut while being focused on any other editor panels, it will pop up the editor console for you. Just input the command name `r.ProfilerGPU.ShowUI`, and it will appear.

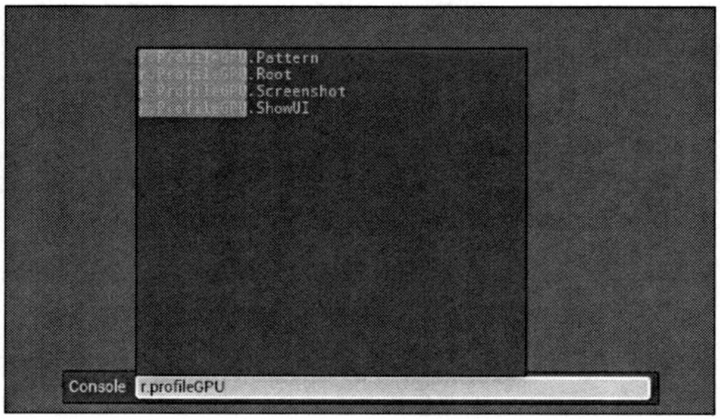

Note that, for some reason, it might not appear on the Mac editor builds, however, it is okay with the Windows editor builds. Sometimes, it might cause you some performance lags, but this is quite normal as it is based on Slate (the UI solution used to build the editor UI), which is rendered in the GPU and has to update every frame in order to display the correct results for you.

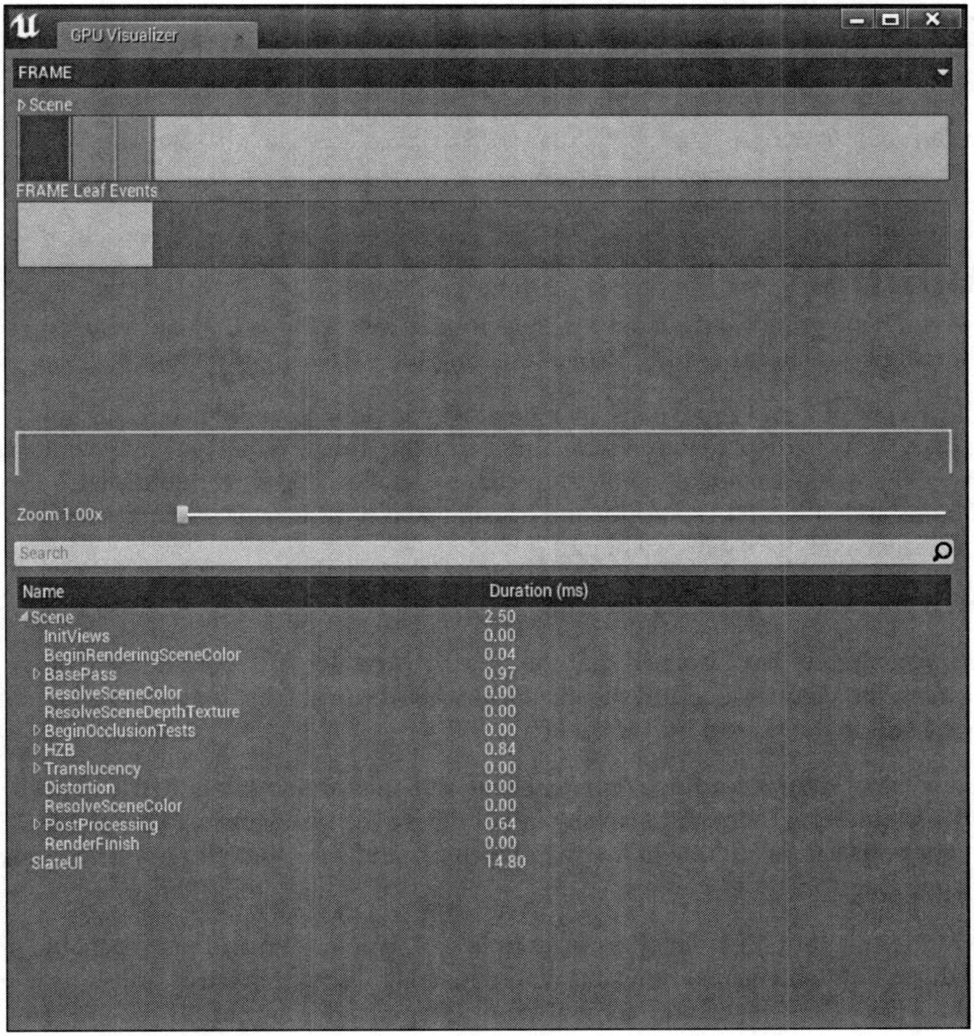

While everything is calculated in milliseconds, you will be able to easily define what causes so much time to be rendered, and therefore, you can start checking the reason and optimizing it. There is no key solution that the GPU Visualizer will provide you in order to fix your bottlenecks, but it will lead you to in the right direction by letting you know what takes more time than usual during the frame.

Recommended

As the topic of the book focuses on the rendering pipeline, the rendering tools, and what can be used to debug and profile the rendering pipeline, we will not discuss other useful tools that are not related to the rendering pipeline. However, there is another powerful tool that comes with Unreal Engine, which is called the **Profiler** (previously used to be called **Stats Viewer**). It focuses more on the overall game performance and gameplay logic, and it is better to read about it if you are interested in the fields of debugging the logic debugging and profiling.

You can refer to `https://docs.unrealengine.com/latest/INT/Engine/Performance/Profiler/index.html`.

Summary

Now you have your hands on all the most important methods that can be used in Unreal Engine in order to control and debug the rendering pipeline.

Console variables and show flags are a great way to debug a build itself, and now you know how to display the console and start using them. While we have mentioned a few of them that are related to the show flags part, the console variable's list is still huge, and you can keep trying and learning about the console variables for the different aspects of game debugging.

What if you want to debug in the editor?

Then, you already have learned that the console variables still work in the editor. However, the view modes and the visualizers are the best way to go as long as you are still in the Unreal Editor itself!

What is better than recording some real-time statistics and loading them in Excel and keep studying them and learning about where the problems occur and why? You got your hands on how to fire the FPS charts and save them for a future usage or debugging.

The hidden editor GPU Visualizer is an Epic tool. It is hidden and not reachable in the editor, but you learned how and where to get it. Using it is fairly simple as it displays the value, but as you know it is not 100 percent accurate.

As we have discussed all the rendering features and how to debug and learn more about the pipeline, I would recommend that you keep optimizing, debugging, and testing all your work. Then, we will move on to the next chapter where we are going to speak more about the scalability in Unreal Engine.

8
The Unreal Scalability Settings

Unreal Engine was built as a cross-platform engine that would help you build your game once and deploy it on a wide range of platforms, including Windows, Max, Linux, Android, iOS, Steam, Xbox One, PlayStation4, Oculus, and many more custom platforms. Each of these platforms has its own hardware limitations, and you'll need to adapt the game performance for the various game needs, such as using a split screen for a multiplayer mode. In a similar case, you will render the whole level more than once, and this has made tuning the graphics and display options the most easiest methods for controlling the performance, without affecting much of the gameplay.

Scalability is not just changing some graphics settings, it is more about the targeted platform and making decisions about gameplay, AI, art, sound, and so on, in order to fit the targeted platform.

Consoles have never been a source of scalability problems as they are fixed and powerful. However, the problem is mostly related to PCs or mobile devices (mostly Android). The number of different setups and device combinations out there made it hard to focus on a single hardware specification. You can have two Android devices from the same company, but each of them can use a different graphics chipset. A PC cannot compare to how much diversity you can find.

This is where the scalability options come into play, and everyone involved in the project has to take part in making some decisions regarding an aspect of the project, as Unreal Engine is one big package that everyone in the project pipeline will be using. It is not only a platform for coding or level designing, but it is used by just 'QA' people, producers, artists, programmers, and pretty much everyone who is involved in an Unreal Engine project.

By the end of this chapter, you will be able to:

- Master the project's render settings
- Understand where to find all the scalability options in the Unreal Engine
- Know how to quickly adjust the game to match the different platforms
- Add a multiplayer split-screen quickly to your projects
- Understand what the **Device Profiles** are and how to use them
- Learn more about the console variables, but this time about what can be useful about adjusting the quality to fit the platform

Now, let's quickly dive into the core of this chapter!

The general rules

There are a few general rules that you can follow and consider in order to quickly adjust the performance to fit the targeted platform:

- As different machines have different setups, this leads to having a faster or slower game. These differences might come from the following things:
  - The GPU or its memory
  - The screen resolution
  - The CPU and its core count
  - The HDD size and latency
  - Memory size and latency
  - The OS version and architecture
- Graphics are generally the easiest to scale where you can do some optimization without affecting the gameplay much. This can be done in the shape of auto adjustment of the settings, or even by exposing some values for the player in the **Option** menu. The things that you can control that have no gameplay effect can be as follows:
  - Texture details
  - Motion blur
  - Anti-aliasing
  - Resolution
  - Frames per second
  - Image quality

- In a multiplayer game, a player might have the advantage of a higher frame rate, which gives them a faster response time by just changing some variables via the console variables. A console variable can offer an enormous amount of values than needed for the scalability. Some multiplayer games fix this problem by giving the control to the server administrator to override those settings in order to give all the players the same number of chances without any advantages.
- Keep in mind that a combination of console variable settings can lead to problems, so having the server control the whole thing is worth it.
- Try to document and communicate changes over time.
- Scalability on the low end means that more players can play the game. Scalability on the high end means that the game can look better, especially in screenshots and tests.
- Documenting the low, recommended, and high specifications will make life easier for the whole team.
- Test on a variety of platform specs:
    - Low, medium and high GPU
    - Low and high CPU
    - Low and high memory
- Understand that some hardware might only be slow for some features, for example, with the amount of objects, materials, lights, and so on. It is not necessarily that the hardware is slow in general.
- Understand in-engine profiling tools, such as the GPU profiler, the console variables, and the profiler (Stats Viewer):

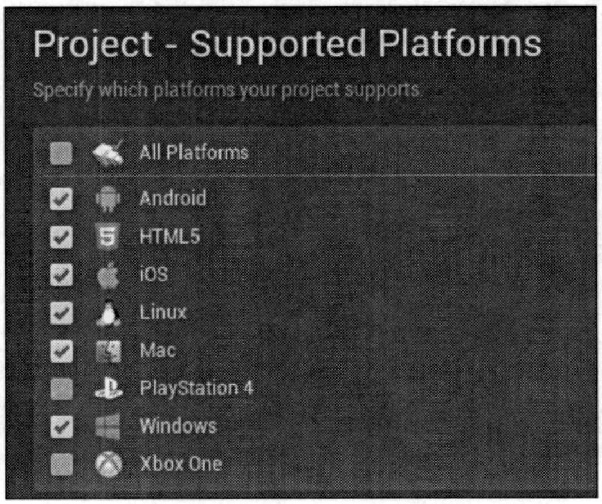

The render settings

Even before diving more into the project, I think that it is the time to discuss one of the most important options provided by Unreal Engine--the render settings, which are located in the project's **Settings** window.

While the render settings are something important, I decided to discuss it here with the scalability options as they have a huge impact on the platform you are going to target, and based on this, you can enable, disable, or even balance some options.

The render settings can be found in the project **Settings** window, which can be accessed from the **Edit** menu.

As with any of the other project's **Settings** provided in Unreal Engine, the options you will find here are the global options, which means that they will be applied to the whole project and not only to a specific level or a specific area of your game.
The **Rendering settings** options contain the following:

- **Mobile**: This is the option that will only apply to mobile platforms (currently, Android and iOS only).
  - **Mobile HDR**: This option can be used if the mobile needs to render in full HDR. Disabling this option is good for a better performance on the old devices. You can also disable it in games that do not require lights at all, such as 2D games.
- **Culling**: Not everything should be displayed on the screen; sometimes, there are things that are far away from the view, and it is not necessary to keep them rendered in the pipeline. Here is a list of some options and parameters that will help you control the culling:
  - **Occlusion Culling**: This allows occluded meshes to be culled and not rendered.
  - **Min Screen Radius Lights**: This is the screen radius where the lights are culled. A larger value can improve the performance but will cause some light to pop off when it affects a small area of the screen.
  - **Min Screen Radius for Early Z Pass**: This is the screen radius where the objects are culled for the early Z pass. The larger values can improve the performance, but the very large values can degrade the performance if large occluders are not rendered.
  - **Min Screen Radius for Cascaded Shadow Maps**: This is the screen radius where the objects are culled for cascaded shadow map depth passes. The larger values can improve the performance but will produce some artifacts, those artifacts came from the fact that it will stop casting shadow.
  - **Warn about no precomputed visibility**: This displays a warning when no precomputed visibility data is available for the current camera location. This can be helpful if you make a game that relies on the precomputed visibility, such as a first person game on a mobile device.
- **Textures**: This could be a source of troubles on some devices, but if that's the case, then you probably need to do some tweaks with the textures settings.
  - **Texture Streaming**: This enables the texture to be streamed based on what is visible on the screen.

- **Use DXT5 Normal Maps**: Toggle this to use DXT5 for normal maps, otherwise, the BC5 will be used. Keep in mind that this does not support all the hardware and changing this setting will not have any effect until you restart the editor.

- **Lighting**: Rendering is all about lights, and here are listed a set of lighting options that will help you to get the good balance between the quality and the performance.
    - **Allow Static Lighting**: Toggle this to allow any static lighting to be generated and used, just like lightmaps and Shadow Maps. Games that only use the dynamic lighting should disable this option in order to save some static lighting overhead. This setting is one of those that requires an editor to restart in order to work effectively.
    - **Use Normal Maps for Static Lighting**: Toggle this to allow any static lighting to use normal maps for lighting computations.
    - **GBuffer**: Toggle this to enable the usage of GBuffer.
    - **Generate Mesh Distance Fields**: Toggle this to distance fields of static meshes that are needed for **Distance Field Ambient Occlusion** (**DFAO** if you still remember), which is used to implement the Movable Skylight shadows and Ray Traced Distance Field Shadows on direction lights. Enabling this option will increase the mesh's build times and the memory usage. This option needs an editor to restart in order to work.
    - **Distance Field Penumbra Size**: This value represents the size of the uniform penumbra produced by the static shadowing.
    - **DBuffer Decals**: This is the decal feature (experimental yet).

- **Tessellation**: Tessellation is one of the most complex and recent features in the real-time rendering graphics; it allows you to get details on demand only. Here are the render settings that are related to the tessellation implementation in the Unreal Engine:
    - **Adaptive pixels per triangle**: If the adaptive tessellation is enabled, this option will try to tessellate the mesh so that each triangle contains the specified number of pixels. The tessellation multiplier specified in the material can increase or decrease the amount of tessellation.

- **Postprocessing**: The post processing effects are one of the most complex and wanted features. While each effect has its own unique set of options, the whole post processing pass has its own parameters too. Here is a list of the parameters that control the post processing in general, regardless of the effects used:

  - **Separate Translucency**: This allows translucency to be rendered to a separate render targeted and composited after a depth of field. This will prevent the translucency from appearing out of focus.
  - **Custom Depth Pass**: Toggle this for the custom depth pass to tag primitives for postprocessing passes. Enabling this option can save memory but may cause hiccups the first time the feature is used.

- **Translucency**: Sometimes, the translucent objects behave incorrectly or give unwanted results, especially when they overlap. Here is a list of options that is meant to allow you to do some tweaks to fix those issues. I would recommend that you never make any changes in this section unless you have a real problem:
  - **Translucent Sort Policy**: This is the sort mode for translucent primitives that affects how they are ordered and how they change the order as the camera moves.
  - **Translucent Sort Axis**: This is the axis where the sorting will take place when the previous value (**Translucent Sort Policy**) is set to **Sort Along Axis**.

- **Default Postprocessing Settings**: As discussed before, the post processing are enabled by default for any project, but here you can choose which to be enabled or disabled by default.
  - **Bloom**: Toggle this for the bloom post-processing effect.
  - **Ambient Occlusion**: Toggle this to the Ambient Occlusion post-processing effect.
  - **Ambient Occlusion Static Fraction (AO for baked lighting)**: Toggle this to the AO for baked lighting post-processing effect.
  - **Auto Exposure**: Toggle this to the auto exposure post-processing effect.
  - **Motion Blur**: Toggle this to the motion blur post-processing effect.
  - **Lens Flares (Image based)**: Toggle this to the lens flares post-processing effect.
  - **Anti-Aliasing Method**: Toggle this to the anti-aliasing post-processing effect or select its type.

- **Optimizations**: Having depth means that you already have a Z-pass (no wonder, it is 3D rendering), but this pass might cause some problems, especially with animated objects. It is something that happens everyday, but the options listed here are to help you in case you have these depth issues:
  - **Early Z-pass**: This checks whether to use only a depth pass to initialize Z culling for the base pass.

- **Movables in early Z-pass**: This checks whether to render movable objects in the early Z-pass.
- **Clear Scene**: This controls how the scene is cleared before rendering.

- **Editor**: Optimizations for render settings are not only required for the game, but sometimes, the editor itself needs to tweak some in order to run fast. Here are the settings that will make your editor render faster in some cases:
  - **Wireframe Cull Threshold**: This is the screen radius where the wireframe objects are culled. The large values can improve the performance when viewing the scene in wireframe.

The scalability options

Unreal Engine has lots of options that you can tweak in order to distribute your game with different platforms and/or different configurations. These options are not listed in one place, however, the majority of the options are listed in the scalability **Settings** menu. A majority of these options are found in the **Settings** menu, which you can go to from the toolbar.

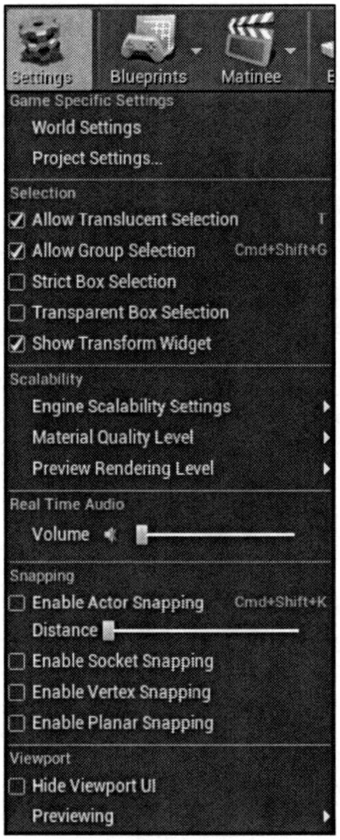

In general, the supported scalability options in the Unreal editor are explained in the following sections.

The Engine Scalability Settings

This option contains a majority of the effective options. These options can be generally found among a lot of commercial engines, but Unreal has more control over them. As you can see, once you hit the **Engine Scalability Settings** from the previously mentioned menu, it will pop up a small window. The window is self-explanatory; in fact, any value can be set to a level of four different quality values. Pick the ones that make your performance run well on the targeted devices.

All the adjusted values in this menu can be found in the `BaseScalaiblity.ini` file, which is located in the `[UE4_InstallPath]/Engine/Config` folder.

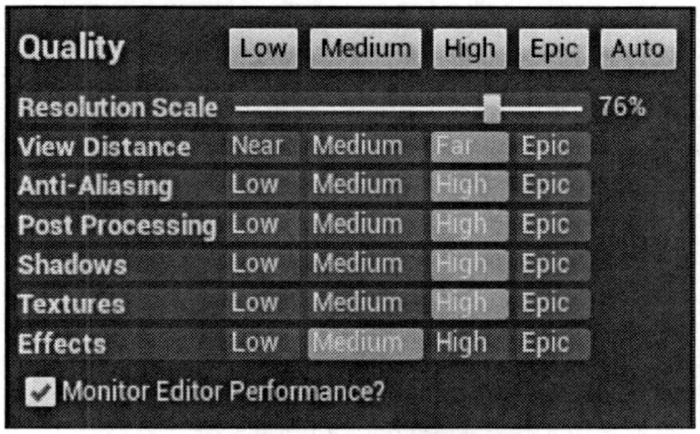

- **Resolution Scale**: The slider gives you the chance to render the game in a lower resolution. Basically, it is a percentage of the full resolution. Keep in mind that this technique will not be applied to the UI.
- **View Distance**: This culls the objects based on their distance to the viewer.
- **Anti-Aliasing**: This adjusts the anti-aliasing quality level regardless of its type, which is the same as using the `r.PostProcessAAQuality` console command.
- **Post Processing**: This adjusts the quality of the post-processing effects.
- **Shadows**: This adjusts the quality of dynamic shadows.
- **Textures**: This adjusts the textures' filtering mode.
- **Effects**: This adjusts the quality of the other different types of effects, such as the **ReflectionQuality**, **SceneColorFormat**, **DetailMode**, **SSR**, and much more.

The Material Quality Level

It is found in the same place, under the settings menu in the top bar. However, this one is a little different--it has only two options.

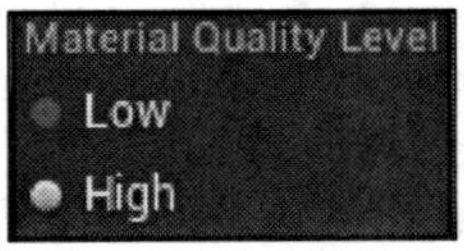

Let's be clear, it does nothing by default. None of the selections will make a difference. However, if you made a logic for it, that will make a difference.

While you are building your materials, you can use a node called **Quality Switch**, and with it, you can connect the two pieces of logic, one less performance intensive than the other.

This means that if you use this mentioned node while building the materials' logic in order to separate the expensive behaviors from the cheap ones, the **Low** and **High** options will disable some expensive material parts that have a minor effect on the final look.

Device Profiles

The **Device Profiles** is one of the most amazing development features in Unreal Editor. It can be found in the **Developer Tools** under the **Window** menu.

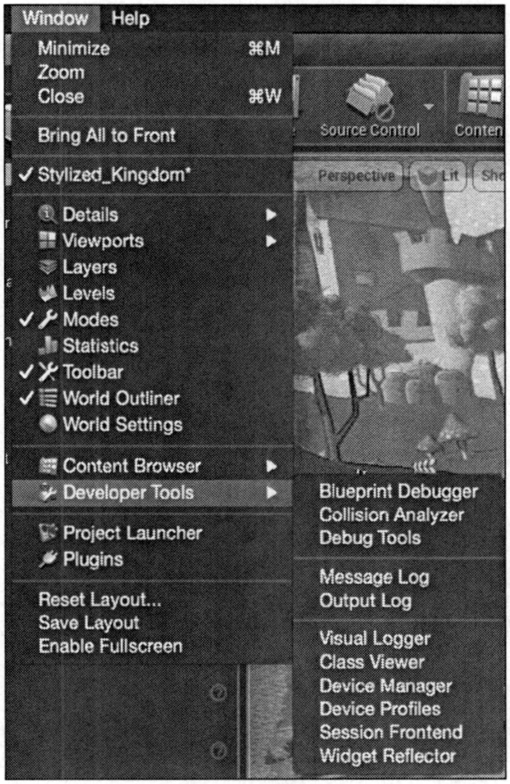

The importance of this window is that it will give you an easy-to-use UI that has direct access to the `DefaultDeviceProfiles.ini` file in the configuration files directory.

Can you imagine changing some text in a configuration text file? It's not easy!

Any changes made to that file will change and set the device specific configurations, which means that it is very critical that you are sure of any changes made there.

For example, you can change the game resolution in the devices to use half of the size or so. It matches the same results that you get from using the console variables (check the last point), but as the console variables require an input process in order to take place, this change in the `DefaultDeviceProfiles.ini` file will be auto triggered in the game. In other words, this will be the default option for the build.

As you can see in the following screenshot, the **Device Profiles** window contains all the supported *Devices* and not only *Platforms*. For each device, there are lots and lots of settings that you can tweak.

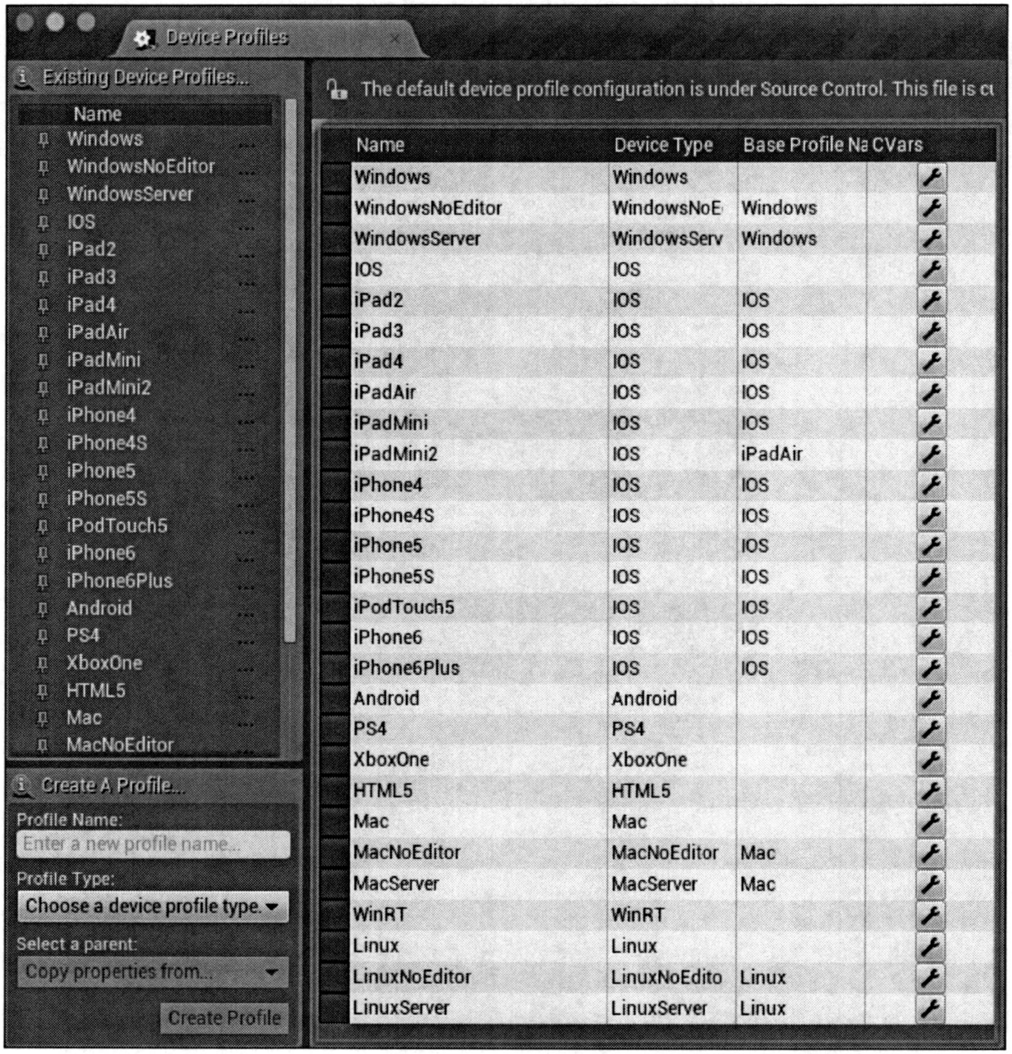

Detail Mode

Every single mesh in your level will have **Rendering** settings attached to it. In the LOD options of these rendering settings, you can set the **Detail Mode** property in order to set the minimum detail level of the mesh. This option gives you an opportunity to fit the models of the LOD levels with the targeted platforms.

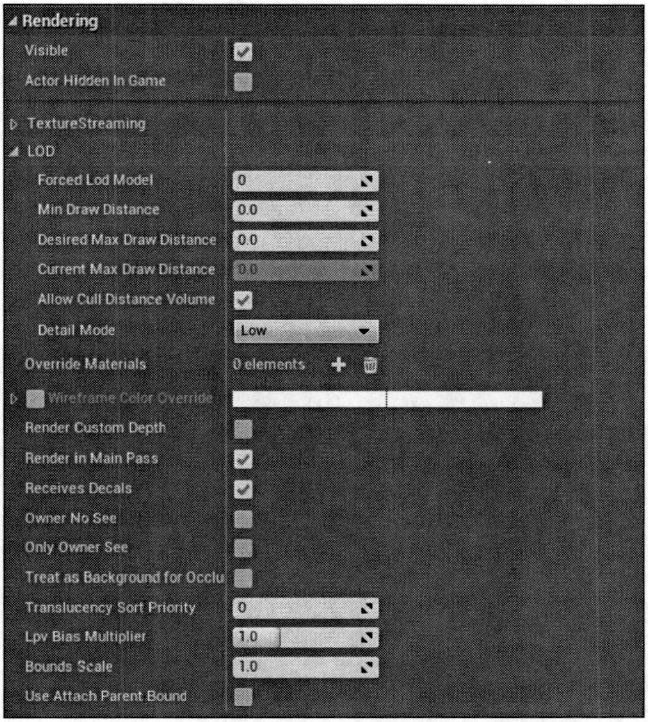

Console variables

Using the console has always been tricky. However, one nice trick is that if you just type `r` in the console, this will filter the commands to display the renderer-related commands. You can use any of them; they are all exposed by their names, and it is easy to figure out the usage of each of them. Usually, they will change in the configuration files of your game.

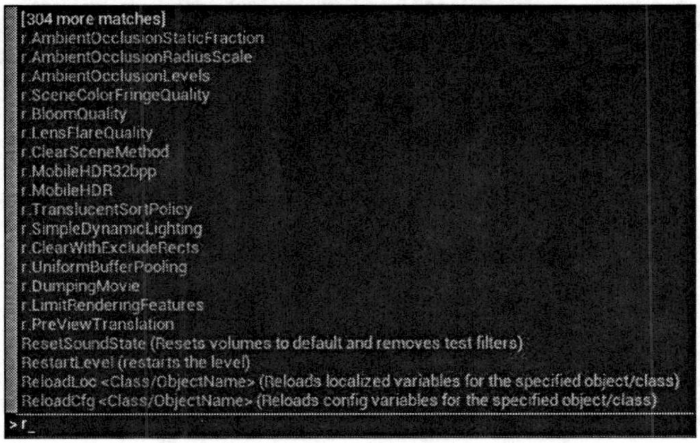

Extending to a multiplayer split-screen

If you want to extend your game even further and scale it and its audience, but in the same platform, probably your best bet would be to add a multiplayer without the need to have a network connection between the player. Regardless of the multiplayer types, we will talk about the local multiplayer split-screen.

While every engine and framework handles this part in their own unique way, it might take you a few minutes or even hours to set up the base of the split-screen. The Unreal Editor gives you a super shortcut that allows you to get it running in seconds.

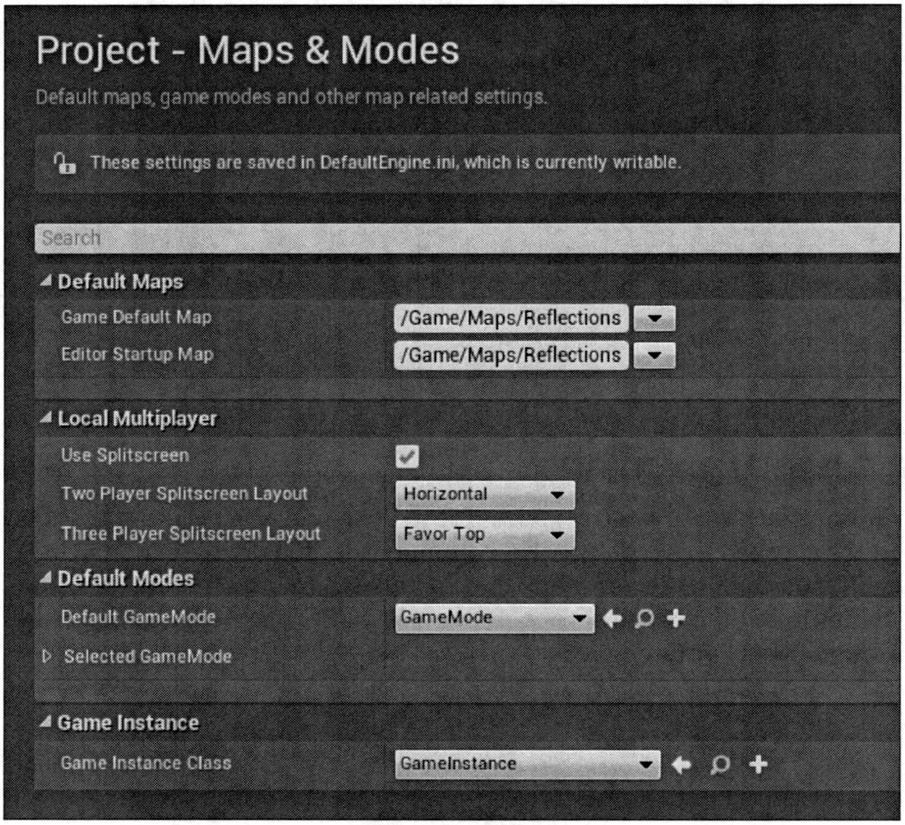

Again, from the project's **Settings**, you can go to the **Maps & Modes** section. Here, you will find a fold out named **Local Multiplayer**, which really implies something.

The options are super easy to digest, but not enough to build something:

- **Use Splitscreen**: This option can be used to check whether the screen needs to be split or not when multiple local players are presented
- **Two Player Splitscreen Layout**: This viewport layout can be used if the screen needs to be split when there are two local players
- **Three Player Splitscreen Layout**: This viewport layout can be used if the screen needs to be split when there are three local players

After setting your options, you'll find that nothing happens. Of course, it needs some gameplay logic, but it is a very simple logic, as it just requires you to use the node called **Create Player** in order to create players, and then the screen will be split for you the next time you run the game. The main idea here is that as long as the feature is enabled in the **Maps & Modes** settings, the screen will keep splitting to match the local player's count.

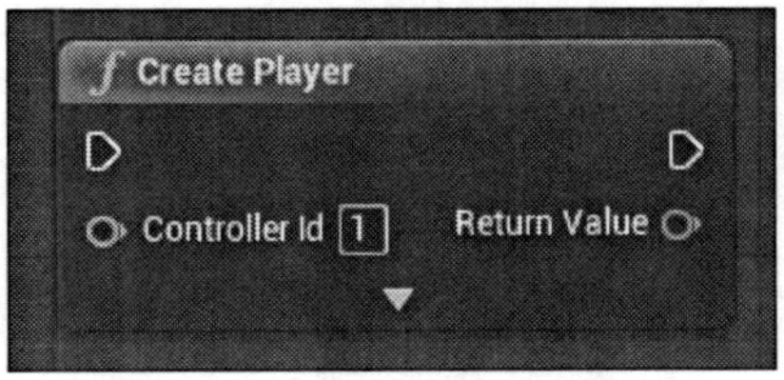

You might still need to add a lot of logic layers later to handle the UI for different screens or even to handle the player's logic themselves, but here the goal is how to scale the game more and get a split screen up and running in the rendering pipeline.

Summary

Apart from understanding the core points of the ways to keep your project scalable for different devices, you now know more about the render settings, what every option can do, and how important it is to change these options based on your targeted platform.

Scalability settings are not resting in one place, different options, and different menus. While they are very easy to understand, you learned where to find them and what they can do exactly for your game.

The splitscreen support is essential, especially when it comes to consoles and the war of multiplayer games. Tons of multiplayer games are competing out there, and you probably thought of building one; now you know how to simply add a support to this in a few seconds.

The device profile is one of the most unique features in Unreal; why would you need to launch the console every time in order to set some variables that are not exposed in the editor, when you can just set some of these variables using the device profile?

Sometimes, using the console is essential even if you have the correct profiles installed, but you might need to keep changing some variables to test which works the best. Then, the console variables that start with "`r`" is your way to go with the rendering pipeline optimizations.

Now, let's go to the next chapter and learn one more rendering feature. It is not essential nor important in all your games, but it is one of those juicy features. Let's go and make our level foggy!

9
Adding Fog to Your Games

How can we speak about rendering without mentioning one of the oldest (but important) rendering features since the rise of 3D rendering. Fog effects have always been an essential part of any rendering engine regardless of the main goal of that engine. However, in games, it is a must to have this feature, not only because of the ambience and feel it will give to the game, but because it will minimize the draw distance while rendering the large and open areas, which is great, performance wise!

The fog effects can be used for a lot of purposes, starting from adding ambiance to the world to setting a global mood (perhaps scary), to simulating a real environment, or even to distract the players.

By the end of this short chapter, you'll be able to:

- Know both the fog types in Unreal Engine
- Understand the difference between both the fog types
- Master all the parameters to control the fog types

Having said this, let's get started!

The fog types

Unreal Engine provides the user with two varieties of fog; each has its own set of parameters to modify and provide different effects. The two supported fog types are as follows:

- The Atmospheric Fog
- The Exponential Height Fog

The Atmospheric Fog

The Atmospheric Fog gives an approximation of light scattering through a planetary atmosphere. It is the best fog method that can be used with a natural environment scene, such as landscape scenes. One of the core features of this fog is that it gives your directional light a sun disc effect.

Adding it to your game

By adding an actor from the **Visual Effects** section of the **Modes** panel, or even from the actor's context menu by right-clicking on the scene view, you can install the Atmospheric Fog in your level directly.

In the **Visual Effects** submenu of the **Modes** panel, you can find both the fog types listed there:

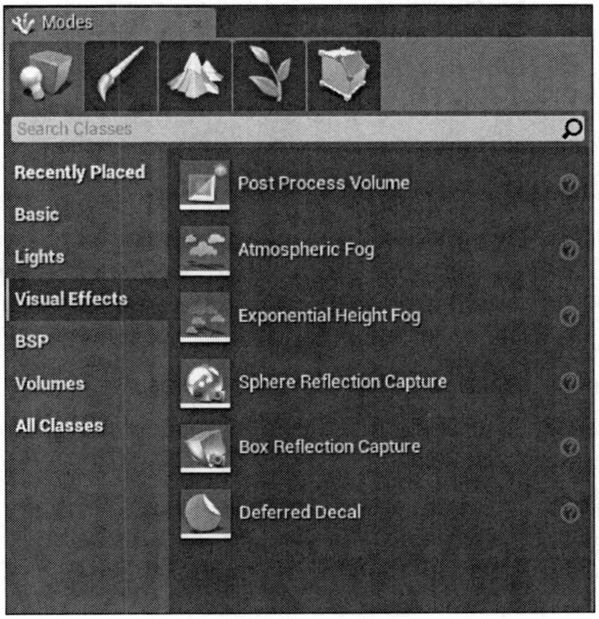

In order to be able to control the quality of the final visual look of the recently inserted fog, you will have to do some tweaks for its properties attached to the actor.

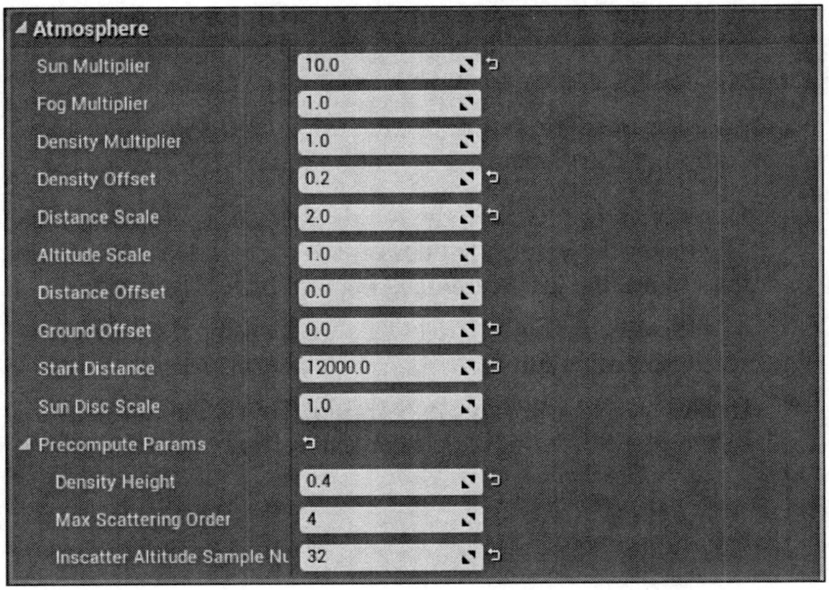

- **Sun Multiplier**: This is an overall multiplier for the directional light's brightness. Increasing this value will not only brighten the fog color, but will also brighten the sky color as well.
- **Fog Multiplier**: This is a multiplier that affects only the fog color (it does not affect the directional light).
- **Density Multiplier**: This is a fog density multiplier (it does not affect the directional light).
- **Density Offset**: This is a fog opacity controller.
- **Distance Scale**: This is a distance factor that is compared to the Unreal unit scale. This value is more effective for a very small world. As the world size increases, you will need to increase this value too, as larger values cause changes in the fog attenuation to take place faster.
- **Altitude Scale**: This is the scale along the *z* axis.
- **Distance Offset**: This is the distance offset, calculated in km, used to manage the large distances.
- **Ground Offset**: This is an offset for the sea level. Normally, the sea level is 0, and as the fog system does not work for regions below the sea level, you need to make sure that all the terrain remains above this value in order to guarantee that the fog works.
- **Start Distance**: This is the distance from the camera lens that the fog will start from.
- **Sun Disk Scale**: This is the size of the sun disk, but keep in mind that this can't be 0, as earlier there was an option to disable the sun disk, but in order to keep it real, Epic decided to remove this option and keep the sun disk, but it gives you the chance to make it as small as possible.
- **Precompute Params**: The properties included in this group need a recomputation of the precomputed texture data:
    - **Density Height**: This is the fog density decay height controller. The lower the values, the denser the fog will be, while the higher the values, the less scatter the fog will have.
    - **Max Scattering Num**: This sets a limit on the number of scattering calculations.
    - **Inscatter Altitude Sample Number**: This is the number of different altitudes at which you can sample inscatter color.

The Exponential Height Fog

This type of fog has its own unique requirement. While the Atmospheric Fog can be added anytime or anywhere and it works, the Exponential Height Fog requires a special type of map where there are low and high bounds, as its mechanic includes creating more density in the low places of a map and less density in the high places of the map.

Between both these areas, there will be a smooth transition.

One of the most interesting features of the Exponential Height Fog is that is has two fog colors: one for the hemisphere facing the dominant directional light and another color for the opposite hemisphere.

Adding it to your game

As mentioned earlier, to add the volume type from the same **Visual Effects** section of the **Modes** panel is very simple. You can select the **Exponential Height Fog** actor and drag and drop it into the scene. As you can see, even the icon implies the high and low places from the sea level.

In order to be able to control the final visual look of the recently inserted fog, you would have to do some tweaks for its properties attached to the actor:

- **Fog Density**: This is the global density controller of the fog.
- **Fog Inscattering Color**: This is the inscattering color for the fog (the primary color). In the following image, you can see how different values work:

- **Fog Height Falloff**: This is the height density controller that controls how the density increases as the height decreases.
- **Fog Max Opacity**: This controls the maximum opacity of the fog. A value of 0 means the fog will be invisible.
- **Start Distance**: This is the distance from the camera where the fog will start.
- **Directional Inscattering Exponent**: This controls the size of the directional inscattering cone. The higher the value, the clearer vision you get, while the lower the value, the more dense fog you get.

- **Directional Inscattering Start Distance**: This controls the start distance from the viewer of the directional inscattering.
- **Directional Inscattering Color**: This sets the color for directional inscattering that is used to approximate inscattering from a directional light.
- **Visible**: This controls the fog visibility.
- **Actor Hidden in Game**: This enables or disables the fog in the game (it will not affect the editing mode).

- **Editor Billboard Scale**: This is the scale of the billboard components in the editor.

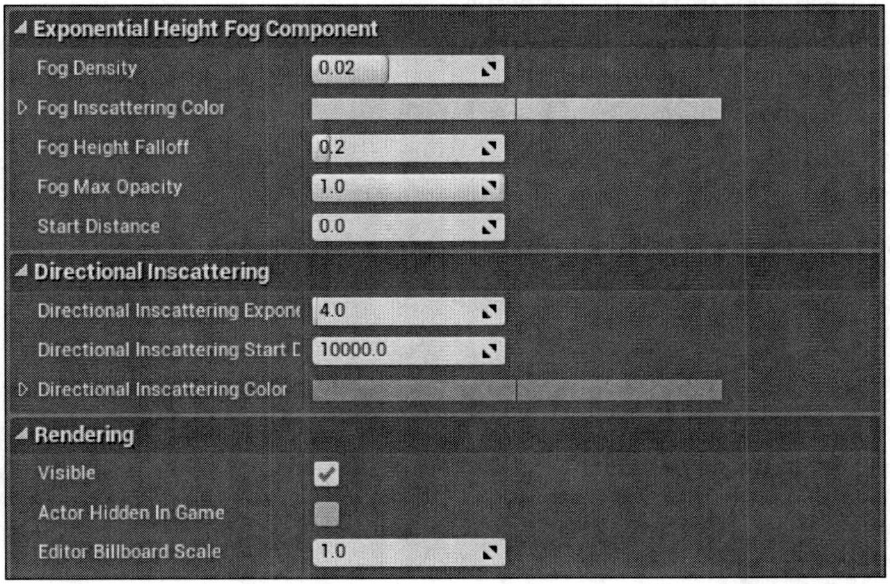

The animated fog

Almost like any other thing in Unreal Engine, you can make some animations for it. Some parts of the engine are super responsive to the animation system, while other parts have limited access. However, speaking of the fog, it has a limited access in order to animate some values. You can use different ways and methods to animate values at runtime or even during the edit mode.

The color

The Height Fog color can be changed at runtime using the **LinearColor Property Track** in the Matinee Editor. By performing the following given steps, you can change the height fog color in the game:

1. Create a new Matinee Actor.
2. Open the newly created actor in the Matinee Editor.
3. Create a Height Fog Actor.
4. Create a group in Matinee.

5. Attach the Height Fog Actor from the scene to the group created in the previous step.
6. Create a linear color property track in the group.
7. Choose the **Fog Inscattering Color** or **Directional Inscattering Color** to control its value (using two colors is an advantage of that fog type, remember!).
8. Add keyframes to the track, and set the color for them.

Animating the Exponential Height Fog

In order to animate the Exponential Height Fog, you can use one of the following two ways:

- Use Matinee Editor to animate the Exponential Height Fog Actor values
- Use a timeline node in the Level Blueprint and control the Exponential Height Fog Actor values

Summary

Now you've got your hands on the last required part of the Unreal Engine rendering tools. You learned about the fog effects and the supported types in the Unreal Editor, the different parameters, and how to use any of the fog types. Now, it is recommended that you go ahead directly to your editor, and start adding some fog and play with its values. Even better if you can start to do some animations for the parameters as mentioned earlier.

Don't just try it in the Edit mode; sometimes, the results are different when you hit play or even more different when you cook a build, so feel free to build any level you made in an executable and check the results.

Now you've learned everything about rendering in Unreal Engine (Not only 4.x but also Unreal 5.x, as the majority of the knowledge you got here will emigrate with you to 5.x when it comes out).

There are certain things that I want to recommend to all the readers, first of all close the book, and go directly to your editor and keep making stuff. Never open the book once you hit a wall. If you keep coming back and forth, it will never stick in your head. So try hard to remember what we discussed and did together, while you were reading, and if your memory can't really help, then you can take a look at the book again. You have my permission now to sneak a look here.

Try to keep reading the release notes in each new Unreal version. Sometimes there are new features added to the engine regarding the rendering systems. Most importantly, they do change the stuff, replace the stuff, or even totally remove the stuff. So in order to save your time to check whether the engine has a new bug, or your work been done incorrectly, it is better to be aware of what has been changed or removed.

If you have any issues relating to the book or the content, I'm always open to answering questions, and it will be easy to find me and shoot me a line.

Make something Unreal. You have massive power in your hands now! However, something Unreal doesn't mean the high-end AAA quality, something basic, such as a solid, with appealing and great visual effects might melt and break hearts!

Recommend this book to your friends.

Index

A

B

C

D

E

F

P

Thank you for buying
Unreal Engine Lighting and Rendering Essentials

About Packt Publishing

Packt, pronounced 'packed', published its first book, *Mastering phpMyAdmin for Effective MySQL Management*, in April 2004, and subsequently continued to specialize in publishing highly focused books on specific technologies and solutions.

Our books and publications share the experiences of your fellow IT professionals in adapting and customizing today's systems, applications, and frameworks. Our solution-based books give you the knowledge and power to customize the software and technologies you're using to get the job done. Packt books are more specific and less general than the IT books you have seen in the past. Our unique business model allows us to bring you more focused information, giving you more of what you need to know, and less of what you don't.

Packt is a modern yet unique publishing company that focuses on producing quality, cutting-edge books for communities of developers, administrators, and newbies alike. For more information, please visit our website at `www.packtpub.com`.

Writing for Packt

We welcome all inquiries from people who are interested in authoring. Book proposals should be sent to `author@packtpub.com`. If your book idea is still at an early stage and you would like to discuss it first before writing a formal book proposal, then please contact us; one of our commissioning editors will get in touch with you.

We're not just looking for published authors; if you have strong technical skills but no writing experience, our experienced editors can help you develop a writing career, or simply get some additional reward for your expertise.

PACKT PUBLISHING

Learning Unreal Engine Android Game Development

ISBN: 978-1-78439-436-3 Paperback: 300 pages

Tap into the power of Unreal Engine 4 and create exciting games for the Android platform

1. Dive straight into making fully functional Android games with this hands-on guide.
2. Learn about the entire Android pipeline, from game creation to game submission.
3. Use Unreal Engine 4 to create a first-person puzzle game.

Learning Unreal® Engine iOS Game Development

ISBN: 978-1-78439-771-5 Paperback: 212 pages

Create exciting iOS games with the power of the new Unreal® Engine 4 subsystems

1. Learn about the entire iOS pipeline, from game creation to game submission.
2. Develop exciting iOS games with the Unreal Engine 4.x toolset.
3. Step-by-step tutorials to build optimized iOS games.

CPSIA information can be obtained
at www.ICGtesting.com
Printed in the USA
FSOW02n1431041215
13922FS

9 781785 289064